Pan African Nationalism in the Americas
The Life and Times of John Henrik Clarke

Pan African Nationalism in the Americas
The Life and Times of John Henrik Clarke

Editors
James L. Conyers, Jr.
Julius E. Thompson

AFRICA WORLD PRESS
TRENTON | LONDON | CAPE TOWN | NAIROBI | ADDIS ABABA | ASMARA | IBADAN | NEW DELHI

AFRICA WORLD PRESS
541 West Ingham Avenue | Suite B
Trenton, New Jersey 08638

First Printing 2004

Typesetting: Jerusalem Typesetting
Cover design: Ashraful Haque
Photo pages layout: Damola Ifaturoti

Cover and interior photgraphs courtesy of the Schomberg Center for Research in Black Culture, The New York Public Library.

Library of Congress Cataloging-in-Publication Data

Pan African Nationalism in the Americas : the Life and Times of John Henrik Clarke / edited by James L. Conyers, Jr. and .

p. cm.
Includes bibliographical references and index.
ISBN 1-59221-293-X -- ISBN 1-59221-294-8 (pbk.)
1. Clarks, John Hendrick, 1915. 2. Historians--United States--Biography 3. African American histroians--Biography. 4. African Americans--Historiography. 5. Africa--Historiography. 6. Pan-Africanism--Historiography. 7. Black nationalism--America--Historiography 8. African diaspora--Historiography. 9. African Americans--Intellectual life. I. Conyer, James L. II. Thompson, Julius Eric.

E175.5.C59P36 2004
973'.04960730092--dc22

2004001776

This book is dedicated to
the memory
of
Frederick Bruce Pierce

TABLE OF CONTENTS

CHAPTER 4: AFRICANA HISTORIOGRAPHY

CHAPTER 5: NARRATIVES

CHAPTER 6: PAN AFRICANISM

INTRODUCTION

In the process of discovery and probe, a researcher occasionally comes to a point, when their query is periodically halted or deferred, to measure a barometer of humanistic and ethical qualities of the subject matter. Likewise, John Henrik Clarke spent over five decades of his life working to: write, preserve, teach, and provide service to advance the field and function of Africana Studies. Still his mission propelled soul and spirit to transcend the social and political dimensions of Africana people in world history. Even with many of the contributions he made to the world African community, there are detractors who refer to him by labeling his intellectual, pedagogical, and community service activities. On the other hand, Clarke is an instrument and paragon of social change in Americana history and culture. This refers to his consistent quest to seek alternatives to advance the cause of Africana people.

In an historical perspective, Clarke was raised in the deep south of Alabama and then he migrated to the northen metropolis of New York city. Equally important, while living in the Harlem community, he was able to make the geographical and ideological transitions to a major metropolis and the philosophical repertoire of a Black renaissance period – which attempted to describe and evaluate the Africana experience from an Pan Africanist perspective.

Still, the concept of Africana agency addresses the central ideas of Clarke. He queried and outlined a mandate for African people on an international tier to be self governing, while simultaneously, being cognizant of narrating and gauging data from a systems analysis. In this sense, African people would not study issues in an isolated manner, but rather, develop a paradigm to study parcels in a global context. In short, the goal of this exercise is to locate and identify linkages and patterns of subordination between other cultural and ethnic groups with that of people and descendants of Africa. In closing, the process of organizing this volume is two-fold: first, for researchers to develop query and studies that examine African phenomena on an international basis and second, for scholars to locate the intellectual and literary ideas of John Henrik Clarke, in place, space, and time. Indeed, his work has provided a base for us to advance more critical thought concerning Africana agency and stratification.

Akwaaba, Medassi, Yimhotep

James L. Conyers, Jr., Ph.D.
Director, African American Studies Program
University Professor of African American Studies
University of Houston
April 6, 2004

Chapter 1

Critical and Reflective Essays on John Henrik Clarke

John Henrik Clarke and Issues in Afrikan Historiography: Implications of Pan Afrikan Nationalism in Interpreting the Afrikan Experience in the United States

Ahati N.N. Toure

In some sense it appears quite obvious, but the struggle of the Afrikan in the United States for liberation has always converged around the issue of the Afrikan's origins, around his/her relation to the Afrikan continent. Whether s/he has followed the route of integration or maintained the older, ancestral path of nationalism, the question of Afrika and Afrikan humanity has been central and inescapable. Even the Afrikan who politically and culturally embraced Europeanization and identification with Europe and who rejected Afrika could not altogether escape Afrika. In the intellectual struggle against white supremacist propaganda and domination, in which history served as the primary theater of combat, that proved altogether impossible, for Afrika was implicated in his/her very being.[1] The European's cultural and intellectual war against Afrikan people, their propagation of the vicious fabrication that the Afrikan was a savage, a being altogether devoid of history, had to be confronted squarely. It was a challenge that could not be ignored, for at the very root of his/her identity Afrika stood, inescapable, unmoveable. Hence, even when the Afrikan had decided against Afrika, the defense of Afrikan humanity could not be completed without the vindication, or at the very least a cognizance, of Afrika.

The European's psycho-cultural war on Afrikan humanity was genocidal, unremitting, ruthless; the Afrikan became the object of fantastic, indefensible, and ahistorical claims designed to buttress an overweening European arrogance and depraved self-image.[2] A few examples will suffice. Afrikans, according to the enslaver and white supremacist Thomas Jefferson in 1783, were intellectual inferiors, in imagination "dull, tasteless, and anomalous" despite their long contact with the so-called civilizing influence of whites.[3] Nearly three quarters of a century later, United States Supreme Court Chief Justice Roger Taney noted in the infamous 1857 Dred Scott vs. Sandford decision that Afrikans in America at the time of the Constitution's authorship "had for more than a century before been regarded as beings of an inferior order, and altogether unfit to associate with the white race, either in social or political relations." Afrikans were, in fact "so far inferior, that they had no rights which the white man was bound to respect; and that the negro might justly and lawfully be reduced to slavery for his benefit."[4]

Deeply agitated by the fact some fellow Europeans were apostatizing from white supremacist orthodoxy, John Campbell in his 1851 refutation, *Negro-Mania: Being An Examination of the Falsely Assumed Equality of the Various Races of Man*, countered "I take it for granted that no dark race of man has ever been equal to the white race." Indeed, insisted Campbell, "Equal numbers ceteris paribus, the dark race must submit to the fair, the two cannot exist together in the same community on terms of equality – I speak not here of the justice or injustice of the matter, I speak only of fact! the whole history of the world proves it." With a shrillness bordering on hysteria, Campbell continued: "never at any given time from the most infinitely remote antiquity until now, has there ever appeared a race of negroes, that is men with woolly heads, flat noses, thick and protruding lips, who has ever emerged from a state of savageism or barbarism, to even demi civilization."[5]

The so-called liberator, Abraham Lincoln, some few years later agreed with Campbell, declaring in a political campaign debate with Stephen A. Douglas that "I am not, nor ever have been in favor of bringing about in any way the social and political equality of the white and black races." In his view this was because of the "physical difference" between the two peoples. He added: "there must be the position of superior and inferior, and I as much as any other man am in favor of having the superior position assigned to the white race."[6]

European scholars in the United States and in Europe were also unified in their contempt for Afrikan humanity. Georg Hegel, the noted 19th century German philosopher and political theorist, asserted (without, of course, having ever set foot in Afrika) Afrikans were immoral, cannibalistic, savage, inhuman, exhibiting "the natural man in his wild and untamed state. We must lay aside all thought of reverence and morality – all that we call feeling – if we would rightly comprehend him; there is nothing harmonious with humanity to be found in this type of character."[7] As a result, offered Hegel, enslavement by Europeans was preferable to "their lot in their own land."[8] In 1863, Louis Agassiz, Harvard University zoologist and eminent polygenist concurred, declaring (no doubt based upon his scientific expertise) the prospect of social equality for Afrikans with Europeans was "impracticable," the "natural impossibility" of such a thing "flowing from the very character of the negro race."[9]

The list is endless, as this enumerating of white supremacist insults could be extended *ad nauseum*. But it is little wonder, then, that in the 19th century there was among Afrikan intellectuals and activists in the United States a vigorous, primarily cultural and political, debate on the question of Afrika and the Afrikan's relationship to the homeland and to the European's society. And it is no wonder, under the steady, pernicious, and mind-bending onslaught of anti-Afrikan propaganda, that many chose to repudiate identification with Afrika. A few examples here, too, will suffice. For his part Richard Allen, bishop and founder of the African Methodist Episcopal Church – at one point in his career an active promoter of emigration to the newly-founded Haitian republic – repudiated identification with and repatriation to the Afrikan homeland. In an 1827 editorial in *Freedom's Journal*, the first Afrikan newspaper published in the United States, Allen, who had created his own church because the Europeans had excluded him from theirs, declared that while we Afrikans "were *stolen* from our mother country and brought *here*," Afrika, to him, was a land of "Heathens." This was in stark contrast to America, he asserted, a land "colonized by as *wise, judicious*, and *educated* men as the world afforded." To Allen, "This land which we have watered with our *tears* and our *blood*, is now our *mother country* and we are well satisfied to stay where wisdom abounds and the gospel is free."[10] [emphasis author's]

Nineteen years later Frederick Douglass declared his unequivocal preference for the United States over Afrika by remarking: "The black man (unlike the Indian) loves civilization. He does not make very great progress in civilization himself, but he likes to be in the midst of it, *and prefers to share its most galling evils, to encountering barbarism*." Douglass's commitment to America was unswerving. "We have grown up with this republic, and *I see nothing in her character, or even in the character of the American people, as yet, which compels the belief that we must leave the United States*."[11] [emphasis added]

Like Douglass and Allen, the fiery 19th century abolitionist Henry Highland Garnet – until he later reversed his position to became a staunch advocate of Afrikan repatriation – was adamant in his rejection of the Afrikan homeland.

> We must… cherish and maintain a national and patriotic sentiment and attachment. Some people of color say that they have no home, no country. I am not of that number. It is empty declamation. It is unwise. It is not logical – it is false.… *America is my home, my country, and I have no other.… I love my country's flag,* and I hope soon that it will be cleansed of its stains, and be hailed by all nations as the emblem of freedom and independence.[12] [emphasis added]

Pan Afrikan nationalists, on the other hand, embraced identification with and even repatriation to the homeland. Among them was perhaps the first to change his name in recorded Afrikan history in the United States, Paul Kofi (spelled Cuffee at the time), a wealthy 19th century Boston shipowner who financed the repatriation of U.S.-held Afrikans to Sierra Leone. Kofi had discarded his enslaver's name, Slocum, in favor of his father's name, Kofi, a Ghanaian (Akan, Ewe) name that means a male born on Friday. "Be not fearful to come to Africa, which is your country by right," he wrote to those he had left behind. "Africa, not America, is your country and your home."[13]

The same conviction held for John Russwurm, who along with Samuel Cornish in New York City established the first Afrikan newspaper in the United States in 1827. By 1829 he had become an advocate of repatriation when he asked, rhetorically, "can any consider it a mark of folly, for us to cast our eyes upon some other portion of the globe… where the Man of Colour freed from the fetters and prejudice and degradation, under which he labours in this land, may walk forth in all the majesty of his creation – a new born creature – a Free Man!"[14] The first Afrikan to graduate from Bowdoin College in Maine, Russwurm eventually emigrated to Liberia to become the nation's first superintendent of schools and founder of its first newspaper.

Thirty years later, Pan Afrikan nationalists began to explore the possibility of settling in other areas of West Afrika. Elombe Brath, one of the leading Pan Afrikanist revolutionary activists and intellectuals in the United States, notes that Martin Robison Delany, accompanied by Robert Campbell, a Jamaican-born Afrikan nationalist, formed the Niger Valley Exploring Party, traveling in 1859 to the Niger River area of Yorubaland in what is now Nigeria to attempt a repatriation effort there.

> Their mission was to attempt to negotiate treaties with indigenous leaders to secure land where they could develop a settlement for Afrikan repatriates

> from the U.S. A key element in their plan was to engage in the production of cotton, which they would then sell on the world market at cheaper prices than that sold by the slave plantation owners in the U.S. By accomplishing this, they hoped to undercut the profitability of the american slave system and thus destroy its value as an industry that would continue to hold Black people in bondage.[15]

That effort was undermined, however, by British imperial expansion in the area. The activists, deemed to be representatives of the "Afrikan race in America," had initially reached agreements with the rulers of Lagos and Abeokuta. But by 1861 the British had taken control of Lagos and effectively sabotaged the resettlement effort.[16]

Some 22 years later the movement to return to the Afrikan homeland had not died. The fiery, razor-tongued Henry McNeal Turner, a bishop of the African Methodist Episcopal Church, dismissed objections to Afrikan repatriation as originating from "the riff-raff white-man worshippers, aimless, objectless, selfish, little-souled and would-be-white negroes" to whom "the white man is all in all, therefore it is useless to attempt to be anybody, especially where the white man does not hold sway." Turner ridiculed "the nonsensical jargon that the climate of Africa is against us, we can't live there, the tropics are no place for moral and intellectual development, coming from the mouths of so-called leaders, [as] simply ridiculous," adding "If I were so ignorant, I would hold my tongue and pen and not let people know it."[17]

Significantly, these political and cultural movements among 19th century Afrikans reflected two fundamentally different approaches to liberation struggle in the United States, and they would be reflected, as well, in 20th century Afrikan historiography, which constituted a critical extension of the liberation struggle into the intellectual and academic spheres.[18] From the beginning Afrikans defined liberation as ending European white supremacist colonial domination. But while universally agreeing on the goal, they historically divided over its definition, defining liberation – the goal of overcoming white supremacist colonial domination – in two fundamentally different ways.

One definition was and remains to end white supremacist colonial domination by achieving the integration or assimilation of Afrikans as equals and as Europeans within the mainstream of European culture in the United States. This means that like Irish-Americans, Italian-Americans, German-Americans, etc., the Colored-, Negro-, Black-, Afro- and now African-American struggles for recognition and acceptance as a subset of the European people, as an ethnic group among American European ethnic groups. The "African-American" seeks full participation in the social, political, economic, and cultural arrangements of the society. This definition of liberation is called integrationism.

The other definition was and remains to end white supremacist colonial domination by achieving cultural, political, economic, military, and territorial independence from the European people of the United States. This means the Afrikan recognized and asserted the human right to reclaim the independence s/he enjoyed before capture and forcible removal from Afrika. The Afrikan sought independence from the United States and its European people either within the territorial United States, other countries in the Americas, or on the Afrikan continent itself. This definition of liberation is called nationalism.

Thus, one group of Afrikans defined liberation as rejecting identification with Afrika. Instead, they identified themselves as Americans, and as belonging to the European people called Americans and to the country these Europeans created, in which country they were rejected. The other group saw themselves as Afrikans and as belonging to the people and continent of Afrika. At the very least, these Afrikans saw themselves as never belonging to the European people called Americans, or to the country they created, in which country they were held prisoners.

This cultural tension informed the Afrikan's push for and recognition of the strategic importance of historical inquiry, which was never separated from these divergent political goals. Hence, the Afrikan's exploration of the meaning and importance of history was never merely an intellectual or academic exercise. Its historiographical significance would always be highly political, a national project in the struggle for human rights of the highest order. The task of discovering the truth of history and the Afrikans' role in the world was intended to validate Afrikan humanity, to discern the Afrikan's past, and to extrapolate his/her future role in the world community. It was by all means a pursuit of the truth, for the Afrikan historian in the United States rejected white supremacy as a grotesque lie. Truth was a weapon in the Afrikan's arsenal, a means by which to pursue one or the other goal of the liberation struggle.

It is into this context that John Henrik Clarke was born and to which he would make his seminal contribution to the Afrikan's understanding of his/her gift to, and place and destiny in the world. Born 1 January 1915 in Union Springs, Alabama, Clarke came to the earth plane in the wake of a tremendous push by Afrikans to take the liberation struggle to the arena of historical inquiry. His birth followed by only 32 years George Washington Williams's publication in 1883 of his two-volume *History of the Negro Race in America From 1619 to 1880.* He was born a mere 20 years after William Edward Burghardt DuBois, the first

Afrikan to earn a Harvard University Ph.D., published his dissertation, *The Suppression of the Afrikan Slave Trade to the United States, 1638–1870*, the first in the Harvard historical series. And he arrived in the same year that Carter Godwin Woodson, another Harvard-trained historian, established what is now the Association for the Study of African American Life and History with the declared mission of restoring Afrikan people to the missing pages of America's and the world's history.

One of the most brilliant scholars of Afrikan world history, Clarke possessed a prodigious, encyclopedic grasp of the global Afrikan experience, and was a fascinating and brilliant lecturer. During his 83 years he traveled Afrika and the world. A confidant and friend of Omowale Malcolm X; the author of the historic charter of Omowale's Organization of Afro-American Unity, an advisor to Osageyfo Kwame Nkrumah, editor of the legendary *Freedomways*, the journal of civil rights era activism, Clarke was an editor, writer, poet, journalist, and literary critic, a political activist and revolutionary, a Pan Afrikan nationalist, a formidable intellectual, historian, and scholar. He authored some 38 or more articles in academic, intellectual, political, and popular journals and magazines. He edited at least 17 books on subjects ranging from Marcus Garvey and Malcolm X to South Afrikan apartheid, slavery and the slave trade, and Pan Afrikanism and the liberation of southern Afrika. He authored at least 11 books on topics ranging from poetry to Afrikan world history and Afrikan liberation struggle. His lectures – one of his great gifts was his ability to present the scope and breadth of Afrikan world history with incomparable clarity and power – were innumerable.

Clarke's training in history took place in the 1930s in New York City under the guidance of Arthur Alphonso Schomburg, Willis N. Huggins, and Charles C. Seifert, who "literally trained me not only to study African history and the history of Black people the world over but to teach this history." Indeed, Arthur Schomburg "is responsible for what I am and what value I have in the field of African history and the history of Black people all over the world."[19] In a further explanation of his historical training, Clarke reveals "Arthur Schomburg taught me the interrelationship of African history to world history. Willis N. Huggins taught me the political meaning of history. William Leo Hansberry, in his lectures when he came over from Howard [University in Washington, DC], taught me the philosophical meaning of history."[20] Clarke also supplemented this training some two decades later with studies at New York University and the New School of Social Research (both in New York City), at Pacific Western University, and at the University of Ibadan (in Nigeria) and the University of Ghana. Throughout the 1960s he taught in community centers throughout Harlem, New York. He lectured at the City University of New York's Hunter College for 17 years, becoming an associate professor in 1970, and chaired its Department of Black and Puerto Rican Studies, retiring at age 70 as professor emeritus in 1985.

What is significant about Clarke's career as a historian was his concern with examining the nature of Afrikan history in a way that differed significantly from the classic approach of "African-American" or "Black American" historiography. Whereas that historiography was principally concerned with explicating the Afrikan experience in the United States as an *American* experience, Clarke's approach was to see the Afrikan experience in the United States as an *Afrikan* experience, centered in and flowing from the history of the Afrikan continent itself. "Slavery is only one factor in African history and that too is often misunderstood. For most of the years African people have been in the world, they have been a free and self-governing people," he wrote. "Africans were great makers of culture long before their first appearance in Jamestown, Virginia."[21] Being in America, for Clarke, was being away, in exile, from home. The primary obligation, allegiance and identification for Afrikan people, regardless of geographical location, was with Afrika, and not the nations in which they find themselves, and in which, also, for the most part, they are aliens. This is because Afrikans were a nationality unto themselves. Their nationality and national allegiance lay not in the foreign countries in which they were in exile. Clearly, for Clarke this decided absence of loyalty to the country of residence included the United States.

> We must stop killing ourselves about belonging to mother countries not of our making. Languages not of our making. Stop worshipping gods not of our choosing and realize that wherever we are on the face of the earth, we are an Afrikan people. No matter where our bodies are, our heartbeat, our future, our political being is in Afrika. We are an Afrikan people wherever we are on the face of the earth.[22]

To the contrary, Black American historiography saw the genesis of the Afrikan identity in the United States in the English enslavement of Afrikans in Jamestown, Virginia, in 1619, viewing it as an *American* identity. Although survey histories by distinguished historians such as John Hope Franklin's classic, *From Slavery to Freedom*, or Benjamin Quarles's *The Negro in the Making of America*, begin with an origin in medieval West Afrika, the Afrikan is, nonetheless, declared to belong and to be committed to America. Wrote Franklin in his first edition, published in 1947: "it must be admitted that the effect of acculturation on the Negro in the United States has been so marked that *today he is as truly American as any member of other ethnic groups that make up the American population.*" Franklin's historiographical objective was to "*tell the story of the process by which the Negro has sought to cast his lot with an evolving American civilization.*"[23] [emphasis added] Fourteen years earlier, the eminent and pioneering Carter G. Woodson, in his otherwise seminal classic, *The Mis-Education of the Negro*, took a similar stance when arguing for an American identity, positing: "We are not all Africans... *because many of us were not born in Africa*; and we are not all Afro-Americans *because few of us are natives of Africa* transplanted to America."[24] Benjamin Quarles observed 36 years later that "If, strictly speaking, there is no such thing as Negro history, it is because *his past has become so interwoven into the whole fabric of our* [American] *civilization....* Except for the first settlers at Jamestown, *the Negro's roots in the original thirteen colonies sink deeper than those of any other group from across the Atlantic.*"[25] [emphasis added] Quarles saw the emerging significance of Afrika in the modern world as a basis for arguing the admission of Afrikans in the United States into the European mainstream. "And in our own times the emergence of freedom-minded nations in Africa would seem to make it advantageous for Americans to view afresh the historic role of their colored fellows."[26]

Earl Thorpe in his *Black Historians: A Critique*, further underscores this nexus between a defense of Afrika and the integrationist impulse in "African-American" historiography. In his examination of the work of Charles H. Wesley, he notes, quoting him: "Laying down the lines along which the history of the United States and the Western world should be rendered, Wesley declared that '1) History should be reconstructed *so that Africa... shall have its proper place;...* and 4) History should be reconstructed *so that Negroes shall be regarded as Americans* and not simply as slaves *or as an alien part of the* [American] *population.*'"[27] [emphasis added] Nathan I. Huggins agreed. "Afro-American history and American history are not only essential to one another. They share a common historical fate," he wrote in a repudiation of the Afrikan identity. "Afro-Americans, too, are new, a new people brought into being as a consequence of American history, *a new people for whom after several generations in America it was impossible to trace back to any tradition beyond the American experience itself.*"[28] [emphasis added]

Clarke, by contrast, saw the identity of Afrikans in the United States as *Afrikan*, beginning in the prehistory and antiquity of the Afrikan continent. For him the Afrikan experience in the United States represented only one phase of a history and identity independent of Europe that spanned millennia. Here the contemporary struggle against European domination was seen in the context of similar struggles against foreign domination that occurred over a period that began in Afrikan antiquity. This is significant in that, for Clarke, American domination was merely the latest, not the defining, experience of the struggle of Afrikan people against foreign oppression. In a lecture in London, England, titled *African Resistance and Colonial Domination: The Africans in the Americas*, Clarke captured this perspective in a brief introductory statement, summarizing: "I have said and documented that we, as a people, have been under siege for over 3,000 years."[29] Indeed, Clarke observed in another lecture titled *Pan-Africanism and the Future of the African Family*, with Afrikan unification *as a family of peoples* in this millennia-old struggle for sovereignty, the triumph over foreign domination will be complete. "Because of the 3,000 years or more that we were under siege, we have been trying to put that family back together again. Once we put that family back together, and it takes hold successfully, we will walk on the stage of world power and be what we once had been and never again be dependent on any people."[30]

It is for this reason that Clarke's approach emphasized a global and Pan Afrikanist focus that explored and assumed organic interconnections between the regional histories of Afrikans in the Americas and on the Continent. In this case, Afrikan history was not seen merely as the history of peoples *on* the Afrikan continent, but the history of the peoples *of* the Afrikan continent; Afrikan history obtained *wherever Afrikans from the Continent* found themselves. While the center for Afrikan history remained in Afrika, Afrikan history was, nonetheless, a history of the Afrikan peoples in the world – or, the extension of the influence of Afrika, through its peoples, into the world. Hence, he would say,

> We are not a minority. Between the Caribbean islands and South America and Afrikan people in the Pacific and in Afrika itself we constitute a major portion of the population of the earth. In the 21st century there may be, or more than likely will be, a billion Afrikan people on the face of the earth. We might be the second, if not the first, the largest ethnic group in the world. And we have to put ourselves together as a family. We have to see ourselves as a family.[31]

As a scholar concerned with world civilizations, Clarke addressed the role of the Afrikan, and Afrika, in world history and in intercourse with non-Afrikan peoples over millennia. "In approaching this subject," he posited, "the first thing you need to know is that for thousands of years before the existence of Europe, what we know as Africa was the world.... We have not talked enough about our life as a people before the European contact and the negative impact of the European presence."[32] In this he did not differ with integrationist scholars, who were equally concerned with the reinsertion of the Afrikan, and Afrika, into the history of the world.[33] The differences lay in the interpretation of the significance of that history for Afrikan national destiny. Stanford Lewis in his stimulating and pathbreaking essay, "African Resistance: A Look at Some 20th Century African Americans Whose Scholarship Sought to Reclaim and Restore Ancient Kemet to Africa," noted the differences in an examination of the writings of 13 Afrikan scholars in the United States on the question. His analysis led him to group them into three basic schools of thought – what he called Vindicationists, Ethiopianists, and Afrikan Infusionists – that divided along the lines of integrationist and nationalist approaches in historiographical interpretation.[34]

For Vindicationist scholars, notes Lewis, the chief concern was an integrationist vision of Afrikan antiquity that tied "racial mixing" to social progress, establishing, as well, a model and teleology for the Afrikan's destiny in the United States that accorded with the integrationist quest to effect an assimilation into the European mainstream as cultural equals. In the Vindicationist vision,

> the classical Kemetic Nile Valley was inhabited essentially by a mixed race or mulatto population, that there occurred there a mixing of white, Black and others that was the greatest of any known society. Despite such mixing, these people created and prospered as human beings. *In this sense, the social and racial conditions presumed to exist in ancient times could be used as a standard for racial equality for the discriminated and minority African population in America. The social conditions that existed in ancient times were seen as similar to modern American society* with the difference being that the Europeans are in the majority in the United States. *The challenge, then, was to discover whether the Europeans of America could not only create a technologically great society, but one in which racial harmony and equality could be achieved.*[35] [emphasis added]

Interestingly, Lewis found that Ethiopianist scholars, although "clearly opposed to the mixed race emphasis of the vindicationists," agreed on the essential significance of the history. The Ethiopianists, he observes, "retreat from the racial ambiguity that ancient Kemet posed to the more certain ground of Ethiopia. Insofar as Ethiopia (or Nubia-Kush) was indisputably African, they were able to refute the Hamitic Hypothesis, which argued a mulatto (vindicationist) or caucasoid (white supremacist) origin of African civilization. The genius of Africa, under this formulation, remains indisputably Black."[36] But, he adds:

> In short, the Ethiopianist school, not unlike the vindicationists, argued that the Ethiopian contribution to European civilization serves as proof not only of the European indebtedness to Africa and to Africans, but as proof of African humanity *and as a rationale for non-discriminatory inclusion within Euro-American society. In this sense, the policy aim of the Ethiopianist school – to promote the liberality of European culture – is identical to the vindicationist objective.*[37] [emphasis added]

The Afrikan Infusionist school, however, differed significantly in focus. "The African Infusionist scholars reject the notion that the Nile Valley was an experience in racial integration between Europeans and Africans," writes Lewis. "To the contrary, they argue that the ancient Kemites and their culture originated in the heart of Africa and flowed up the Nile. In addition, cultural influences came through Kemet to the outside world from the African interior. Thus, Nile Valley civilization was a product of the infusion of African cultures."[38] He adds:

> What is significant about this position is that the ancient Kemetic culture is seen as important in revitalizing and giving guidance and focus to contemporary African American culture.... The Infusionists argue that ancient Kemetic civilization originated from the south and that the people and culture were African. Because of this example from antiquity, Africans have the ability to emulate the achievements of their ancestors. *These achievements must be focused to create an African worldview that rejects the epistemological hegemony of European culture. The rejection of European culture extends to the Christian religion, an overall Eurocentric worldview and European rule. The call is for cultural and political independence.*[39] [emphasis added]

Clarke, too, shared what Lewis describes as the Afrikan Infusionist position, "emphasizing the indigenous Southern African origin of the ancient Egyptians, who were equally, 'Africans.'"[40] Indeed, he maintains "Egypt was not a singular civilization but a composite civilization which was composed of all of the cultures and ethnic elements of that entire valley. Egypt was not a civilization in itself, but a culmination of a number of civilizations, all of them originally coming from the south."[41]

As a nationalist, Clarke also analyzed the implications of Afrikan history for the struggle against European white supremacist colonial domination and urged the possibility of victory based on the fact of the achievements of the Afrikan past. A central theme of the implications of that past was the imperative of nation-building, of constructing a destiny in which Afrikans would reclaim their sovereign status, wresting it from the stranglehold of European domination in the United States and in the world. This achievement must be based firmly in a cultural revolution that draws from the wellsprings of Afrikan tradition, he argued. The success of the quest for the Afrikan's reclamation of national sovereignty is rooted in cultural re-Afrikanization and in a concomitant de-Europeanization or psycho-cultural de-colonization. This includes, indispensably, the much maligned matter of Afrikan traditional religion. "When a people laugh at your gods, they have you one way, and when they train you to laugh at your gods, they have got you another way," he admonished. "I have said, repeatedly, that not only is Africa in need of a cultural revolution, but there will never be a true cultural revolution until an African head of state prays to an African god in public, without apologizing for it."[42]

> No state institution or society within the whole of the Afrikan world will ever be successfully run on a European model. In throwing off European dominance and pursuing state independence, Africans the world over should have reexamined all religious concepts and concepts of governance that they inherited from their former European rulers. All political, cultural, and religious institutions should have been reappraised and a concept should have been adopted relevant to the needs of African people and not the needs of their colonial masters. The values of a traditional African way of life should have been reexamined and reconsidered.[43]

As with the Afrikan Infusionists Lewis examined, Clarke's vision was for complete sovereignty for Afrikans colonized in the United States. "We are a conquered people. We are a colonized people within the United States," he observed. And the urgent task of liberation struggle was to "understand that our history is Afrikan and" to understand, as a consequence, "what we have to do to rescue our people from dependency." The destiny of the Afrikan in America was to see to it that every "component that makes a nation, we must have someone trained to do it well."[44] Afrikan people in the United States must be engaged in a strategic effort to restore sovereignty to themselves, he urged. "We're going to have to understand that nobody has any vested interest in Afrikan people coming to power. ... So we have to do some serious thinking about our world position."[45]

As a revolutionary, a Pan Afrikan nationalist and a socialist, Clarke was concerned with the ways in which Afrikan history could assist a colonized people in understanding their condition and the means by which they may recapture sovereignty in all spheres – political, economic, social, cultural, and spiritual. This, in fact, was the central purpose of Afrikan history: the preparation of the Afrikan to understand the acquisition, enhancement and management of power. For Clarke "the new reality is that African people must be educated to regain *the main thing they lost during slavery and colonialism, the control of the state and their own destiny,*" he wrote. "The main purpose of education is to train the student to be a proper handler of power.... *Education that fails to equip you to handle some form of power is irrelevant* and not education at all."[46] [emphasis added]

Re-Afrikanization, independence, and national sovereignty are the national destiny of the Afrikan in the United States and in the world, Clarke urged, and it is to this national destiny that he dedicated his life during his 83 years on the planet. The uncorruptible and indefatigable spirit of struggle, the defiant and unyielding commitment to revolution, the grand and uncompromised vision of self-determination, were the legacy he bequeathed us. Indeed, for Clarke, the history of Afrikan national achievement was a source for much optimism despite the ravages of European white supremacist colonial domination, because past achievements pointed to present and future potentialities. In that spirit, in a speech on the crisis in the Afrikan family, he commented on the implications of white supremacist indoctrination on the Afrikan psyche, its crippling effect on revolutionary vision and struggle. Still, because of the clarity and depth of his historical consciousness, he could not help but sound a concluding note of optimism.

> One of the great crimes of oppression is that it suspends your ability to dream. It suspends your ability to fantasize. There are black people who can't even fantasize ruling a state. But if you cannot even dream of ruling a state, if you can't even see it in your fantasy, you will not see it in your reality. And you can rule a state much better than many states are being ruled today.[47]

END NOTES

1. One notes a simple commentary in Benjamin Quarles's *The Negro in the Making of America* (New York: Macmillan Publishing Company, 1969), p. 32. In examining the transferability of skills from free Afrika to enslaver America, he observes: "In Africa the handicrafts of the native tribes – weaving, pottery, carving in wood, ivory, and bone – were fashioned with surprising technical finish. African Negroes had been among the first peoples to work in iron and gold, metal forging being one of their oldest arts. *Bondage in the New World did not erase these ancestral skills in the handicrafts.... Thus the craft work of colonial America reflected the art work of Negro Africa, an art that today has won a distinctive place in modern* [read European] *esthetics.*" [emphasis added]

   Even John Hope Franklin in the preface to the first edition of his nearly 50-year old classic survey of Afrikan history in the United States, *From Slavery to Freedom*, noted in 1947 that "I have undertaken to bring together the essential facts in the history of the American Negro *from his ancient African beginnings* down to the present time." [emphasis added]. See John Hope Franklin and Albert A. Moss, Jr. *From Slavery to Freedom: A History of African Americans* Seventh edition (New York: Alfred A. Knopf, 1994), p. xxxi.

2. See John Henrik Clarke, *Who Betrayed the African World Revolution? And Other Speeches* (Chicago: Third World Press, 1994), p. 157. Of European imperialism, including its scholarship, he observes: "In order to justify the slave trade, the Europeans created an African people in their minds who never actually existed. They created a people with no known culture and no known contact with a civilized way of life.... When today one looks at the fight against Black Studies and the revival of history to reflect the contributions of non-European people to the cultures of the world, we are seeing the results of almost a thousand years of anti-human propaganda in favor of Europeans.... Of all the people in the world, Africans are the greatest sufferers from the anti-history campaign launched by the Europeans. Their campaign literally reversed human history."
3. Philip S. Foner, *Basic Writings of Thomas Jefferson* (New York: Halycon House, 1950), p. 145.
4. As quoted by Imari Abubakari Obadele, *America The Nation-State: The Politics of the United States from a Nation-Building Perspective* (Baton Rouge, LA: The House of Songhay, 1990), pp. 174–175.
5. John Campbell, *Negro-Mania: Being An Examination of the Falsely Assumed Equality of the Various Races of Man* (Miami: Mnemosyne Publishing Co., Inc., 1969; reprint Philadelphia: Campbell and Power, 1851), pp. 6–7.
6. As quoted by T.F. Gossett, *Race: The History of an Idea in America* (New York: Schocken Books, 1965), p. 254.
7. Georg W.F. Hegel, *Philosophy of History* (London: The Colonial Press, 1900), pp. 94–95.
8. Ibid., p. 96.
9. As quoted by Stephen Jay Gould, *The Mismeasure of Man* (New York: W.W. Norton, 1981), p. 48.
10. Deidre Mullane, ed., *Crossing the Danger Water: Three Hundred Years of African-American Writing* (New York: Anchor Books, 1993), pp. 72–73.
11. Frederick Douglass, *The Negro's Right to Remain in America*, a speech in the 27 March 1846 issue of the *Liberator* in Philip S. Foner, ed., *Frederick Douglass: Selecetions From His Writings* (New York: International Publishers, 1945), pp. 53–54. His statement is later repeated in 1853 in *Proceedings of the Colored National Convention Held in Rochester July 6th, 7th and 8th, 1853* in Howard Holman Bell, ed., *Minutes of the Proceedings of the National Negro Conventions, 1830–1864* (New York: Arno Press and The New York Times, 1969), p. 36.
12. As quoted by Mary Frances Berry and John Blassingame, *Long Memory: The Black Experience in America* (New York: Oxford University Press, 1983), p. 399.

13. As quoted by Vincent Harding, *There is a River: The Black Struggle for Freedom in America* (New York: Vintage Books, 1981), p. 65.
14. Mullane, *Danger Water*, p. 71.
15. Elombe Brath, "The Crisis in Nigeria." *Nation Time* 3 (Fall 1998): 8. *Nation Time* is a quarterly newspaper published out of New York City by the New Afrikan Liberation Front, an umbrella organization for the New Afrikan independence movement in the United States. For a further discussion of Delany's Afrika mission, see Victor Ullman, *Martin R. Delany: The Beginnings of Black Nationalism* (Boston: Beacon Press, 1971), pp. 211–246. On page 224 Ullman quotes Delany concerning his efforts to secure a place for Afrikan repatriation in these terms: "I have determined to leave my children the inheritance of a country, the possession of a territorial domain, the blessings of a national education, and the indisputable right of self-government."
16. Ibid.
17. Edwin S. Redkey, ed., *Respect Black: The Writings and Speeches of Henry McNeal Turner* (New York: Arno Press and The New York Times, 1971), pp. 56–57.
18. The emergence of Africana Studies is superbly illustrative of this point. Although the discipline is not history *per se*, it is firmly grounded in, and a certain product of, the Afrikan history movement in the United States and is, therefore, of relevance here. The following quotations, which serve to bear this out, are from various scholars in the field writing in James L. Conyers, Jr., ed., *Africana Studies: A Disciplinary Quest for Both Theory and Method* (Jefferson, NC and London: McFarland & Company, Inc., Publishers, 1997), pp. 95, 126, 131, 143. James E. Turner in his essay, *Africana Studies and Epistemology: A Discourse in the Sociology of Knowledge*, writes that "As a methodology, history, in Black Studies, constitutes the foundation for theoretical construction of an analysis of the fundamental relationship between the political economy of societal developments and the racial divisions of labor and privilege, and the common patterns of life chances peculiar to the social conditions of black people. *Basic to the teleology of Africana Studies is the application of knowledge to promote social change.*" James B. Stewart in *Reaching for Higher Ground: Toward an Understanding of Black/Africana Studies* concludes his essay with the thought that "the refinement of the Black/Africana disciplinary matrix *is critical for the salvation of human civilization and for ushering in the multicultural world that DuBois envisioned.*" James L. Conyers in *African American Studies: Locating a Niche in the Public Sphere of Higher Education* quotes Nathan Huggins in remarking that to "'understand Afro-American Studies... *it is necessary to consider both higher education and the American civil rights Movement.*'" Finally, Delores P. Aldridge in her essay, *Womanist Issues in Black Studies: Towards Integrating Africana Womanism into Africana Studies*, notes "Black or Africana Studies began as a field of study in the 1960s in the wake of the civil rights movement and in the midst of

pervasive campus unrest. *From the outset it had both an academic and social mission.*" [all emphases added]

19. John Henrik Clarke, ed., *New Dimensions in African History: The London Lectures of Dr. Yosef ben-Jochannan and Dr. John Henrik Clarke* (Trenton, NJ: Africa World Press, Inc., 1991), p. 137.
20. Clarke, *Who Betrayed?*, p. 117.
21. Ibid., p. 6.
22. Kwaku Person-Lynn, *John Henrik Clarke: The Knowledge Revolutionary* (1998). http://www.usafricaonline.com/JohnHenrikClarke.html. See also Clarke, *Who Betrayed?*, p. 54. He writes: "Because our origin is Africa, our political heartbeat should be in tune with Africa. No matter where we live on the face of the earth, we should proclaim ourselves an African people. That is our nationality, no matter what nation we were born in and what nation we choose to live in."
23. Franklin and Moss, *From Slavery to Freedom*, p. xxxii.
24. Carter Godwin Woodson, *The Mis-Education of the Negro* (Washington, DC: The Associated Publishers, Inc., 1969), p. 200.
25. Quarles, *The Negro*, p. 7. August Meier, commenting in an introduction to Benjamin Quarles's *Black Mosaic: Essays in Afro-American History and Historiography* (Amherst: University of Massachusetts Press, 1988), pp. 9–10, observed: "This theme of the centrality of blacks to the American ethos and its fulfillment, along with the optimistic view that in the end the spirit of the Declaration of Independence would be fulfilled, are explicitly expressed in nearly all of Quarles's works."
26. Ibid., pp. 7–8.
27. Earl Thorpe, *Black Historians: A Critique* (New York: William Morrow and Company, Inc., 1971), pp. 136–37. Thorpe defines Afrikan history in the United States thus: "*Black history is American history* with the accent and emphasis and point of view, attitude and spirit of Afro-Americans.... *Black history is that American history* which, until the 1960s, was viewed by white America with contempt and disdain or ignored altogether, just as black people themselves were viewed and treated.... *The central theme of black history is the quest of the Afro-American for freedom, equality and manhood.*" [emphasis added] See also Earl E. Thorpe, *The Central Theme of Black History* (Durham, NC: Seeman Printery, 1969) and James L. Conyers, Jr., *Charles H. Wesley, African American Historiography and Black Studies: An Historical Overview* in James L. Conyers, Jr. and Alva p. Barnett, eds., *African American Sociology: A Social Study of the Pan-African Diaspora* (Chicago: Nelson-Hall Publishers, 1999). With respect to Wesley's remarks on American identity, Douglass in 1853 put forth the position in quite similar language: "We are Americans, and as Americans, we would speak to Americans. We address you not as aliens nor as exiles ... but we address you as American citizens asserting their rights on their own native soil." See Sterling Stuckey, *Slave Culture: Nationalist*

Theory and Foundations of Black America (New York and Oxford: Oxford University Press, 1987), p. 224.

28. Nathan I. Huggins, *Integrating Afro-American History* in Darlene Clark Hine, ed., *The State of Afro-American History: Past, Present, and Future* (Baton Rouge and London: Louisiana State University Press, 1986), pp. 160–61.
29. Clarke, *New Dimensions*, p. 24.
30. Ibid., p. 98.
31. Dr. John Henrik Clark and Dr. Ivan Van Sertima, *The Black Family* (Highland Park, NJ: Journal of African Civilizations, Audio Division, 1987). Clarke wrote in *New Dimensions*, p. 31: "No matter where you are and no matter what religion you might belong to, and no matter what kind of schooling you have gone through, you are distinctly an African person. You are a supporter of some loyal feelings for every African person that walks this earth, and if you have confusion about that, you have confusion that is detrimental to the freedom of your own people."
32. Clarke, *New Dimensions*, p. 97.
33. See Clarke, *Who Betrayed?*, p. 156. He writes: "African history is as old as world history. In fact, African history is the essence of world history. In order to understand African history in its true light, it may be necessary to place Africa at the center of world history and to start the rest of human history from that center."
34. Stanford Lewis, "African Resistance: A Look at Some 20th Century African Americans Whose Scholarship Sought to Reclaim and Restore Ancient Kemet to Africa." *The Western Journal of Black Studies* 19 (1995): 90–104. Lewis grouped the scholars as follows: in the Vindicationist school are W.E.B. DuBois, Carter G. Woodson, Alfred G. Dunston, Jr., St. Clair Drake, J.A. Rogers, Frank M. Snowden, Jr., and George G.M. James. In the Ethiopianist school are Drusilla D. Houston, John G. Jackson and William Leo Hansberry. In the Afrikan Infusionist school are Jacob H. Carruthers, Yosef A.A. ben-Jochannan, and Chancellor Williams.
35. Ibid., p. 96.
36. Ibid., p. 99.
37. Ibid.
38. Ibid., p. 101.
39. Ibid.
40. Clarke, *New Dimensions*, p. 5.
41. Clarke, *Who Betrayed?*, p. 86. Lewis in *African Resistance*, p. 96, notes the archeological evidence for this history, writing: "This position of the Ethiopian parentage of ancient Kemetic civilization is consistent with evidence discovered in 1964… Published in an article in the *New York Times* titled "Ancient Nubian Artifacts Yield Evidence of Earliest Monarchy," the research by Professors Keith Seele and Bruce Williams of the Oriental Institute of the University of Chicago found that:

    "Evidence of the oldest recognizable monarchy in human history, preceding the rise of the earliest Egyptian kings by several generations, has been discovered in ancient artifacts from ancient Nubia in Africa.... The discovery is expected to stimulate a new appraisal of the origins of civilization in Africa, raising the question of to what extent later Egyptian culture may have derived its advanced political structure from the Nubians. The various symbols of Nubian royalty are the same as those associated, in later times, with Egyptian kings.

"The new findings suggest that the ancient Nubians may have reached this stage of political development... several generations before the earliest documented Egyptian king.

"Williams, in an article in the *Journal of African Civilizations*, called the discovery significant because the research had established Nubia as 'a birthplace of pharaonic civilization several generations before the rise of the first historic Egyptian dynasty.'"

42. Clarke, *New Dimensions*, p. 102. Clarke added: "I was and still am a great admirer of Julius Nyerere, but after he started kissing the Pope's ring, I began to question how one who condemns white people in the morning can worship them in the evening, without seeing this as a contradiction of what he stands for."
43. Clarke, *Who Betrayed?*, p. 155. This admonition, of course, applies equally to Afrikans in the United States, whose attachment to their American rulers, as can be seen from the citations of 20th century historians and 19th century political figures, is no less passionate and debilitating to liberation than for those Afrikans whose European colonial masters are British, French, Belgian, Dutch, Portuguese, Spanish, et al.
44. Clarke and Van Sertima, *Black Family*.
45. Ibid.
46. Clarke, *Who Betrayed?*, pp. 165–166.
47. Clarke and Van Sertima, *Black Family*.

John Henrik Clarke and Africana History: A Bibliographical Essay

James L. Conyers, Jr.

Introduction

The discipline of Africana Studies was veered in toil. In this battle, African Americans have steadily recommended a descriptive and evaluative analysis of scrutinizing the black experience from an Afrocentric perspective. Additionally, this concise pronouncement gives framework and ample meaning in the manner of studying the life and historical works of John Henrik Clarke. Clarke's endowments to the field of Africana history are extensive, focusing on African Civilizations. Community Studies on Harlem, New York; American Negro Short Stories; William Styron's Nat Turner; Black Titan; a biographical study of W.E.B. DuBois; and African World history are but a few of the titles and themes of the twenty-eight books he has either edited or authored.

As we commiserate his loss this year, we were bestowed in having the scholar rigor, steadfastness, and common-sense lucidity of one of the leading African thinkers in the Pan African world. I confine my analysis to the Pan African world inasmuch as, as we read and study the works of Clarke, it becomes obtrusive that many of us are just embarking to hear and reverberate his teachings on African world history. Equally important, the broader population of our society would find Clarke's analysis, colloquial training in history, and analytical explication view of the Pan African world as convalescent and partisan. Nonetheless, Clarke can readily be considered one of the most philoprogenitive (i.e., prolific) black historians groomed and socialized by the African American proletariat. For contextual clarification, Clarke used the term *proletarian* from an Afrocentric perspective, which does not articulate communism, but rather the emphasis is drawn to African Socialism-nationalism.

In contemporary times, the term *Afrocentric perspective* refers to the deep structural and critical examination of the Africana diasporic and continental experience, based on the cultural and historical experiences of Blacks. Although this term is used readily in the contemporary genre of critical and political theory, the interpretative analysis has a genesis that goes back to the late 1800s. During that period of time, African Americans used expressions such as folk culture, southern culture, and retention of African culture, with emphasis on the collective prism of Black American life, culture, and history. Essentially, the Afrocentric perspective is not a counter point of view but rather an alternative analysis of examining issues and schema of race, gender, class, ethnicity, policy, and language. Overall, the meaning centers on the fact that Clarke, like many of his contemporaries, may have not coined this term but was indeed precursory of critically analyzing and examining the black experience. Simply put, Clarke and other noted black historians such as Charles H. Wesley, Carter G. Woodson, Lorenzo Greene, Joel A. Rogers, Malcolm X, Fannie Lou Hamer, Ruby Dee, and Ossie Davis, can be considered precursors to the Afrocentric movement. To be straight forward, the concept of precursor acknowledges the transition and development in ideological repertoire from one generation to the next.

Research Query and Analysis

Query and a researchable problem statement center around the idea of two issues:

(1) Ideological repertoire; and (2) Alternative perspectives and analysis in examining the creation, consequences and systematic subordination of Africana diasporic and continental people. In reference to *ideological repertoire*, what is implied is to examine the cosmology in which Clarke operates from and presents in his scholarly writings. Equally important, *alternative perspectives* and views address how Clarke consistently applied a macro analysis of studying the causal explanations, models effect, and problems imposed on Africana people. Therefore, in this study, the theoretical construct employed is interdisciplinary, located within the contours of Africana Studies; the method is sociological, focusing on the use of secondary sources; and the analysis is Afrocentric, in the way of seeking to define, enumerate, and describe Africana people from their own primary base of identity.

Again, with emphasis to Clarke, he labored most of his life publishing, debating, teaching, and advocating for a collective global Pan Africanist perspective. Therefore, the process of collecting data in this study focused on selected essays written by Clarke and *The Oral History Biography of John Henrik Clarke*, written by Barbara Adams. Hence, this essay seeks to conduct a bibliographical study centered around the thematic approaches of Africana History, Black Nationalism/Cultural Nationalism/Pan Africanism, and the Social Construction of Race. Moreover, a qualitative assessment is necessary in this study, in the attempt to locate Clarke's writings on the aforementioned thematic approaches and to foster praxis from these ideas and works. Table 1.0 is an illustration of the scientific method and approach used in this study.

Table 1.0 – Theory, Methodology, and Analytical Framework

Theory	Ujimaa Paradigm: Emphasis is on Collective Work and Responsibility. An extracted variable from the Nguzo Saba, the implementation of this theoretical construct measures the phenomena on the basis of cosmology, ontology, axiology, epistemology, social ecology. The centerpiece of the analysis is located from an Afrocentric perspective.
Methodology	Secondary Analysis: Emphasis is on the use and review of secondary sources.
Analysis	Afrocentric Perspective: Emphasis is on describing and evaluating the ascribed phenomena, based on the historical and cultural experiences of Africana diasporic and continental people.

Again for contextual clarification, the term *scientific approach* applies to the theoretical paradigm employed and the procedure for collecting data; it is not to be confused with the articulation of scientism, which refers to: "the ideological use of science, defined by Eurocentrically, as an activity which sanctions all thought and behavior; that is, science becomes sacred, the highest standard of morality."

Social Ecology and Biographical Profile

The focus of this study is a bibliographical essay on selected articles and the *Oral History Biography of John Henrik Clarke*. Organizational structure of this essay focuses on thematic approaches. In order to examine the scholarship of Clarke, we need to locate him regarding his social ecology. *Social ecology* refers to the examination of social and environmental factors that shaped Clarke's views, norms, mores, and shared values. In this sense, we study him as a representative of his community rather than as an isolated individual who makes a contribution to world history. Clarke was born in Union Springs, Alabama on January 1, 1915. He was the son of Jon and Willella Mae Clarke. Later on, he moved just across the state border to Columbus, Georgia, where he attended grade school and high school. The time period of 1915 is an era of blacks beginning to migrate northward out of the deep of the south. Reviewing in a historical perspective, the period of 1877–1900 is what Rayford Logan refers to as the Nadir. Pertaining to the cessation of black history, 1901–1917 is referred to as the Age of Booker T. Washington. Others have used the term post bellum Blues 1865–1915, with reference to and emphasis on African American folklore, movements, and organizations. Conclusively, the essential point is that the historiography of this period shaped and formatted the ideas and philosophies of John Henrik Clarke. In reference to African American historiography, the period 1915 witnessed the following events and occurrences:

- Booker T. Washington dies on November 14, 1915;
- The NAACP protests against the showing of D.W. Griffith's "Birth of a Nation";
- Bishop Henry McNeal Turner, a black Pan Africanist dies;
- The United States Supreme Court, in Guinn v. The United States, outlaws the "Grandfather Clauses" used by southern states to deny blacks the opportunity to vote;
- Carter G. Woodson establishes the Association for the Study of Negro Life and History; also, the Journal of Negro History becomes the scholarly organ of the association;
- John Hope Franklin, the other noted and senior black historian in the United States, is born on January 2, 1915, in Rentiesville, Oklahoma; and Margaret Walker is born the same year, on July 7 in Birmingham, Alabama.

(As a side-bar note to the reader, John Oliver Killens is born on January 14, 1916, in Macon, Georgia; Dudley Randall is born on January 14, 1914, in Washington DC; Gwendolyn Brooks is born on June 7, 1917, in Topeka, Kansas; and the Noble Drew Ali establishes the Moorish Science Temple in Newark, New Jersey in 1913.)

Relative to American historiography, the following events and issues were taking place:

- It is the middle of the Woodrow Wilson presidential administration;
- "Birth of a Nation" premiered on March 3; this film justified the existence and advocacy of the KKK;
- President Wilson vetoes a bill indicating that immigrants have to pass a literacy test;
- The United States Supreme Court rules in the Coppage v. Kansas case that states do not have the right to deny hiring of an individual affiliated with and holding union membership;
- United States Marines occupy Haiti one day after the assassination of President Vilbrun Guillame Sam, and the United States signs a treaty on September 16th, making this country a protectorate of the US;
- Secretary of State William Jennings Bryan resigns from office regarding irreconcilable differences with President Wilson;

The historiography of African Americans and Americans has some overlap; however, the central point is that adversity, struggle, and perseverance appear to be common themes of the black experience in America during this period of time. Referencing to Clarke, Table 1.1 is a biographical profile of the subject.

Table 1.1 – Social Ecology and Profile of John Henrik Clarke

Year	Event
1915	Born to parents, John and Willella Clarke, in Union Springs, Alabama.
1933	Comes to New York City and begins studying creative writing at the League of American Writers.
1941–45	Military service in the United States Air Force during World War II; serves as a sergeant-major.
1948–52	Attends New York University.

1949–55	Executive Board Member of the Association for the Study of Afro-American Life and History.
1956–58	Attends the New School for Social Research; periodically teaches classes on Afro-American and African history.

Year	Event
1958–60	Assistant to Director of the Pittsburgh Courier, and feature writer.
1961	December 24th, marries Eugenia Evans.
1967	Member of board of directors of Langston Hughes Center for Child Development.
1967–70	Carter G. Woodson Visiting Professor in African History, Cornell University.
1969	Member of the Advisory Board of the Martin Luther King Jr. Library Center.
1969–73	Serves as President of the African Heritage Studies Association.
1970	Honorary Doctorate L.H.D. from the University of Denver.
1970–85	Serves as Associate Professor of Africana and Puerto Rican Studies at Hunter College, City University of New York.
1985	Serves as Professor Emeritus of Black and Puerto Rican Studies at Hunter College.
1992	Honorary Doctorate Litt. D. from the University of District of Columbia.
1993	Receives an Honorary Doctorate from Clark-Atlanta University.

Overall, the emphasis and purpose of using the social ecological summary of Clarke is to locate him in place, space, and time. Appropriately, this conjuncts with analysis, to study his works in a collective capacity. Hence, Clarke is the representative factor of an intellectual tradition of black historians and scholars who addressed the conventional wisdom of the Eurocentric hegemonic perspective and simultaneously offered an alternative Pan Africanist perspective.

Africana World History

History can be defined as the sum expression of human events shaped in the image and interests of the historian. Thus, when the term Africana world history is used, we are then referring to the study of Africana continental and diasporic phenomena, from an Afrocentric perspective. Congruently, Clarke approached Africana world history from a macro analysis, illustrating the patterns of subordination and colonialism among Africans throughout the global world. Ironically, when many of us read history in general, there is the procedure of examining history in local or communal levels, without drawing parallels and overlap with similar or other historical experiences.

Clarke's interest in history was mentored by Arthur Alfonso Schomburg. Schomburg was one of the most prolific bibliophiles in the United States. At the time of Clarke's arrival in New York, Schomburg's residency was in Harlem, New York, and during this period he was anchored at the 135th street New York Public library. In contemporary times, the 135th Street New York Public Library has been renamed to the *Schomburg Center for Research in Black Culture.* As a bibliophile, Schomburg was a collector and avid reader of Africana world history. It is believed that, this is the starting point to focus in Clarke's critical perception and interpretative analysis in examining Africana continental and diasporic culture within the framework of historical writings. Elinor Des Verney Sinnette describes the mentoring relationship between Schomburg and Clarke in the following manner:

> Two of the students John Henrik Clarke and Kenneth Clark, developed a special attachment to the well-liked curator and would themselves become recognized for their contributions to the black cause. A shy southern youth, John Clarke has read Schomburg's "The Negro Digs Up His Past" while still living in his hometown, Columbus, Georgia. When he arrived in New York City in 1932, one of the first places he visited was the 135th Street Branch Library to make an appointment with Arthur Schomburg. Told that an appointment was not necessary, Clarke climbed the three long flights and introduced himself to the curator. On that first visit, Schomburg began to direct Clarke's reading and became his first history teacher. Schomburg emphasized the need for Clarke to read books on world history if he wanted to develop better understanding of black history. Over the years Schomburg not only continued to guide the young Clarke in his reading and provide answers to his probing questions, he also served as one of Clarke's surrogate fathers. Many times, not content with the information he had obtained after a long

> day's reading, Clarke would accompany Schomburg to the subway, seeking additional insights. Never showing disinterest, the curator would use those few moments at day's end to satisfy the questions of his young inquisitor.

Simply put, Clarke, in the tradition like other lay historians, such as Schomburg and Joel Rogers developed a craftsmanship of examining and writing history from the macro to the micro, as it relates to Africans throughout the world. He writes about the inter-relationship of this macro and micro analysis this way: "In most cases, what is called 'African History' is only the history of Africa's contact with Europe, beginning with the slave trade. What is called 'Negro History' is generally the history of American slavery and subsequent effects." In another essay titled, "The Origin and Growth of Afro-American Literature," he discusses this issue again, in more contemporary terms and clarity, by stating:

> Contrary to the misconception which still prevails, the Africans were familiar with literature and art for many years before their contact with the western world. Before the breaking up of the social structure of the West African states Ghana, Mali, and Songhai, and the internal strife and chaos that made the slave trade possible, the forefathers of the Africans who eventually became slaves in the United States lived in a society where university life was fairly common and scholars were beheld with reverence.

Moreover, when Clarke assumed the presidential chair of the African Heritage Studies Association in 1969, becoming the organizations first national president, his aim and objective was to establish a study of Africana world history from a Pan Africanist perspective. Initially, this organization was affiliated with the African Studies Association. Consequently, because of the continual pattern of a scientific colonial view employed to study African phenomena, Clarke and some of his contemporaries opted to establish their own organization. Karenga notes that Clarke set out several fundamental goals for AHSA, such as:

1. To examine every aspect and approach to the history and culture of African people;
2. To project AHSA ideas and philosophies into as many organizations addressing issues and concerns of African people.
3. To challenge and query those individuals who claimed to have expertise on African history;
4. To use African history as a tool of analysis to effect the unity and collectivist of African people world-wide;

5. To establish an alternative epistemology placing emphasis on a critical Pan Africanist perspective (i.e., Afrocentricism and Cultural Nationalism)
6. To define African heritage in the context of understanding the inter-relationship and overlap of the Africana continental and diasporic experience.

As we aggregate the collective vocation of Clarke, his strategic and tactical planning in advocating a global Pan Africanist perspective was utilitarian and presented a common-sense approach to examining the creation and consequences of African people encountering subordinate group status. Lastly, he consistently challenged the accountability and responsibility of black scholars' breadth, depth, and scope of study, by writing:

> Because history is both topical and ancient and cannot be separated, there is no way to talk about Africana Studies without looking again at the roots of world history and the interplay among the histories of various peoples. The black historian, who knows his people's history and its relationship to the history of the world, should start with the bold assertions that Africa is the basis of world history, and that African people are the mothers and fathers of mankind. Black scholars, the world over, must be courageous enough to make this assertion and prepare themselves to prove it academically.

Black Nationalism, Cultural Nationalism, and Pan Africanism

The concept of nationalism can address at least five topologies of thought: (1) Cultural; (2) Religious; (3) Economic; (4) Bourgeois Reformism; and (5) Revolutionary Black Nationalism. However, in order to keep structure and organization of this study, I will focus on three schools of thought in nationalism. As we continue to discuss the thematic approaches outlined in this study, I will briefly offer working definitions for the terms: Black Nationalism; Cultural Nationalism; and Pan Africanism, with relevance to John Henrik Clarke.

In general the term Black Nationalism, refers to: an ideological repertoire that attempts to describe and evaluate the social, political, religious, cultural, and economic conditions of African Americans. Conditionally, this implies that an overthrow of the existing power apparatus has to come about in order for their to be functional change. Cultural Nationalism can be defined as: "black people having distinctive culture, life styles, values, philosophy, which are essentially different from those of white people. According to some cultural nationalists, black culture is but one of the many subcultures that make up pluralistic American society. Another variation stresses the superiority of black culture over (white) Western culture." Even more important, the concept of Pan Africanism provides a macro analysis of Black and Cultural Nationalism. Moreover, there are two basic functions of Pan Africanism: (1) global – the focus on the unification of Africans throughout the diaspora; and (2) continental – the focus being on the unification of Africans on the continent.

Clarke's ideas, philosophy, and research centered around a global Pan Africanist perspective. In an essay he wrote titled, "Towards Pan Africanism: The Third International Congress of Africanists," illustrated the praxis in Pan Africanist ideology which Clarke referred to, in March of 1974. Here we see delegations of Africans representative from the continent and the global world addressing issues such as: social and cultural development; neglected dimensions of life, history, and culture; economic and political development; existence of apartheid and racism; and the study of African history. This time period of the post sixties witnessed a cultural resurgence in Black pride, identity, and cultural affiliation with continental and Caribbean African communities.

In his essay titled, "The New Afro-American Nationalism," published in 1961, he identified four cluster groups in New York city that made significant contributions to the nationalist movement. Table 1.2 illustrates these organizations by name, leadership, year founded, and nationalist topology.

TABLE 1.2 – John Henrik Clarke's Analysis of Cutting Edge Black Nationalists Organizations During the Civil Rights Movement

Name	Leadership	Year	Topology
Nation of Islam	Elijah Muhammad	1932	Religious/ Economic
Muslim Brotherhood	Talib Ahmed Dawud	1950	Religious
United African Nationalist Movement	James R. Lawson	1948	Cultural/ Political
The Universal African Nationalist Movement	Benjamin Gibbs	1941	Cultural/ Economic
Cultural Association for Women of African Heritage	Aminata Moseka (a.k.a., Abby Lincoln)		Cultural/ Political
The African Nationalists Pioneer Movement	Carlos Cooks	1941	Cultural/ Economics

Again, in Clarke's writing, we see the emphasis on addressing the practicality and tactical planning of cultural nationalism, with the long term vision and scope of global Pan Africanism as the crux for his social and political views. Probably Clarke's best illustrative examples of discussing the concept of black nationalism and Pan African Africanism is his descriptive analysis of Marcus Garvey and Malcolm X. He cites Malcolm X's definition of black nationalism as:

> Our political philosophy will be black nationalism. Our economic and social philosophy will be black nationalism. Our cultural emphasis will be black nationalism. Many of our people aren't religiously inclined, so the Muslim Mosque, Inc., will be organized in such a manner as to provide for the active participation of all Negroes in our political, economic, and social programs, despite their religious or non-religious beliefs. The political philosophy of black nationalism means: We must control the politics and politicians of our community. They must no longer take orders from outside forces. We will organize and sweep out of office all Negro politicians who are puppets for outside forces.

Throughout the years Clarke views and philosophies changed, however, he remained steadfast and consistent regarding the contributions of Marcus Garvey and Malcolm X to the intellectual development and synthesis of Black Nationalism and Pan Africanism.

In closing on the issue of Clarke's view, opinions, and philosophies concerning the conceptual framework of nationalism, he identified the institutional and social policy structures of the maintenance, advancement, and transitional phases of racism and racialism, practiced in the United States and other foreign countries.

Social Construction of Race

In contemporary times the concept and idea of race has been deconstructed to have meaningless purpose, cause or consequence. Racism can be defined as the doctrine supporting the idea that one race is superior to others. Racialism then can be defined as: one who advocates and believes in racism, whereas they appear to be unconscious of their socialization to be a racist and believe, they think therefore they exist (i.e., racial discrimination, denying the opportunities to equal access to scarce and valued resources). Citing a cliche from John Mbiti, whose analysis is continually xenocentric, his analysis regarding the African conceptualization of existence is practical, whereas he says, I am Because We Are and Because We Are Therefore I am.

Thus, in discussing the issue of the continual systematic subordination of Africana people, few have engaged in dialog of substantial merit. Substantial merit, whereas, through the layers of deconstructed literature, history and philosophy, the casualties of black oppression have not been addressed with balance. Moreover, these points of discovery are relative to the life, works, and interpretative analysis of Clarke. It is as a result of the continual pattern of the employment a Eurocentric hegemonic perspective that scholars such as Clarke and his contemporaries were not so much concerned with revisionist history, but rather, alternative views and perspective aligned within a global Pan Africanist methodology.

Furthermore, then, the concept of the social construction of race is valuable, however, short sighted in examining variables surrounding dual labor markets, dual consciousness, and the suppression of black culture. Most of the sociological studies in America does not query or adequately explain how past occurrences of racism, prejudice, and discrimination advance a self-fulfilling cycle that perpetuates an informal economy on an international and domestic level.

CONCLUSION

As I wrap up this essay, again the effect set forth, was to examine thematic approaches in the structure of a bibliographical essay. The discussion of the relevance, significance, and purpose of African American history is one of debate that has existed over the last century. Equally important, to discuss or examine the works of a black historian who dismissed and did not accept the conventional wisdom of the Eurocentric hegemonic perspective, becomes a tier of controversy and struggle in itself. Thus, the struggle, courage, valor, and commitment to the race is exemplified by Clarke and others – allows black scholars to exist and work within academies of higher learning in contemporary times. Fervently, this issue needs to be addressed as scholars present a de-passe attitude and loss of memory concerning those who have come before us and the dues and sacrifices they made in principal and merit and their loss of monetary and social exposure. Lastly, Clarke's name has to be kept alive within the academies of higher learning within the curricula, within faculties memory and ethos, and within the mission and thrust of Africana Studies. Yaa Asantewaa – Nzuri Sana-Yimhotep!

ENDNOTES

1. John Henrik Clarke, "The New Afro-American Nationalism," *Freedomways*, Fall 1961, pp. 294.

2. Marimba Ani, Yurgu: *An African-centered Critique of European Cultural Thought and Behavior*, Trenton, New Jersey: African World Press, 1994, pp. xxvi. Ani in this book has produced a critical and invaluable study examining the philosophy and intellectual thought of European culture.
3. Alton Hornsby, *Chronology of African American History*, Detroit: Gale Research Incorporated, 1991, pp. xxviii–xxix.
4. Jeffrey C. Stewart, *1001 Things Everyone Should Know About African American History*, New York: Main Street Books, Doubleday, 1996, p. 254. Stewart's book is a reference work that examines African American history and culture. An insightful text that reviews in chronology and context the African American experience.
5. Alton Hornsby, Editor, *Chronology of African American History*, Detroit: Gale Research Incorporated, pp. 66–67.
6. *Chronicle of America*, New York: Dorling Kindersley, 1995, pp. 586–589.
7. Maulana Karenga, *Introduction to Black Studies*, Los Angeles, California: University of Sankore Press, 1997.
8. Elinor Des Verney Sinnette, *Arthur Alfonso Schomburg: Black Bibliophile and Collector*, Detroit: The New York Public Library and Wayne State University Press, 1989, pp. 182–83. This article identifies the mentoring relationship between Schomburg and Clarke. Also, the author points out the curricula emphasis and direction of Clarke critical analysis and insight in examining the black experience.
9. John Henrik Clarke, "Black Power and Black History," *Negro Digest*, February 1969, p. 13.
10. John Henrik Clarke, "The Origin and Growth of Afro-American Literature," in Molefi Kete Asante and Abu Abarry, *African Intellectual Heritage*, Philadelphia: Temple University Press, 1996, p. 218.
11. Maulana Karenga, *Introduction to Black Studies*, Los Angeles: University of Sankore Press, 1993, pp. 29–30. The Karenga text is considered by many as one of the leading intellectual studies conducted on African Americans. Moreover, his citations on Clarke illustrate the irreconcilable differences among the constituency which established the African Heritage Studies Association. Briefly, to mention from this organization grew other cluster groups such as the Association for the Study of Classical African Civilization.
12. John Henrik Clarke, "Africana Studies: A Decade of Change, Challenge, and Conflict," p. 32, in James E. Turner, Editor, *The Next Decade: Theoretical and Research Issues in Africana Studies*, Ithaca, New York: Africana Studies and Research Center, Cornell University, 1984.
13. Raymond L. Hall, *Black Separatism in the United States*, Hanover, New Hampshire: University Press of New England, 1978.
14. John Henrik Clarke, "Towards Pan Africanism: The Third International Congress of Africanists," *Black World*, March 1974, pp. 71–76.

15. John Henrik Clarke, Editor, *Malcolm X: The Man and His Times,* Trenton, New Jersey: Africa World Press, 1990, p. xxi.
16. Ellis Cashmore, *Dictionary of Race and Ethnic Relations,* New York: Routledge Press, 1996, p. 305.

John Henrik Clarke's Rebellion in Rhyme

Raymond R. Patterson

In the Introduction to *Rebellion in Rhyme: The Early Poems of John Henrik Clarke*, published in 1948 and republished in 1991, Clarke writes, and I quote:

> Most of the poems in this volume were written when I was between the age of 18, in the summer of 1933, and the age of 26, in the summer of 1941. These poems reflect my early beginnings as a social thinker and as a young man, straight out of the South during my early years in Harlem reflecting on the African condition and the awareness learned from associating with a diversity of politically-left movements and the revival of the Garvey movement during the Italian-Ethiopian War, 1930-1936. I was a member of the Harlem History Club then functioning out of the Harlem YMCA on 135th Street. I was active in the National League of Negro Youth and, for a short period, in the Young Communist League. I was discovering the world and social change and wondering what role my people would play in the change for a better world. The writing of these poems at this juncture in my personal development was a form of therapy, a ventilation of my inner self, an airing of my grievances and a celebration of the fact of my being alive. (p. xi)

Clarke goes on to say that most of the poems in the collection (many of which first appeared in publications like *Crisis*, *The Chicago Defender*, and *The Pittsburgh Courier*) were written "on the spur of the moment, with little rewriting," except for two poems, "Sing Me a New Song" and "Meditations of a European Farmer." (pp. xi–xii)

"Meditations of a European Farmer" is typical of the poems in the collection. Its nine lines of rhymed verse present the thoughts of a farmer whose fields have been ravaged by war and who wonders if the land which once provided "shelter and bread," will survive the onslaught. By contrast, "Sing Me a New Song" is in free verse and is the longest of the 98 poems in the book.

A reading of this poem and a look at some of its references should enrich our understanding of John Henrik Clarke during his early beginnings as a social thinker.

Sing Me a New Song
Sing me a new song, young black singer,
Sing me a song with some thunder in it,
And a challenge that will
Drive fear into the hearts of those people
Who think that God has given them
The right to call you their slave.
Sing me a song of strong men growing stronger
And bold youth facing the sun and marching.
Sing me a song of an angry sharecropper,
Who is not satisfied with his meager share
Of the produce that he squeezed from the earth
While watering the earth with his sweat and tears.
Sing me a song of two hundred million Africans
Revising the spirit of Chaka, Moshesk and Menelik,
And shouting to the world:
"This is my land and I shall be free upon it!"
Put some reason in my song and some madness too.
Let it be the kind of reason
Frederick Douglass had,
When he was fighting against slavery in America.
Let the madness be the kind of madness
Henri Christophe had when
He was driving Napoleon's army from Haitian soil.
Sing me a song with some hunger in it, and a challenge too.
Let the hunger be the kind of hunger
Nat Turner and Denmark Vesey had,
When they rose from bondage and inspired
Ten thousand black hands to reach for freedom.
Let the challenge be the kind of challenge
Chrispus Attucks had
While dying for American Independence.
Don't put "I ain't gonna study war no more" in my song.
Sing me a song of people hungry for freedom,

Who will study war until they are free!

The title of the poem, which is repeated in the first line, addresses a "young black singer." It implies that the old song is no longer adequate. The speaker has a clear idea of what new song is needed and what its content should be. The new song should have thunder, challenge, reason, madness, hunger challenge, challenge, and more challenge. In seven stanzas these symbols are given specific references in literary works, historical events and figures, as well as circumstances and ideas touching the Black struggle for freedom in America, Africa and the Caribbean.

We can only speculate on the identity of the young black singer addressed in the poem, or on the specific old song being rejected. The tradition of militancy and protest in the Harlem Renaissance poetry of Langston Hughes, Claude McKay and others still survived in post-Depression African American poetry of the 1940s, but it was muted. A less socially and politically oriented poetry, like that of a Countee Cullen, however, enjoyed national recognition. Two important exceptions to this were Gwendolyn Brooks's 1945 collection, *Street in Bronzeville*, and three years earlier, in 1942, Margaret Walker's award-winning volume *For My People*. The title poem of Walker's book could have been the seed for Clarke's "Sing Me a New Song." In its concluding lines, Walker writes, "Let the martial songs be written, let the dirges disappear. Let a race of men now rise and take control."

Perhaps the old song with its absence of militancy that Clarke rejects can be seen in an Arna Bontemps poem, "The Day Breakers," published in the influential 1925 anthology, *The New Negro*, edited by Alain Locke.

The Daybreakers
We are not come to wage a strife
With swords upon this hill;
It is not wise to waste the life
Against a stubborn will.
Yet would we die as some have done:
Beating a way for the rising sun.

In tracing sources, we are more secure in concluding that Clarke's call to "Sing me a song with thunder in it" reflects his knowledge of Frederick Douglass's 1852 speech, *The Meaning of the Fourth of July for the Negro*, condemning Americans who claim ignorance of the realities of slavery: "For it is not light that is needed, but fire; it is not gentle shower, but thunder." Clarke wants a song that would also challenge ignorance and strike fear in the hearts of those who use biblical scripture to justify slavery.

The second stanza of Clarke's "Sing Me a New Song" calls for "a song of strong men growing stronger." This is a clear reference to Sterling A. Brown's well-known poem, "Strong Men," first published in his 1932 collection *Southern Road*. The poem has as its epigraph a line from poet Carl Sandburg, "The strong men keep coming on." It recounts a brutal history of African Americans, from enslavement in Africa, to proscription in the slums of contemporary America, and how their survival has been sustained by song. It ends with the hopeful refrain:

> One thing they cannon prohibit –
> The strong men... coming on
> The strong men gittin' stronger.
> Strong men.... .
> Stronger.... .

Clark no doubt first heard the song of "bold youth facing the sun and marching" in the Langston Hughes poem "Youth," appearing in Alain Locke's *The New Negro*:

> Youth
> We have tomorrow
> Bright before us
> Like a flame.
> Yesterday
> A night-gone thing,
> A sun-down name.
> And dawn-today
> Broad arch above the road we came.
> We march!

Clarke's song of the angry sharecropper dissatisfied with the small share of what his labor produced is the song he must have heard in Sterling A. Brown's poem "Old Lem," published in 1939. It begins:

> I talked to old Lem
> and old Lem said:
> "They weigh the cotton
> They store the corn
> We only good enough
> To work the rows;

They run the commissary
They keep the books
We gotta be grateful
For being cheated;

"Sing Me a New Song's" third stanza turns to Africa. It calls for "a song of two hundred million Africans." The song must *revise* the spirit of Chaka, the 19th century Zulu military genius who unified the peoples of South Africa and held back European colonial expansion; Moshesk, the Basuto leader and founder of the Bantu Confederation, whose 1862 military alliance with the British enabled his South African nation to resist encroachments by the Boers and Cecil Rhodes; and Menelik, no doubt Menelik II, the emperor of Ethiopia who in the 1895 Ethiopian-Italian War defeated the Italian Army attempting to invade his country.

Clarke uses the word *revise* in his instruction to the "young black singer." It is not enough to revive the spirit of past leaders. The lessons of history must be used in the new song. The cruelty of Chaka in achieving his goals, the mistake of a Moshesk in allying with a colonial power that later overwhelmed him, and the decision of a Menelik II to allow the defeated Italian Army to withdraw, only to have it return in 1935 and conquer his country, should not be in the new song.

Nevertheless, the song should not be completely rational. "Put some reason in my song and some madness too," the poem declares. The fourth stanza offers Frederick Douglass's eloquent arguments against slavery as an example of the reason needed. The madness is that of Henri Christophe, the 19th century revolutionary Haitian leader who helped overthrow slavery and defeat Napoleon's invading army, but who eventually committed suicide.

Besides thunder, challenge, reason and madness, the song must have "some hunger in it, and a challenge too." The hunger must be for freedom, like that which inspired Nat Turner, the Virginia slave who in 1831 planned and led a bloody insurrection; and Denmark Vesey, a free South Carolina black who, over a period of several years planned a wide-spread slave rebellion to begin July 1822, but was discovered before his plans could be carried out. The challenge in the song must be that of a Chrispus Attucks, the runaway slave and seaman and martyr of the American Revolution, who died in the Boston Massacre at the front of an angry crowd protesting the British occupation of Boston.

"Don't put 'I ain't gonna study war o more' in my song," declares the final stanza of the poem - in other words, no spirituals, no sorrow songs. The challenge t biblically sanctioned oppression sounded in the opening stanza of the poem is repeated in this rejection of a passive acceptance of oppression. "Let the marital songs be written, let the dirges disappear," said the poet Margaret Walker. "Sing me a song," echoes Clarke, "of a people hungry for freedom,/ Who will study war until they are free!"

The word *rhyme* in the book's title, *Rebellion in Rhyme,* may suggest Clarke's feelings about the literary quality of the poems. However, the alliterative linking of *rebellion* with *rhyme* makes an important statement. It asserts a connection between rebellion, a social/historical activity, and rhyme, a literary/cultural pattern. It places the struggle for freedom within a pattern represented by art and culture.

Rebellion in Rhyme joins artistic creation and activism, and is John Henrik Clarke's legacy as a poet. It reveals his early thinking and forecasts concerns he would have throughout his career. He believed that knowledge and scholarship must serve in the ongoing struggle for freedom. His role as an editor at *Freedomways: A Quarterly Review of the Negro Freedom Movement* was consistent with this. The Summer 1963 issue, "Harlem: A Community in Transition," which he edited, contains articles of analysis and social criticism along with work by James Baldwin, Sterling Brown, Langston Hughes, and his own short story, "Revolt of the Angels."

His Introduction to *American Negro Short Stories,* published in 1966, observes that the writers included in the anthology "have questioned and challenged all previous interpretations of American Negro life. In so doing they have created the basis for a new American literature." (p. xix) Similarly, his editing in 1968 of *William Styron's Nat Turner: Ten Black Writers Respond,* is consistent with this aim of challenging false interpretations of black life. The book is a trenchant response to distortions of history by William Styron in depicting Nat Turner for his 1967 Pulitzer Prize novel, *The Confessions of Nat Turner.*

John Henrik Clarke instructs his "young black singer" to "Sing Me a New Song." Long before he became Director of the Heritage Teaching Program of Harlem Youth Opportunities Unlimited, and decades before achieving recognition as a distinguished historian, writer, editor, activist and university professor, Clarke set a task for black youth, to write a song to inspire a people hungry for freedom. It is the task Black poets of the 1960s and '70s attempted to fulfill. Clarke's *Rebellion in Rhyme* challenges us today. Its most successful poem, "Sing Me a New Song" is the primer of a great teacher.

Chapter 2

Black Nationalism

Black Power and Black History

John Henrik Clarke

Reprinted from: *Negro Digest*, February 1969, pp. 13–20.

> It is not really a "Negro revolution" that is upsetting the country. What is upsetting the country is a sense of its own identity. If, for example, one managed to change the curriculum in all the schools so that Negroes learned more about themselves and their real contributions to this culture, you would be liberating not only Negroes, you'd be liberating white people who know nothing about their own history. And the reason is that if you are compelled to lie about one aspect of anybody's history, you must lie about it all. If you have to lie about my real role here, if you have to pretend that I hoed all that cotton just because I loved you, then you have done something to yourself. You are mad.
>
> – James Baldwin from "A Talk to Teachers," December 1963

Figuratively speaking, the concept of Black Power and Black History are twins that were fathered by the same historical experience. This concept was created to counteract another concept: that the people of African descent had no history worthy of respect. The Europeans who started the slave trade and the colonial system that followed needed to propagate this concept in order to justify their action.

The present day young black militants are asking, in many ways, why the word *history* is so limited when it is applied to their people. They are beginning to learn (belatedly) that history, depending on how it is manipulated, can be either an instrument of oppression or of liberation. In most cases, what is called "African History" is only the history of Africa's contact with Europe, beginning with the slave trade. What is called "Negro History" is generally the history of American slavery and subsequent effects.

The Europeans who started the slave trade in the fifteenth century had to forget – or pretend to forget – all they had previously known about Africa's contribution to the development of mankind.

The present-day Black Power and Black History advocates are trying to restore what the slave trade and the system of economic oppression took away. Their fight has long roots and it was not started by Stokely Carmichael or H. Rap Brown.

In a formal sense the concept of Black Power started in the nineteenth century, concurrent with the many attempts to restore Black men to an honorable place in history. The concept of Black Power confuses most people because they are looking for a complicated system. Black Power means no more or less than the right to determine your own destiny, starting with the control of your own communities. This is the same thing that every ethnic group in America has – or is trying to get. Black Power without a respect for Black History is meaningless. Until the essential manhood of a people is respected, no power in their hands is effective.

In a speech made in Cuba last year, Stokely Carmichael, while addressing himself to the subject "Black Power and the Third World," said this:

> Since 1966, the cry of the rebellions has been "Black Power." In this cry, there was an ideology implied which the masses understood instinctively. It is because we are powerless that we are oppressed and it is only with power that we can make the decisions governing our lives and our communities … Black Power is more than a slogan; it is a way of looking at our problems and the beginning of a solution. Because our color has been used as a weapon to oppress, we must use our color as a weapon of liberation. This is the same as other people using their nationality as a weapon for their liberation… This coming together around our race was an inevitable part of our struggle. We recognize, however, that this is not the totality, only the necessary beginning.

Then, while emphasizing the need for the cultural restoration of a people he said:

> Black Power recognizes that while we are made to feel inferior, this is only that we can be easily exploited. Color and culture were and are key in our oppression, therefore our analysis of history and our economic analysis are rooted in these concepts. With power we will take our birthright, because

> it was with power that our birthright was taken from us... Black Power not only addresses itself to exploitation, but to the problem of cultural integrity.

The nineteenth century black militants, and some before them, were saying essentially the same thing in different ways.

The fight against the distortion and suppression of the true history of the Africans and Afro-Americans was started long before the Civil War by "free Negroes" and escaped slaves who had learned to read and write.

The back-to-Africa idea has been a recurring theme in the lives of Black Americans for more than a hundred years. The thought was strong during the formative years of the Colonization Society and some of the most outstanding Black men of the eighteenth and nineteenth centuries came under its persuasion. In the middle of the nineteenth century, while the issue of slavery was being debated in most of the country, the feeling for Africa among American blacks was growing stronger. Publications like Freedoms' Journal and Douglass Monthly, edited by Frederick Douglass, called attention to the plight of the people of Africa as well as Black Americans.

As far back as 1881, the renowned scholar and benefactor of West Africa, Dr. Edward Wilmot Blyden, speaking on the occasion of his inauguration as President of Liberia College, sounded the note for the organized teaching of the culture and civilization of Africa and decried the fact that the world's image of Africa was not in keeping with Africa's true status in world history. I quote from his address on this occasion:

> The people generally are not yet prepared to understand their own interests in the great work to be done for themselves and their children. We shall be obliged to work for some time to come not only without the popular sympathy we ought to have but with utterly inadequate resources.
>
> In all English-speaking countries the mid of the intelligent Negro child revolts against the descriptions of the Negro given in elementary books, geographies, travels, histories...
>
> Having embraced or at least assented to these falsehoods about himself, he concludes that his only hope of rising in the scale of respectable manhood is to strive for what is most unlike himself and most alien to his peculiar tastes. And whatever his literary attainments or acquired ability, he fancies that he must grind at the mill which is provided for him, putting in material furnished by his hands, bringing no contribution from his own field; and of course nothing comes out but what is put in.

Dr. Eric Williams places the origin of this Revolution in historical perspective and calls attention to its early development:

> When, in 1492, Columbus, representing the Spanish monarchy, discovered the New World, he set in train the long and bitter international rivalry over colonial possessions for which, after four and a half centuries, no solution has yet been found. Portugal, which had initiated the movement of international expansion, claimed the new territories on the ground that they fell within the scope of a papal bull of 1455 authorizing her to reduce to servitude all infidel people. The two powers (Spain and Portugal), to avoid controversy, sought arbitration and, as Catholics, turned to the Pope – a natural and logical step in an age when the universal claims of the Papacy were still unchallenged by individual and governments. After carefully sifting the rival claims, the Pope issued, in 1493, a series of papal bulls which established a line of demarcation between the colonial possessions of the states: the East went to Portugal and the West went to Spain.

Though the announcement of the fact came much later, the European "scramble for Africa" and subsequently, Asia and North America started with this fact. The labor and raw materials of Africa, Asia, South America and the Wet Indies financed the European Industrial Revolution.

The Africans who were brought to the new World against their will were dehumanized, and in most cases, deculturalized. They were neither respected Africans nor accepted New World Americans. They were renamed, and became a marginal branch of the human family now referred to as Negroes. The Europeans needed a rationale for their actions and a rationale was created with supporting concepts. The cruelest concept ever devised by the mind of man was created to support the slave trade and the colonial system that followed – the concept of race and the assumption that there are superior and inferior races. The Africans were depicted as a people without a history who had never properly handled power and who, certainly, had made no contribution to the development of human cultures. And thus the seeds of the present-day conflict were planted.

Black History and Self-Identity

The American Federation of Teachers Conference on "Racism in Education" held in Washington, DC on December 8, 9, and 10, 1966, set in motion much of the present action and the debate about Black History and how it should be taught in the public schools.

The noted actor, Ossie Davis, addressed the conference on the first day. His opening remarks were: "Those of us who are concerned, who are caught up, who really want to be involved in the revolution, must be prepared at this conference to tear aside our most private thoughts and prejudices... ."

The tone or the conference had been set. For two days more than 1,500 teachers and educators examined and indicated the American educational system. They were told that a curtain of ignorance hangs over the school systems of this nation and that our children are not being educated to face the realities of this nation and this world. Cases of deliberate distortion of the role that the Black Americans have played in the making of this country were pointed out. And it was further stated that everyone from professional textbook writers to missionaries had participated in this distortion.

Ossie Davis cited the English language as a basic transmitter of prejudice. In his speech entitled, "The English Language is My Enemy," he said that he counted 120 synonyms for the term "blackness" in Roget's Thesaurus, half of which were grossly unfavorable.

Davis argued that right from the time a black child learns the English language he learns 60 ways to despise himself, and a white child learns 60 ways to aid and abet the crime.

Keith E. Baird, a New York school teacher, who followed Ossie Davis, talked about the importance of ethnic identification for Afro-Americans. Mr. Baird, who is a teacher of languages spoke of the respected place in history, as celebrated in the Jewish holiday of Hanukkah of the Maccabees of Biblical times. He also pointed out that in the process of ethnic identification, not only a person's individual attributes are considered, but the "cultural identification of this group."

Baird presented to the conference a resolution that he urged it to adopt, the wording of which was:

> To say that the slavery-connected word "Negro" should be abandoned, and in its place the words "Afro" or "African-American" be applied to persons of African descent in the United States in all places where such reference to ethnic descent is appropriate.

At a later conference session concerning resolutions, this one was unanimously adopted.

In his presentation, Mr. Baird had defined what the cry for Black History is about – it is about the search for a people's identity and their need for a new image of themselves. The Black Americans are trying to locate themselves on the map of human geography. This explains the growing preference for the words "Black African" and "Afro-American." These words show how the Black Americans relate to a land, a history and a culture.

In a number of other conferences sponsored by the local branches of the American Federation of Teachers and the UFT, the teachers agreed on plans to implement courses in Black History. The main conferences were held in Detroit (May 11–13, 1967) and in Chicago (March 22–24, 1968), and conferences in Denver and St. Louis followed. While many of the white teachers clearly admitted that racism is rampant in the American educational system, very few of them had any basic plan concerning what to do about it. Their reluctance to commit themselves to the correction of this racism caused a lot of black teachers to form separate organizations, some within the framework of the American Federation of Teachers and the UFT. The Chicago Black Teachers Caucus was one. In New York City the Afro-American Teachers' Association was another.

Still another organization, the Conference of Afro-American Educators, which met in Chicago in June 1968, shows the best potential of becoming a nation-wide force to affect change in the educational system. At this conference Donald Freeman, who renamed himself Baba Lamumba, defined education as it relates to black people:

> What we understand by education is the application of all one's knowledge for the benefit of the collective which in turn will benefit each individual within the collective. To this end what must constitute a basic part of one's education is the understanding of people rather than things. We realize that once people understand themselves, their knowledge of things is facilitated, that the exclusive knowledge of things does not guarantee knowledge of people and in fact contributes to the erosion, disintegration, and destruction of the creativity of man.
>
> Therefore, education must (1) teach Black people who they are, (2) teach Black people what they are fighting for, (3) teach Black people who they must identify with, (4) teach Black people where their loyalty must lie, (5) teach Black people what must be done, (6) teach Black people how to do it, and (7) teach Black people that the destinies of all Black people are inseparably linked whether we are in North, Central, or South America, the West Indies, Europe, Asia, or Africa.
>
> Now there must be a complete unity of all aspects of one's life and in particular education must be indelibly linked with one's life processes for the benefit of each Black man and woman and all Black people. Those who have knowledge primarily from books must be linked with those who have knowledge from the streets and vice versa to confront and solve all the problems of Black people. Education must assure that all of what one learns

> can be and will be applied to concrete practical problems and their solutions. If our people can throw Molotov cocktails in white stores, we can certainly throw Molotov cocktails in our minds. Mathematics, physics, electronics, sociology, religion and other sciences must not be viewed as abstractions, but comprehended as the concentrated experiences of man's inter-relationships with man, nature and the universe to mold and control his own destiny.

It is obvious that the American educational establishment is not ready to correct itself and implement these suggestions that it would consider extreme. This would not only be tantamount to correcting itself, it would also be tantamount to repudiating itself. At the base of the grievance of the Black teachers and growing numbers of black people is the fact that they have been educated or miseducated in a system that has yet to acknowledge that they are an integral part of American or Western Civilization. Both the clamor for Black Power and Black History are the clamor of people to enter the mainstream of a society and to institute dynamic social reform – or to replace that society. The most far-reaching reforms will be in the field of education. Control is the key word in the school situation because it implies power to act in one's best interest at a time and a place of one's choosing. The educational establishment could digest or tolerate decentralization because the school system would still be run in the main by the educational establishment, which is a force operating outside the local community. When community control is added to decentralization, a whole new area of power is defined. This means that the community will have the right to hire and fire teachers and to control the massive budget of the school system that is now a major American industry.

In an address in Ann Arbor, Michigan on May 25, 1968, Dr. Grace Boggs said in effect that the question of Black control of the schools has now become a question of survival for all black people. Urban school systems are disintegrating before their eyes to the point where their actual physical and mental safety are at stake. Black children and their parents have lost the traditional respect for the teachers and principals of their schools because of the growing alienation between the school and the community. The mass media, principally television, have taught these children to become suspicious of most large establishments, especially police forces and governmental agencies that make promises which they do not keep.

Many of the white teachers in the large educational systems in cities like New York, Detroit, Philadelphia, Chicago, and Los Angeles, come to the system with preconceived notions about the ability of the Black child to learn. Instead of teaching him they spend a lot of time convincing themselves that the children are unteachable. They do not bring their best teaching ability to these communities because they do not respect the children or the community enough to do so. In addition to being poor teachers for the Black community, these teachers are not even good baby-sitters. In a lot of cases they are arrogant, unfulfilled and insecure people, long overdue for analysis. Very often the Black child and the Black community become whipping-boys for their neuroses. Community control would mean that these teachers can be transferred or fired, once their lack of qualifications have been proven.

There is no attempt to drive all white teachers out of any Black community. However, teachers who fall within the above description will not be secure under any form of community control.

Keith E. Baird, director of the Afro-American History and Cultural Unit of the Board of Education, gave the following explanation of decentralization and community control at the Summer Forum at Columbia University in August of 1968 on the Black Experience.

> I am going to talk about decentralization in the public schools and its implications. I use the term "decentralization" largely because it is the one that is generally used. Now, most words that begin with this prefix "de-" suggest a kind of fall from grace, and I think that discussion about the changes that are being sought in the school system suffer somewhat from this semantic difficulty. I rejoice, however, to see that in this booklet the "Decentralization" means re-forming the present school system in New York City into largely autonomous school districts, joined with the central education agency into a city-wide federation.
>
> Now this is a fairly decent and workable definition, but what does it actually mean in terms of the "Black Experience," the context in which we have come together to discuss this matter? We seem to have two separate questions before us: "decentralization" and "community control." Of course the two are not necessary.

Now there is no problem about white people controlling the schools, because that, of course, is what has always happened. The schools are run by white people: the majority of the teachers are white, and the people who administer the schools are in great part white. Thus we have what are essentially white schools, reflecting white interests, a white self-concept, and white culture. The question of community control comes in because certain enclaves, certain new ethnic enclaves, will not be having greater control, or at any rate be in a better position to exercise control over the schools their children go to—proved, of course, that the rules and regulations of the New York City Board of Education actually permit this to happen.

Thus we come to what is really the crux of the situation, namely, the control of schools in Afro-American and Puerto Rican areas by the Afro-American and Puerto Rican communities, particularly because these communities have not been significantly represented until now at the policy-making level in educational affairs. What community control boils down to is simply this: are we or are we not going to let Black people and Puerto Rican people really tell teachers what to do? Especially, tell white teachers what to do? And so on. That is really what this whole thing boils down to, and we may as well face up to it.

Because most of decentralization and community control talk in New York City is centered around IS 201 in Harlem and Ocean Hill Brownsville in Brooklyn, it would be well to show the essence of the background f this conflict.

The crucial issue of the IS 201 controversy is the poor quality of education in-ghettos such as Harlem.

From the first through the twelfth grade, and increasingly larger proportion of ghetto youth perform below their grade level in reading and math. Eighty-seven percent of the pupils in the Harlem school district are below grade level. Better than two-thirds of the pupils drop out before graduation from high school. Daniel Schreiber, the former assistant superintendent of District 4, in which IS 201 is located, verified these figures.

The parents of school district 4 were willing to accept the promise of the Board of Education that integration would help solve the problem of poor education for their children.

When 201 was proposed as a junior high school as far back as 1958, parents objected on the grounds that construction of the a school at the proposed site would create another segregated school. As late as 1965, Dr. Bernard Donavan maintained that 201 would be an integrated school. He even alluded to having the school related to a University accompanied by special programs. By February of 1966, Daniel Schreiber maintained that 201 would be integrated, but by this time, "integrated" had come to mean representative groups of black and Puerto Rican children.

As early as March 28, community representatives were demanding the establishment of a community group to which teachers would be responsible in addition to the demand for an integrated school. Parents' opposition to the Board of Education's response (or lack of response) to these demands canceled the scheduled opening of 201 for the spring term of 1966. The school district was gerrymandered without the consultation of the community to create a student body of Puerto Ricans and Negroes.

"Integration" gives way to "quality education." By the end of the summer, the Board of Education had to admit that it had no plan for truly integrating I.S. 201. The parents, realizing that the Board of Education had no intention of integrating the schools of Harlem focused attention on the basic problem of improving the quality of education in Harlem with the realization that it would in reality have to be segregated.

There is agreement between the parents and the Board of Education that the Board has failed to integrate the Harlem schools. There is also agreement between the parents and the Board that the quality of education in Harlem is low. The disagreement lies in the means used to improve education in Harlem upon the Board of Education whose present structure system to meet the needs of the ghetto community. The composition of the board, how its members are selected and its source of power indicate the distance that exists between the body that makes educational policy and the community for whom the policy is made.

The Ocean Hill-Brownsville decentralization experiment in Brooklyn, New York was spoiled by success. The Local School Board, consisting mainly of parents from the community, took their jobs seriously and asked that a number of teachers who they deemed incompetent by transferred. This move seemed to have shocked and angered both the Board of Education and the head of the United Federation of Teachers. This abrupt exercising of power by the Local School Board and their Unity Administrator came unexpectedly.

The two large black ghettos of Brooklyn merge at Ocean Hill. Its inhabitants include a growing number of Puerto Ricans. Nothing of a dynamic nature was expected of these slumdwellers.

In September 1966, the controversy around IS 201 in Harlem had a profound effect on the Ocean Hill-Brownsville school district. That month a group of parents in Harlem demanded that the Board of Education respect their right to select the principal for IS 201. These parents were asking, for the first time, to have a voice in the administration of the schools in their community. The contagious cry for community control was not spreading beyond Harlem. It did not bypass the Ocean Hill-Brownsville School District in Brooklyn.

After some protracted agitation, the Board of Education allowed the people of Ocean Hill to form an administrative unit, with the understanding that the Board would relinquish some of its authority to this unit. The Administrative Unit and the local Governing Board succeeded thought it would use. This is the basis of their trouble with the Board of Education never thought it would use. This is the basis of their trouble with the Board of Education and the United Federation of Teachers.

The dispute between the people of Ocean Hill-Brownsville on one side and the Board of Education and United Federation of Teachers on the other side might well be a sad indication of what will soon be a national crisis in education. The cry for Black Power and Black History has rekindled a long smoldering fire that will, no doubt, affect major changes in the educational, political and economic structure of the United States.

The New Afro-American Nationalism

John Henrik Clarke

Reprinted from: *Freedomways*, Fall 1981, pp. 285–295

The February, 1961, riot in the gallery of the United Nations in protest against the foul and cowardly murder of Patrice Lumumba introduced the new Afro-American Nationalism. This nationalism is only a new manifestation of old grievances with deep roots. Nationalism, and a profound interest in Africa, actually started among many Afro-Americans during the latter part of the nineteenth century. Therefore, the new Afro-American nationalism is not really new.

The demonstrators in the United Nations gallery interpreted the murder of Lumumba as the international lynching of a black man on the altar of colonialism and white supremacy. Suddenly, to them at least, Lumumba became Emmett Till and all of the other black victims of lynch law and the mob. The plight of the Africans still fighting to throw off the joke of colonialism and the plight of the Afro-Americans, still waiting for a rich, strong and boastful nation to redeem the promise of freedom and citizenship became one and the same. Through their action the UN demonstrators announced their awareness of the fact that they were far from being free and a long fight still lay ahead of them. The short and unhappy life of Patrice Lumumba announced the same thing about Africa.

Belatedly, some American officials began to realize that the foreign policy of this country will be affected if the causes of the long brooding dissatisfaction among Afro-Americans are not dealt with effectively. Others, quick to draft unfavorable conclusions and compound misconceptions, interpreted this action as meaning there was more Afro-American interest in African affairs than in the affairs of the United States. Both interpretors seemed to have missed a vital point – the United States has never had and official policy based on the granting of complete citizenship to Afro-Americans, nor has the United States ever had an official policy based on the complete elimination of, or approving of the complete elimination, of colonialism in Africa.

Patrice Lumumba became a hero and a martyr to Afro-American nationalists because he was the symbol of the black man's humanity struggling for recognition. The life of Patrice Lumumba proved that he was a product of Belgian paternalism and misrule in the Congo. In more favorable circumstances, he might have become one of the most astute national leaders of the twentieth century. When the Congo emerged clearly in the light of modern history, he was its bright star. Lumumba was a true son of Africa and was accepted as belonging to all of Africa, not just the Congo. No other personality in African history has leaped so suddenly from death to martyrdom.

This is why Lumumba was and is still being extolled – this "best son of Africa," this "Lincoln of the Congo," this "Black Messiah," whose struggle was made noble by his unswerving demand for centralism against all forms of Balkanization. His effort was made heroic by his unyielding resistance to the forces of neo-colonialism which finally killed his body, but not his spirit. The spirit of Patrice Lumumba will roam over the African land for many years to come. This spirit was a natural choice to rekindle the flame of Afro-American nationalism.

Harlem has always been the incubator for black nationalism in the United States. Presently this nationalism is being hampered by too many organizations and too many leaders with conflicting programs. Some of these "leaders" are self-seeking money changers who have found a haven, and a bonanza in the African nationalist movement. The major nationalist groups and their programs are briefly outlined here:

Nation of Islam: A nation-wide organization, dating back to 1930, led since 1933 by Elijah Muhammad, born Elijah Poole in Georgia sixty-three years ago. Headquarters in Chicago, Temple No. 7 in New York is led by 35-year-old Minister Malcolm X. The Black Muslim movement is presently the most dynamic force for protest and change in the United States. Of all the Afro-American nationalist groups this is the one that is most feared by white people. More about them later.

Muslim Brotherhood: This group claims to be the authentic Muslim and is hostile to the Nation of Islam group, whose followers are massive and growing fast. The hostility between these two groups has been overplayed by the press. Muslim Brotherhood is led by Talib Ahmed Dawud, husband of singer Dakota Staton.

United African Nationalist Movement: This group was started in 1948 by James R. Lawson, formerly an official in the Harlem Labor Union. Lawson's many enemies insist that his movement is mostly on paper. This accusation notwithstanding he continues to be one of the most active of the Harlem group of nationalists. He maintains liaison with most of the African missions at the United Nations, he says, "to exchange information, ideas and techniques and to coordinate demonstrations in the common cause."

The Universal African Nationalist Movement: This organization has been led by Benjamin Gibbons for over twenty years. This is one of the numerous groups that was formed after the breaking up of the major "Back to Africa" movement – The Universal Negro Improvement Association, after the decline of Marcus Garvey, who was the most colorful and the most effective of all African nationalists of the 20th century. This group still uses Garvey's old slogan, "Africa for the Africans – those at home and those abroad."

Cultural Association for Women of African Heritage: This group is important because it represents the entry of Afro-Americans from the entertainment field into the nationalist movement. Headed by a dynamic personality, singer Abby Lincoln, who participated in the demonstration at the UN. In defense of her group, she says, "We Afro-Americans will be heard by any means you make it necessary for us to use." She is without reservation in denouncing, "crumb-crunching, cocktail-tipping Uncle Tom leadership paid by colonialists."

The African Nationalist Pioneer movement headed by Carlos Cooks, is the most active of the splinter nationalist groups born out of the breaking up of the Garvey Movement. Other groups in this category are: The Garvey Club, United Sons and Daughters of Africa, and The First African Corps. The most active of the new nationalist groups are: Liberation Committee for Africa, On Guard Committee for Freedom and the Provisional Committee for a Free Africa.

The National Memorial Book Store, operated by Lewis H. Michaux is the main gathering place for Harlem nationalists. It is called the Home of the Common Sense and Proper Propaganda, Headquarters of Back to Africa Movement. The backroom of the bok store contains a collection of pictures of the great personalities in the history of Afro-Americans. The area in front of the store has been renamed "Harlem Square."

Of all the nationalist groups in the United States, the Nation of Islam, called the Black Muslims, are the most written about and most misunderstood. The interpreters of this group have not been able to decide whether the movement is religious or political. In a recent interview with Malcolm X, he said to me: "Our religion is mainly trying to find a way for the black man to get some heaven while he is down here on earth."

To accomplish the above mentioned objective, the Black Muslim movement will have to be both religious and political. It will have to be a spiritual, political and an economic force.

A recent convert to the Black Muslim Movement, explaining why he joined the movement, and the basis of its appeal to an increasing number of Afro-Americans, said: "I am a man of forty years of age. I fought against people who were supposed to be this country's enemies in the Second World War, and my father fought in the First World War. I have been a patriotic citizen and I always obeyed this country's laws. Yet, I have never been able to feel like a citizen or a man. I was a 33rd degree Mason and I have been a deacon in two different churches. I am a first class cabinet maker and I've had my own shop for nearly ten years. In spite of all of this, white people still treat me as if I was a boy. The Muslims have taught me that I am a man – a black man – and that's something I can feel proud of."

This convert has stated the case for the Black Muslims, in capsule. The drama of this search for dignity, definition and direction is old, the cast of characters is new. To some extent the Black Muslims are a latter-day version of the Garvey Movement, with a new sounding dogma which is basically the same as Marcus Garvey's. To the Black Muslim the American promise and the American dream have grown sour without fulfillment. They have lost faith in the United States as a democratic nation.

The Black Muslims in the United States have created what is essentially a proletarian movement. This is the largest movement of this nature to emerge among Afro-Americans since the heyday of Marcus Garvey and the collapse of his "back to Africa" dream.

In the following quote from Eric Lincoln's book, *The Black Muslims in America,* he explains why the Black Bourgeoisie "leaders" have been a complete failure with the Afro-Americans who make up the growing Black Muslim Movement.

> "Organizations such as the NAACP and the National Urban League, for all their virtues, have not caught the imagination and adherence of the Negro masses. Their memberships tend to comprise middle and upper-class Negroes and whites, in each case the least disprivileged of their race. The Black Muslims, by contrast, are undeniably a mass movement. From their present base of more than 100,000 members, they are reaching for the support of the entire Negro lower class – and ultimately, of all other black Americans."

With this program it can be clearly seen that the Black Muslims have flung down a challenge to all other existing Afro-American organizations. How this challenge is answered will determine the future of the people of African descent in the Western World.

Religious Convictions Involved

The explainers of the new Afro-American Nationalism have given most of their attention to the black nationalist splinter groups, heirs to the once powerful Garvey movement, and the Black Muslims. In taking this all too narrow approach, they have neglected another vital manifestation of the new Afro-American Nationalism. Afro-Americans are turning away from both Christianity and Islam. There is a growing tendency to study and adhere to religions and customs that originated in Africa.

The most notable trend in this direction can be observed in the rise of Voodoo cults in Harlem and other large Afro-American communities. The name of the cult, like the cult itself, is of West African origin. In Africa these cults were once predominant among the Fon people of Dahomey and the Yoruba people of Western Nigeria. This African religion, now being reintroduced is not new to the people of African descent in the Western world. In Janheinz Jahn's book, *"Muntu, The New African Culture,"* he gives the following report of the early manifestations of Voodoo in the slaves who were brought to England, the West Indies and the United States:

> "The reason why it (Voodoo) was the religious conception of Dahomey in particular that came to prevail in Haiti is apparent from a London report of 1789 which tells us that ten to twelve thousand slaves were exported yearly from the Kingdom of Dahomey. The English exported only seven to eight hundred of these, the Portuguese about three thousand and the French the remainder. In other words more than six to eight thousand a year were shipped to the French Antilles, above all to Saint Dominique, as the principal French colony of Haiti was then called."

Moreau de Saint-Mery, a relative of the Empress Josephine, wrote several volumes on the plantation life of the transplanted African in the West Indies. He describes, among other things, a Voodoo ceremony.

"According to the Arada Negroes, Voodoo means a great supernatural being, a snake that knows the past and the present and through the medium of the high priestess foretells the future. These two are called King and Queen, Master and Mistress or Papa and Mama." The meeting takes place, he says, only secretly and at night, far from profane eyes. The initiated put on sandals and wrap themselves in red clothes... Sacrificial gifts are brought, the King and Queen receive them. The receipts are used to meet the expenses of the community and assist needy members. Then follows an oath similar to that at the opening of the meeting and 'As fearful as the first,' an oath of secrecy and obedience."

In a recent announcement to his Afro-American brothers, Ofuntola Oserjeman, the self-proclaimed Priest of the Yoruba Temple of New Oyo (Harlem's new African name) called for a return not only to African religions, but to an African way of life in its entirety. In his message he says:

> "We must Africanize everything! Our names, our hats, our clothes, our clubs, our churches, our religion, our schools, home, furnishing, businesses, holidays, games, arts, social functions, political parties, our manners and customs, etc., etc., etc.
>
> "Begin with yourself today. You have nothing to lose or fear. It is as natural for persons of African descent to take and maintain the customs, dress and traditions of their motherland, as it is natural for persons of European descent to continue European customs in America. It is distinctly unnatural and degrading, even ridiculous, for persons of African decent to have and keep European customs and habits forced upon them during their enslavement. Our liberation must be complete. Every technique of slavery must be wiped out. We must begin with our so-called leaders. Support Africanization! Note to men: adopt the African look; cut the brim off your hats you will look like you should, and less like an imitation. Change!"

And thus the Afro-Americans' search for identity continues. The search is both heroic and pathetic. In growing numbers Afro-Americans are turning back to old African religions and ways of life at a time when some Africans are beginning to turn away from them. The new African-minded Afro-Americans are accepting the old African religions and ways of life, literally, at a time when the Africans are accepting these religions and ways of life, selectively and with some reservations.

All African life is now going through a period of transition and modernization. An attempt is being made to preserve the best of old African ways of life. In increasing numbers, Africans with a western education and a western oriented religion, principally Christianity, are beginning to feel spiritually unfulfilled. Now, with new insight, Africans are looking back and reevaluating the worth of old African ways of life, while concurrently looking forward to the building of modern and industrialized African states. Therefore, the direction and predicament of the African and the Afro-American is basically the same – being both progressive and regressive. Distance, years of separation and alien ways of life imposed by rulers not of their choosing, have created misunderstanding and a lack of coordination of effort between these two African people. This fact notwithstanding, the Africans and the Afro-Americans are traveling different roads to the same ultimate goal – the realization and projection of themselves as full-fledged and dignified human beings. The African heritage of history and culture is being reclaimed. The notion that Europe and North America represents the only accomplishment that can be called a civilization is no longer accepted and believed. The European concept of the Africans and the North American concept of the Afro-American is now being both questioned and challenged.

Among the Afro-Americans, particularly, very often the question is awkward and the challenge is ill-prepared. This is due, in part, to the fact that the new nationalist movements among Afro-Americans are led, mainly, by aroused proletarians unlike the nationalist movements in Africa, whose leadership consist of a more articulate, educated elite. The new Afro-American nationalism was born, and is growing without the encouragement of the so-called "Negro leadership class."

The new Afro-American nationalists, with all their awkwardness and inadequacy, have learned a lesson and discovered a great truth that still eludes the "Negro leadership class" referred to here. They have learned the value of history and culture as an instrument in stimulating the spiritual rebirth of a people.

The cultural heritage of a people is directly related to their history. There can be no true understanding of the people of African origin in the United States until there is a better understanding, and more respect for, their African background. The culture of a people is the fuel that feeds the fires of their ambition, pride and self-esteem. There can be no meaningful advancement without this stimulation. A people must take pride in their history and love their own memories in order to fulfill themselves. This is the lesson, I believe, the new Afro-American nationalists are trying to learn and teach.

I think I can bring the picture clearer into focus by paraphrasing a statement made by Saunders Redding at the first "American Negro Writers Conference," in March 1959.

"A people's ultimate purpose is to use their gifts to develop their awareness of themselves in order to become a better instrument for living together with other people. This sense of identity is the root by which all honest creative effort is fed. A people's relation to their culture is the same as the relation of a child to its mother's breast."

In spite of the charlatans and money changers who occasionally invade the camps of the new Afro-American nationalists, their influence continues to spread. Their numerous and conflicting programs leave much to be desired. There is a hunger among Afro-Americans for a new and more dynamic leadership. This hunger often drives them from one inadequate leader to another. The smug middle class leadership of organizations like the NAACP and the National Urban League have missed (or misjudged) the new tempo of restlessness among the Afro-American newly alerted masses. They still seem to think of this group as being uneducated, unwashed and unorganized – worthy of being led but not worthy of being touched or listened too. The American dream and the American promise of full citizenship with dignity, after being so long delayed, is now being discarded as a hope and an objective by large numbers of Afro-Americans. Africa has become the magic word and the new hope. There is now, in Harlem, an African oriented political party. This party – called the New Alajo Party, recently sent out the following summons to action to its present and potential followers.

"UNITY, ACTION, POWER"

> "The re-Africanization of the black people of America has begun. Like yeast in a hot oven we are suddenly beginning to rise. Each person must do his part.
>
> "In traditional Africa every person of 14 years of age must join a society to learn the culture, history, and political aims of his nation and his people. For 100 years blacks in America have grown old with little or no knowledge of themselves or political aims to which they should aspire. Now, for the first time the *Alajo Party* has a school for the training of our people and their leaders.
>
> "All leaders must be educated by their own people in their own aims. Our present leaders are not. That is why our power is wasted. The U.S. owes us millions of dollars in indemnity for slavery. We must have a strong leadership to collect this money which is due to each family. You and your friends should join the *Alajo Party* now to petition the U.S. to pay its debt to us."

Admittedly, the chances of collecting this vast indemnity are thin indeed. That is not the important point here. The fact that this issue has been placed on the agenda of things desired by the Afro-Americans and a demand has been made for its consideration represents a new and extreme approach to the plight of the people of African origin in the western world. This approach also represents a concession. There is now a growing number of Afro-Americans who have given up all hopes of ever being completely integrated American citizens.

The Priest Rev. Ofuntola Oserjeman Adefunmi, of the Yoruba Temple Ogboni (Keeper of ancestral customs) is also chief and founder of the Alajo Party. According to his literature:

> "By his initiation into the Priesthood of the Orisha Vudu Religion, he is the first of the blacks of America to return whole-heartedly to the culture and traditions of Africa. He is bound therefore to uphold and establish the national customs of his Ancestors. He and the members of his party, and all who join them are adding new glory to the pageantry of West African civilization, as the sacrifice, not for barren integration or separation but to restore Africans, born in America, the foundations of their cultural genius."

The position of Priest Rev. Adefunmi (like it or not) is clear – much clearer that the position of the moderate Black Bourgeoisie "leaders," who are not leading. The Afro-American today represents a revolutionary force in the United States. Again, I think I should emphasize, the leadership of this force is basically proletarian. By proletarian I do not mean communist. The new Afro-American nationalists, like the African nationalists, are gravitating toward a form of African Socialism. This new African Socialism will be nothing more than a rehash and an updating of the old communal Socialism that existed in Africa for more than a thousand years before the European Karl Marx was born. An increasing number of thinking Africans and Afro-Americans are now looking back at their history and culture, and within themselves, for the spiritual and philosophical stimulus for their survival and direction.

On this matter the position of the new Afro-American nationalists is extreme, and presently there is no apparent middle ground. The Yoruba Temple nationalists represent a more articulate manifestation of this extreme position. Unlike most of the other Afro-American nationalists, they have created a sizeable body of literature explaining their point of view.

"The Yoruba Temple," the Priest Rev. Adefunmi explains, "is the advance guard for the change now being felt in the minds of every awaking Afro-American. It is farther ahead in its program for the future of the Afro-American than any society of its kind. In fact it is the only society of its kind in America. It is the only society which is the same in West Africa, Cuba, Haiti, Trinidad and Brazil, because it is African through and through.

"The soul of the black is his religion. The Yoruba Temple does not believe we can ever fully succeed by trying to be Negroes, Arabs, or Jews. To be first class Americans we would have to be Europeans first. We have wasted 100 years trying to act and be like Europeans (Americans). This is ridiculous when you stop to think what foolishness that is. There is only one thing we can be – Africans, because that is what we were meant to be – face it!"

Well! Let's brace ourselves and face it. So far as the greater number of Afro-American nationalists are concerned, the showdown is now. The issue is clearly joined. In spite of the diversity and contradictions in words and objectives, all of the Afro-American nationalists basically are fighting for the same thing. They feel that the Afro-American constitutes what is tantamount to an exploited colony within a sovereign nation. Their fight is for national, and personal liberation. No people are really free until they become the instrument of their own liberation. Freedom is not legacy that is bequeathed from one generation to another. Each generation must take and maintain its freedom with its own hands. In this regard the Afro-American nationalists have moved far ahead of the articulate beggars of crumbs, now being called "leaders." They feel that the Emancipation Proclamation has always been inadequate. In their fight for a second and more meaningful liberation the Afro-American nationalists have extended the basis of their fight to include the reclaiming of their African heritage. In identifying their fight for national liberation with the new resurgence of Pan-Africanism (actually and Afro-American creation) the Afro-American nationalists have realized the importance of Pan-Africanism not only as an instrument for the unification of Africa, but as a broader means for the unification of all people of African descent the world over. In taking this historical step they have turned away from a leadership that was begging and pleading to a more dynamic leadership that is insisting and demanding.

The Black Family in Historical Perspective

John Henrik Clarke

(Extension of keynote address, given at the Second National Conference of Pan-African Studies on the Black Family, the University of Louisville, Louisville, Kentucky, March 27–29, 1975.)
Journal of Afro-American Issues, Vol. 3, No. 3 & 4, Summer/Fall 1975, pp. 336–342

Because all history is a current event that is forever repeating itself, much to our sorrow, the best way to look at the present status of the Black family is to look at some of the main currents of history that brought this family into being. According to all of the information on the subject that is now known, mankind, the family as a functioning unit and as the first organized society, started in Africa. It is from this base that I have chosen to look at the Black family in historical perspective.

The greatest achievement of the first Black families was, in a different time and setting, the same as the greatest achievement of Black people today – their survival. In a pamphlet, "The African Contribution,"[1] the writer, John M. Weatherwax draws a graphic picture of how the early African families survived and made a contribution to the future of mankind. He says: "These early Africans made hooks to catch fish, spears to hunt with, stone knives to cut with, the blow gun, the hammer, the stone axe, canoes and paddles, bags and buckets, and bows and arrows."

The last few hundred thousand years of the early prehistory of mankind is called the Old Stone Age. This age may have lasted a half-million years. John M. Weatherwax tells us further that "the bolo, stone knives, paddles, harpoons, bows and arrows, blow-guns, the hammer and the axe – all invented first by the Africans – were the start of man's use of power."

In their quest for survival, African families laid the foundation for aspects of modern-day culture. It is the making of tools that sets man apart from and, in a sense, above all living creatures. Africans started mankind along the tool-making path. Some of today's machines, such as automatic hammers, gas engines and long-range missiles, have the roots of their development in the same mechanistic approaches to power started by the early Africans. Every time we light a match, take a bath in water heated by gas, or cook a meal in an oven, we continue a process started by the African: the control of fire. What we call the tribe or the clan developed in Africa. These were families coming together for protection. When a great leader and defender of his tribe died, he became a deity. Regard for him, appreciation for his services to his people, and efforts to communicate with him became a form of worship and the basis for some of the early religions.

Nearly all of the world's religions have their basis in Africa. These religions are salvation-oriented and they predate similar religions in other countries and cultures. On this point I would like to call attention to the book *African Origins of the Major "Western Religions"* by Yosef ben-Jochannan. Christianity was born and developed, largely, on the sail of Africa. This religion held as one of its best-known symbols a Black woman nursing a child. The idea of a virgin other and child had appeared in many ancient civilizations. Its first known appearance was in Africa.

The formation and growth of the world's first families in Africa led to migrations and the peopling of parts of Africa that were without organized societies. Eventually African people migrated to other parts of the earth. Direct descendants of early Africans went to Asia Minor, Arabia, India, China, Japan the East Indies and the Pacific Islands. Some Africans found their way to North and South America and the Caribbean Islands.[2] Africans and people of African descent went also to Turkey, Palestine, Greece and other countries in Europe. From Gibraltar they went to Spain, Portugal, France, England, Wales and Ireland. When Roman writers of history arrived in England, they found there the *Silures*, a people of African descent, ruling Wales and Western England. The *Picts*, who lived in parts of the British Isles, were likewise of African descent. During the migratory period African family life was taking on a new form, setting precedents, and working through new complications in Africa itself. All of mankind would be beneficiaries of the solutions to problems they solved without any assistance from outside.

The first achievement of the early African man and woman was the creation of a functioning family unit. Not only did this major step in human development lay the foundation for the organization of all subsequent societies and institutions, but also the status of women in these societies tells us a lot about the stability of their family structures.

In the first African societies the woman played a major role without demeaning the man or making his role less important. The woman's "place" was not just with her family and in the home.[3] She had a place within the power structure of the society in which she lived. In ancient Africa she often ruled her society with unquestioned power. Many African women were great militarists and often led their countries armies in battle. The Africans had created a society where men were secure enough not to fear women in power.

Societies must be judged by their attitude toward women, children and the family. In the old societies of Africa, and in the new, the attitude was good. African societies, like most non-European societies, were mainly matrilineal. The lineage comes down through the female line and the woman can ascend to power as the head of the state. This proves, if proof is needed, that the women in these old societies developed before Europe was born. In his book, *The Cultural Unity of Black Africa,* the Senegalese writer Cheikh Anta Diop tells us that, "During the entire history of Egypt of the Pharaohs, African women enjoyed complete freedom as opposed to the condition of the segregated Indo-European women of the classical period, whether she was Greek or Roman." He further informs us that "no evidence can be found either in literature or in historical records – Egyptian or otherwise – relating to the ill-treatment of African women by their men. They were respected and went about freely and unveiled, unlike some Asian women. Affection for one's mother and especially the respect with which it was necessary to surround her were the most sacred of duties."

Islam had a profound effect on the structure of African family life. In most cases it changed the matriarchal custom where the lineage came down through the female line to the patriarchal where the lineage came down through the male line. The social organization of Islam did not benefit the women in matters pertaining to power. West Africa was an exception. In this part of Africa, Islam had to adjust to the fact that the women would not give up their power position.

Along the coast of East Africa Moslems often married into the African families that they had converted to their religion. These marriages changed the structure and altered the cultural patterns in large areas of Africa. The Arab slave trade, which used a large number of Black Africans who had been converted to

Islam to help enslave their own people, dealt another tragic blow to the structure of African family life.

In spite of these setbacks, the traditional African family survived. The writer Sheila Smith Hobson gives us this description of the African family in her article "The Black Family Together in Every Sense" (*Tuesday* Magazine, April 1971). She says:

> The African family unit is much larger than that of the Western world... In Africa the traditional family unit includes all relatives; aunts and uncles have just as much authority over children as parents; cousins are treated and thought of as brothers and sisters; and grandparents are given the position of authority and respect...

To me the interesting thing about her description of the traditional African family is that is not any different in design and in composition than my own family when I was growing up in Alabama and Georgia.

The European slave trade began the greatest tragedy in the history of man. The long and forced trek to the so-called new world started, and with it the attendant horrors that were inflicted upon both men and women. This act of protracted genocide and its aftermath lasted for over five hundred years, and its scars have not yet been removed from its victims. This massive unfeeling vandalism greatly affected the African family, whose position of security, prior to this event, was above the families of contemporary Europe.

The African women, valued and respected in their own societies, were assaulted and violated by sailors and slave-catchers before the ships were put out to sea. The men who attached themselves to the slave trade were the scum of Europe. Their status was a gun, their white skin, and the freedom to violate the helpless flowers of African womanhood. Already they had begun to sire the bastard children who would be reduced to the same status as their mothers. The females among these bastard children became favorites and were used as house servants, concubines and prostitutes.

And thus, the African experience in the new world began. In South America and in the Caribbean Islands a semblance of family life and cultural continuity was maintained. In the English colonies that became the United States, life for the Africans was more difficult. These Africans were a part of a cruel and dramatic movement that changed the world forever.

The Africans were brought to South America and the Caribbean Islands to replace the Indians as a labor force.[4] Under the first impact of the European presence, the Indians had died or had been killed in large numbers. The Europeans did not treat the Africans much different than they had treated the Indians. In the first one hundred years after the beginning of European settlement most of the Indians in the Caribbean Islands were extinct and the Indian population in South America had drastically declined. In the meantime, in spite of the brutality, the Africans had increased in both places. They made a partial adjustment to their environment and waited for an opportunity to revolt against it. In large areas of South America and in the Caribbean Islands these opportunities began to come before the end of the first half of the sixteenth century.

The plantation system in South America and in the Caribbean Islands, as mentioned earlier, was radically different from the same system in the English colonies. In America few attempts were made to hold families together. The house slaves were loyal to the house and the master. In most cases, the field slaves were considered to be their enemies. Black families were held together only if it was to the slave owner's benefit or convenience. At first this was not the case, slavery in America had a long development before it reached this tragic point.

The Afro-American historian Lerone Bennett, Jr. is the best authority on this aspect of Black history. His expertise on this subject is astutely reflected in his latest book, *The Shaping of Black America*.[5] This book reflects the flowering of his talent. All of his previous books seem to have been part of the preparation for the writing of this book, his most profound commentary to date of the nature of the Black experience.

Bennett calls his book "an essay toward a new understanding of the long and continuing attempts of Africans and African descendants to possess themselves and the new land." He calls attention to the need for "a new conceptual envelope for Black America history." He says further: "It should be clear by now to almost everyone that understanding the Black experience requires new concepts and a radically new perspective."

At once, Lerone Bennett demonstrates what he means by new concepts and a radically new perspective in the opening chapter of his book called *The First Generation*. Because, as he says, "blacks lived in a different time and a different reality in this country," it should then stand to reason that the honest interpretation of their history requires a different insight and a different frame of reference. The book begins like a good drama promising to lead the reader through an experience that is more than worth the time. The promise begins to fulfill itself before the end of the first page of the first chapter, in the following passage:

> In August, when the shadows are long on the land and even the air oppresses, the furies of fate hang in the balance of black America. It was in August, in

> the eighth month of the year, that three hundred thousand men and women marched on Washington, DC. It was in August, on a hot and heavy day in the nineteenth century, that Nat Turner rode. And it was in another August, 344 years before the March on Washington, 346 years before Watts, and 212 years before Nat Turner's war, that "a Dutch Man of War" sailed up the river James and landed the first generation of black Americans at Jamestown, Virginia.

This Dutch ship and its cargo changed what was to become the United States in such a way that, henceforth, it would never again be the same. The seeds of the only original culture that America can show to the world were arriving on this Dutch ship. Also arriving was the embryo of a conflict that, after more than three hundred years, is still unresolved. Lerone Bennett refers to this cargo as "the black gold that made capitalism possible in America." In this reference he is completely on the case. This cargo of "black gold," and other cargoes that were to follow, made many other things possible. Nationally, it gave America the means to become a world power. Internationally it created the basis for the industrial revolution and the maiden world of science and technology.

Lerone Bennett reminds us that "the drama, which is known as the African slave trade, had been going on for more than one hundred years when the Virginian colony was founded in 1607." These first Africans were not chattel slaves. They were indentured servants. This is a major point that is often missed. Mr. Bennett deals with this aspect of slavery searchingly and very carefully shows how the indentured servant status was transformed into chattel slavery. After the period of indenture, the first generation of Blacks became early Americans in many ways. Some of them became owners of land and slaves. Others became part of the craft and technology class that helped to tame a young and raw America. Labor was needed and this is what these first Blacks meant to the colonies.

The indentured servant system was not created for the Blacks who landed in Jamestown, Virginia. The system was intact long before they arrived. There was a large number of white indentured servants already in the system. Mr. Bennett calls attention to the fact that, in theory, the legal status of the Black immigrants was higher than the first white indentured servants. During and after the period of indenture the first Black families in America came into being.

In spite of the institution of slavery, Black family life did not disappear.[6] It was maintained under difficult circumstances in the South. The Black "freedman" in the North and East fared better and, in most cases, did have a stable family life.

Black family life was totally changed after the Civil War and the end of slavery. A new family structure and new institutions came into being. Some of the troubles of present-day Black America started at this time. In some cases, we modeled our families after white families and our institutions after white institutions.

The betrayal of the period called the reconstruction caused more trouble. The atrocities of the Ku Klux Klan drove many Black families from the rural South to the urban South. The continuation of these atrocities in the cities of the South caused a migration of Blacks out of the South. This move created most of the northern urban ghettoes that we know today. From the first slave ships to the present time, Black families have been looking for better homes, better schools and a way to participate in the social order that rules over their lives. Their problem has always been the same – the lack of power. This is what the Civil Rights, the Black Power and the Black Studies Movements were about. All movements that came before them were about the same thing.

End Notes

1. Weatherwax, John M. *The African Contribution*, Los Angeles, California: Aquarian Spiritual Center Bookshop, 1964.
2. Clarke, John Henrik "The Impact of the African on the New World – A Reappraisal" *The Black Scholar*, February 1973.
3. Weatherwax, *op. cit.*, pp. 22–25.
4. Clarke, John Henrik "On the Cultural Unity of Africa" *Black World*, February 1975, pp. 14–16.
5. Clarke, John Henrik "The Influence of African Cultural Continuity on the Slave Revolts in South America and in the Caribbean Islands," prepared for the Third International Congress of Africanists, Addis Ababa, Ethiopia, December 9–19, 1973, pp. 1–4.
6. Bennett, Lerone Jr. *The Shaping of Black America*, Chicago, Illinois: Johnson Publishing Co., Inc., 1975, pp. 5–38.
7. Blassingame, John W. "Black Autobiographies as History and Literature," *The Black Scholar*, December, 1973. Also see Blassingame, John W. *The Slave Community, Plantation Life in the Ante-Bellum South*, New York: Oxford University Press, 1972.

Candid portrait of historian John Henrik Clarke, at podium, wearing kente cloth sash, ca. 1994.

John Henrik Clarke, historian, college professor and author, 1960s.

Historians John Henrik Clarke (left) and Josef Ben Jochanan (Dr. Ben), ca. 1970s

Author Maya Angelou and historian John Henrik Clarke at Institute for Independent Education Conference and dinner, October 1994.

John Henrik Clarke in his study surrounded by his book collection, 1990s

Chapter 3

Africana Biography and Intellectual Studies

Lerone Bennett: Social Historian

John Henrik Clarke

Reprinted from *Freedomways*, Fourth Quarter, 1965, pp. 481–492

A new generation of restless black Americans gave birth to the present civil rights movement while finding new strength and dignity within themselves. This movement literally demands a re-evaluation of the part that the people of African descent have played in the making of America and the circumstances that brought them here. Among the new writers of the postwar era, Lerone Bennett, Jr. has been the most successful in bringing new insight to this subject.

Lerone Bennett, a native of Clarksdale, Mississippi, belongs to the generation of new black thinkers, who, before and after the Montgomery Bus Boycott, started insisting and demanding their full manhood rights in the United States. This generation literally grew up and matured within the eye of the civil rights storm.

After finishing Morehouse College in Atlanta, Georgia, where he was a schoolmate of Martin Luther King, Lerone Bennett joined the staff of the Atlanta World. Later, after leaving Atlanta for Chicago, he became the Senior editor of *Ebony* Magazine. As an editor he is an active participator in the civil rights movement as well as an astute interpreter of it. He is exceptional as a social historian because, in speaking and in his writing he has developed a method for explaining difficult subject matter without losing any of its importance. Lerone Bennett's talent and interest extend beyond his position as an editor. He is also a poet and short story writer.

The book *Before the Mayflower* introduced Lerone Bennett to a large reading audience. The book grew out of a series of articles which were published originally in *Ebony* Magazine. In his preface to the book, he explains that "the book, like the series, deals with the trials and triumphs of Americans whose roots in the American soil are deeper than those of the Puritans who arrived on the celebrated 'Mayflower' a year after a "Dutch man of war' deposited twenty Negroes at Jamestown." Further, he continues, "this book is founded on the work of scholars and specialists and is designed for the average reader. It is not, strictly speaking, a book for scholars; but it is as scholarly as fourteen months of research could make it."

Before the Mayflower is the first major work of Lerone Bennett. With this book his role as a social historian is firmly established. He has written a clear and concise history of the people of African descent in America that can be understood by readers with no prior knowledge of the subject. In the opening chapter of his book, *The African Past*, he has shown how the African past relates to the early development of what men later called "civilization and culture." He establishes the fact that the Africans who became slaves in the United States had, prior to this catastrophe, lived in a society consisting of a number of well developed independent states that were brought into being long before they knew of the Europeans' existence.

In making an assessment of the revival of interest in African History, the author states: "This re-evaluation has yielded a new perspective on African and human history. Africa, long considered the 'Dark Continent,' is now regarded as the place where man first received light. Ancient Africans, long considered primitive and ignorant, are now revealed as creative contributors to Egyptian civilization and builders of powerful states in the Sudan.

"From Olduvai Gorge in East Africa, from caves in the Sahara and excavations in the Nile Valley have come bits of bone and husks of grain which speak more eloquently than words of the trials and triumphs of the African ancestors of the American Negro."

Elaborating on this point, he further states: "a series of startling discoveries in this area (Olduvai Gorge)suggests that the most important and fascinating developments in human history took place in the Dark Continent. Discoveries by Dr. L.S.B. Leakey and other scholars indicate that man was born in Africa, that he began to use tools here and that his seminal invention spread to Europe and Asia."

In the preface chapter to his book *Before the Mayflower*, Lerone Bennett clearly shows that before the breaking up of the social structure of the West African states of Ghana, Melle and Songhai and the internal strife and chaos that made the slave trade possible, the forefathers of the Africans who eventually became slaves in the United States lived in a society where university life was fairly common and scholars were beheld with reverence.

There were in this ancestry, rulers who expanded their kingdoms into empires, great and magnificent armies whose physical dimensions dwarfed entire nations into submission, generals who advanced the technique of military science, scholars whose vision of life showed foresight and wisdom, and priests who told of Gods that were strong and kind.

In other chapters of his book, Lerone Bennett writes in great detail about the trials and tribulations that the Africans encountered during the slavery era and how they made a contribution to the building of the New World in spite of these drawbacks.

> "Africans helped build Liverpool, Nantes and Newport," he states. "They helped finance the industrial revolution in England. They helped clear the forest in America. They did these things, but they protested every step of the way. Protests began in Africa, where mutinies on ships were common.... In the West Indies and on the mainland, there were many revolts. A long series of conspiracies and revolts culminated in the great Haitian Revolution which played an important part in the abolition of the trade... . The slave trade left a blood-stained legacy. During the four centuries the trade was pursued, it wrecked the social and economic life of Africa, set tribe against tribe and village against village. The trade was no less disastrous in Europe and America where it left a legacy of ill will and guilt and a potentially explosive racial problem."

The stigma of slavery continues to haunt the nation. The guilt that some white Americans feel over slavery moved them more to tears than to action that would eliminate this crucial condition of servitude.

After calling attention to the irony of the black man's participation in the American Revolution – one of history's greatest paradoxes – Lerone Bennett asks his readers to: "Consider the background of the great event. A colony with a half-million slaves decides to go to war in support of the theory that all men are created equal and are 'endowed by their Creator with certain inalienable rights, that among these are life, liberty and the pursuit of happiness.'... Consider the prologue. A bold Negro decides to strike a blow for liberty and becomes the first martyr of the Revolution. Consider the climax. Black men, some of them slaves, enter the lines and sign the Declaration of Independence with their blood."

It is clearly shown here that when the promise of American democracy was made, it was not made to black men, some of whom had helped to make it possible. Thomas Jefferson, the worried slaveholder did not free any of his slaves. In the years following the American Revolution many slaves, both men and women, decided to become the instrument of their own liberation. Starting early in the eighteenth century, one slave revolt followed another until there was no longer any question about the slaves' desire to be free.

In describing the nature of the slaves' resistance to their condition, Lerone Bennett uses a quote from Kenneth M. Stampps' book *The Peculiar Institution*: "The record of slave resistance," he says, "forms a chapter in the story of the endless struggle to give dignity to human life. Though the history of southern bondage reveals that men can be enslaved under certain conditions, it also demonstrates that their love of freedom is hard to crush."

In the chapter of his book called "The Generation of Crisis," Lerone Bennett has written a concise history of the period and the personalities who were the "heroes of the Emancipation." Here we meet Frederick Douglass, one of the great men of the nineteenth century; William Lloyd Garrison, one of the major figures of the abolitionist movement, who had worked closely with Negro abolitionists like James Forten and Charles Lenox Remond. The period saw the emergence of other great black and white freedom fighters such as: William Still, Henry Highland Garnet, Richard Allen, Samuel Cornish, Sojourner Truth, David Walker, Harriet Tubman, Samuel Ringgold Ward and John B. Russwurm.

The war that the nation seemed to have been expecting for a generation came when a group of hot-headed southerners fired on Fort Sumter. The four-year conflict called the Civil War had started. Before it was over, slaves in large numbers joined the Union Army and fought to reunite this country and for their own freedom. At first the Union generals were reluctant to make use of their services. Though the black soldiers entered the war late, they distinguished themselves in many battles and won their share of medals for bravery.

The end of the war created, for a few years, what Lerone Bennett has called "Black Power in Dixie." He describes it in this manner:

> "Never before had the sun shone so bright. An ex-slave, Blanche Kelso Bruce, was representing Mississippi in the United States Senate. Pinckney Benton Steward Pinchback, young, charming, daring, was sitting in the governor's mansion in Louisiana. In Mississippi, in South Carolina, in Louisiana, Negro lieutenant governors were sitting on the right-hand side of power. A Negro was secretary of state in Florida: a Negro was on the state supreme court in South Carolina. Negroes were superintendents of education, state treasurers, adjutant generals, solicitors, judges and major generals of militia. Robert H. Wood was mayor of Natchez, Mississippi, and Norris Wright Cuney was running for mayor of Galveston, Texas. Seven Negroes were

> sitting in the House of Representatives.... Negroes and whites were going to school together... riding in street cars together. An interracial board was running the University of South Carolina where a Negro professor, Richard T. Greener was teaching white and black youth metaphysics and logic."

This hopeful era was shortlived. In 1876 the Reconstruction was betrayed. Jim Crow, already born, grew rapidly and dangerously. Lerone Bennett's picture of this era is sharp and clear.

> "Brick by brick, bill by bill, fear by fear, the wall grew taller and taller. The deaf, the dumb and blind were separated by color. White nurses were forbidden to treat Negro males. White teachers were forbidden to teach Negro students. South Carolina forbade Negro and white cotton mill workers to look out of the same window. In the last decade of the nineteenth century and the first decades of the twentieth, the wall went higher and higher.... In only two other countries, South Africa and Nazi Germany – have men's fears driven them to such extremes."

In a chapter on "Miscegenation in America," Lerone Bennett shows that this is a sex-obsessed nation lacking honesty and adulthood in such matters. "Miscegenation in America," he explains, "started not in the thirteen original colonies but in Africa. English, French, Dutch and American slave traders took black concubines on the Guinea Coast and mated with females on the slave ships."

The concluding chapters in *Before the Mayflower*, "From Booker T. Washington to Martin Luther King, Jr.," "The Bitter Harvest" and the Epilogue, "We Can Not Escape History" are an introduction to the civil rights movements in this century. His insight into the character of Booker T. Washington is singularly astute. This man is both fascinating and frightening. Lerone Bennett describes him as the court of last resort on Negro political appointments in America and white political appointments in the south. "In the critical years from 1895 to 1915, Booker T. Washington was the most prominent Negro in America."

The era of Booker T. Washington is also the era of W.E.B. DuBois, Washington's critic and challenger. After the death of Booker T. Washington in 1915, the towering intellectual figure of W.E.B. DuBois moved to the center of the leadership stage and remained uncontested until the period in the early twenties that witnessed the colorful, brief rise and decline of Marcus Garvey.

Lerone Bennett proves, in the concluding chapters of his book, that the great human drama now being called "The Black Revolution in the USA" has long historical roots and it cannot be fully understood until it is seen in this context.

In the March 1964 issue of *Ebony* Magazine, the first in a series of twelve articles under the general title "Pioneers in Protest" was published. These articles are a biographical continuation of some of the chapters in *Before the Mayflower*. These articles prove, if additional proof is needed, that black resistance movements started early and have had the leadership of some of the most able men and women this country has produced. Benjamin Banneker, scholar and scientist, denounced slavery and the hypocrisy of self-proclaimed patriots who would not join him; Prince Hall, a veteran of the American Revolution, founded the first Negro chapter of the Masons and used this in the fight for civil rights. Richard Allen, an ex-slave, founded the African Methodist Episcopal Church (AME) after Negroes were segregated at service. Frederick Douglas was the noblest of all American black men of the nineteenth century and one of the noblest of all Americans. This great abolitionist's civil rights views are as valid today as they were a century ago. Samuel E. Cornish and John B. Russwurm started a newspaper in order to tell the black man's story from his point of view. John B. Russwurm, talented editor and politician, is generally credited with being the first Negro graduate of an American college (Bowdoin, 1826). Among the white men who helped to create the first freedom movement, Wendell Phillips and William Lloyd Garrison are outstanding. Henry Highland Garnet, a fiery Presbyterian minister, was a leader of the militant abolitionist wing. Sojourner Truth, the first black women to become an anti-slavery lecturer, was also a strong leader in the feminist movements of the 19th century. Harriet Tubman was a pioneer rebel and slave activist who later served as a nurse, scout and spy in the Civil War. John Brown, called "God's Angry Man," was the first white martyr to die for Negro freedom. Thaddeus Stevens and Charles Sumner used the Senate and the House of Representatives as their platform in a collective fight for the full citizenship of the former slaves. W.E.B. DuBois, scholar and protest leader, was the central figure in the development of freedom movements in America and in Africa. He helped organize the National Association for the Advancement of Colored People in 1909 and later became the father of the Pan-African Movement. Speaking of his last years, Lerone Bennett says: "*DuBois was a mountain no American Negro or white man, for that matter, can ignore. It can be said, in fact, that no one can understand the American Negro who does not understand the early DuBois.*"

In this brilliantly written series of biographies, Lerone Bennett commands us to reconsider the lives of these pioneers of protest who would not let a nation forget that it had deprived millions of its citizens of their democratic rights. These pioneers have, in fact, inspired or led a troubled people to the place where they can now, figuratively, at least, sniff the scent of freedom on the threshold of the promised land.

In 1963, Lerone Bennett participated in the historic March on Washington and later wrote an introduction to the book about the March edited by Doris E. Saunders. An excerpt fro his introduction follows:

> "It was the beginning of something and the ending of something.
>
> "It came 100 years and 240 days afer the signing of the Emancipation Proclamation.
>
> "It came like a force of nature.
>
> "Like a whirlwind, like a storm, like a flood, it overwhelmed by its massiveness and finality.
>
> "A quarter-million people were in it, and of it; and millions more watched on TV and huddled around radios.
>
> "There had never been anything like it.
>
> "A TV spectacular, a Sunday picnic, a political convention, an impressive demonstration of Negro unity, a visible expression of resolve, a new concept of lobbying, a living petition, a show of strength, an outburst, a call to the national conscience: the mammoth March on Washington was everything they said it was, and more; and it moved men and women as they had never been moved before."

The March on Washington was the emotional highwater mark of the civil rights movement. A number of personalities, who otherwise would be in conflict, settled their differences, momentarily, and gave this history-making occasion the direction that it needed. The hero and star of the March on Washington was Rev. Martin Luther King. His "I Have a Dream" speech was easily the highlight of the day. He said it would be "fatal for the nation to overlook the urgency of the moment and to underestimate the determination of the Negro" in his book *What Manner of Man*, Lerone Bennett, former schoolmate of Dr. King, has written the most informative biography of the noted civil rights leader and Nobel Prize winner has been published to date.

In my opinion, after *Before the Mayflower*, Lerone Bennet's best book is *The Negro Mood*. His publishers describe the book in the following manner:

> "Here, in concise and provocative presentation, is a lucid analysis of the dominant fact of our age, the migrating Negro mood. In five penetrating essays organized around the theme of "The Negro Mood," Lerone Bennett, Jr., creates an entirely new perspective for an assessment of the explosive fores swirling beneath the surface of the Negro rebellion. Using the basic concepts of community and power, drawing on his vast research in Negro

> history and Negro expressions, the author traces the ascending curve of Negro discontent and tells us why we face the most crucial decision of the history of our country."

For once, we have a book that is exactly what the publisher says it is.

This writer carefully calls our attention to the fact that, "There is," he maintains, "nursery-rhyme approach to the historical process. The Negro rebellion is and outgrowth of migration, urbanization, increasing self-consciousness and increasing alienation. In order to make an adequate response to that rebellion, we must view it within the context of a long history of developing protest and social contention."

In essays like *The Black Establishment; Ethos: Voices From the Cave* and *Tea and Sympathy: Liberals and Other White Hopes*, Lerone Bennett re-examines some of the old dilemmas about the American black man and his relationship to the power structure and to his illusions about himself. The dilemmas are old but Mr. Bennett's insight into them is new and vital.

In the essay "The Black Establishment," Lerone Bennett analyzes the group that Dr. DuBois called the Talented Tenth and E. Franklin Frazier called the Black Bourgeoisie. Both of these classifications are questionable because this black elite has never been genuinely bourgeois, and their talent has always left a lot to be desired. The concept of the Talented Tenth failed because the black elite did not assume the responsibility expected of them. They were too busy imitating the white middle class and retreating from their people. "The Black Establishment," in fact, is an appendage of "The White Establishment."

Lerone Bennett observes that: "The Black Establishment, oddly enough, is not all black. It is a group of Negroes *and whites* who command the power lines in the Negro community: the executive secretaries, the board chairmen (often white), the presidents (often white), and board members (Negro and white) of protest and improvement association; the bishops of Negro denominations and pastors of the largest and most influential churches (the two are not necessarily synonymous); the editors and publishers of major Negro newspapers and periodicals; the leading educators, business and professional men."

The saddest thing about "The Black Establishment" is its abject powerlessness. This is reflected in its inability to make dynamic decisions and translate them into action without the approval of their white advisers.

"The Establishment's word *protest*," Lerone Bennett further observes, "is a mask for inaction. The deepest strain in Establishment protest is sterile and socially irrelevant. Endless debate, polite petitions, the sending of telegrams and letters, the whole ritual of mimeograph machines and typewriters: all this has been a substitute for hard analysis and risky action. The word *risk*: This separates the Establishment and its perennial critics, activists. The Establishment has never been willing to take serious risks. It has never been willing to jeopardize place, position and institutions in adventures for freedom... .The Establishment says officially that the Negro masses cannot be organized, that they are utterly apathetic and demoralized. What this means, unofficially, is that it is impossible to organize the masses around a "responsible," "respectable," "moderate" program – around the Establishment's program, in short... the central weakness of this program – the Establishment's men are too brilliant not to know it – is that men cannot be freed by agents – white or black."

The five well-constructed essays in the book *"The Negro Mood"* call attention to the new realities in American race relations. Mr. Bennett is not afraid to say that our real revolution is ahead of us and what we are now experiencing is only a transitional period on our way to the confrontation that will make the real revolution and determine our survival in this country.

In the "Ethos: Voices from the Cave" Lerone Bennett calls attention to the fact that the Negro rebellion is a cultural as well as social upheaval. "The authentic rebels," he says, "are not demonstrating for something they lack but for something they have, and the feeling is growing that what they have is what America lacks."

What America lacks is a sense of mission and responsibility to all of its people, in a word, a determination to keep its democratic promise irrespective of consequences. To do this, a new and more realistic relationship between blacks and their white liberal allies will have to be established; in fact, the white liberals will have to become radicals. In the essay "Tea and Sympathy: Liberal and Other White Hopes," Lerone Bennett astutely appraises the dilemma of the white liberals and shows how the misguided failings of this group has delayed the essential confrontation and moment of truth that is inevitable. It is not required, finally, that we love each other," Mr. Bennett explains. "What is required is something infinitely more difficult, for us to confront each other. But this is what the white liberals refuse to do. The white liberal is fleeing the truth of his, of our situation. He is seeking personal salvation, not injustice... what moves him is guilt. What the liberal seeks is his last innocence. What the liberal wants, paradoxically, is for the Negro to tell him that his is not as white and as cold as snow."

In essence, the essays in the book "The Negro Mood" are about the changing power relations between blacks and whites. If this were Lerone Bennett's only book, his status as a social historian would still be secure.

Lerone Bennett's importance as a writer is accentuated by his ability to bring new insight to old subjects on the agenda for discussion. His writing is consistently sharp and clear. His article, "SNCC: Rebels With a Cause," (*Ebony* Magazine, July 1965) is a good example of his analytical facility. In this article, Mr. Bennett shows that the Student Non-Violent Coordinating Committee, a product of the sit-in movement, has emerged as the spearhead of the Southern Freedom Movement. He appraises the young developing group as being "the most radical, the most controversial and perhaps the most creative of all civil rights organizations. Tough, abrasive and avowedly revolutionary (in a nonviolent way), SNCC has played a large and unheralded role in a quasi-revolution it wants to make a real revolution."

In a recent special issue of *Ebony* Magazine, August 1965, devoted to *The White Problem in America,* Lerone Bennett, in an article that introduces the issue, shows that "there is no Negro problem in America." In transferring the onus from the victim to the perpetrator, he shows that the problem is where the power is, and, in this country, the power is in the hands of white Americans.

In his latest book, *Confrontation: Black and White,* Lerone Bennett continues his analysis of the development of Freedom Movements and the personalities who made, and destroyed, some of these movements. The chapter entitled "The First Freedom Movement" is the most important, in my opinion, because it gives a capsule history of the long fight for freedom and the men and women who lead that fight. It proves, if proof is needed, that this fight is part of our heritage in this country.

The book ends with this warning: "If we do not stand up and create the America that was dreamed, if we do not begin to flesh out the words on the creed, the commonwealth of Silence will come to a definite and apocalyptic end."

In his writing Lerone Bennett brings the reader face to face with the uncomfortable truth about America's racial conflict. This is the essence of his value as a social historian.

International Aspects of Fanon and His Impact on African Consciousness

John Henrik Clarke

Reprinted from *The Western Journal of Black Studies*,
Vol. 4, No. 2, 1980, pp. 100–104

In preparation for the writing of this paper the writer reread the works of Frantz Fanon, and was reminded that Fanon had grown in stature and in importance since his death in 1961. His book, *The Wretched of the Earth*, is now a classic ideological document for worldwide revolutionary movements. This book had a special impact on the radical Black civil rights activists in the 1960s who were involved in a debate over the concept of violence or nonviolence in their struggle. The writing of Frantz Fanon did not resolve their dilemma, but, at least, it gave them insight into the broader dimensions of their struggle and how it related to the nationalist movements in the awakening colonial world.

This writer thinks that a large number of the readers of Fanon's books missed his message, because they read his works too hurriedly. His message is not just about African consciousness. It is about what people of African descent will have to do to make a new world *social*. Like Dr. W.E.B. DuBois, Fanon was saying that the problem of the twentieth century is the problem of the color line; but that is not the only problem. Black Americans must now consider the culture line and, more importantly, the political line. All of these lines interrelate, and one cannot be completely understood without understanding the others. Frantz Fanon realized that an oppressed people is a wounded people, and they will have to cure their wounds in order to feel whole again. In this case, Fanon is both doctor and patient. When as doctor, he speaks to his patients, who are his people, he is both firm and kind.

The African consciousness of today has long historical roots. The writings of Frantz Fanon give the world a new awareness of this consciousness and accentuated the cultural and political basis of its existence. In order to explain the neglected dimensions of African consciousness, the writer will take an international view of the subject and come back to Frantz Fanon and explain his contribution to it. African consciousness, in the diaspora, is many things, yet, it is a single thing. It is an attempt to repair the damage on African people's lives inflicted by slavery and the colonial system. It is a search for a nationality, and it is one of the many ways that Africans away from home may put their fragmented psyche back together again. This condition is schizophrenic in nature, because Blacks hold an affinity both for Africa and their native lands away from Africa.

Slavery and the colonial system subjected African peoples, the world over, to different forms of estrangement. Those who were born in forced exile, called the diaspora, are estranged from the land and cultures of Africa. Black Americans long for an Africa that they do not fully understand. In their desperate longing they often create an idealistic Africa, in their minds, that does not exist any place, except in the mind. Consequently some of their African consciousness grows out of this dilemma.

In America, African people are a special kind of immigrants. They were made immigrants against their will in a nation of immigrants, where most of the indigenous population (called Indians) have been destroyed. The special, and tragic, status of Blacks is that they are the only immigrants who were invited here. Those who "invited" them waited anxiously for their arrival. They had sent large ships to bring Africans here, manned by well-armed captors. Upon arrival they faced no employment problems. There were plenty of jobs waiting for them. The jobs that they did, without pay, helped to make capitalist America.[1]

Blacks' unrequited love affair with America finally led to the realization that the American dream and the American promise were not made for them. This realization made African-Americans long for Africa again. This longing started in the closing years of the eighteenth century. Early in the twentieth century, three men, Bishop Henry McNeal Turner, W.E.B. DuBois and Marcus Garvey, called attention to a new dream, a new promise, and a new land. The land – Africa – was new because Black Americans had been away from it so long.[2]

In Africa, the Africans educated in the West, or educated in Africa by Europeans, experienced the same kind of estrangement that differed from that of Black Americans only by degree. This estrangement was compounded because Africans were estranged in their own cultural mooring at home. Their dilemma calls attention to a still existing need – the need to have a generation of Africans educated in Africa by other Africans, to serve Africa's needs.

This seems to be a long way around to get to the subject, "International Aspects of Fanon and His Impact on African Consciousness," but the subject is what the writer has been talking about all along. When Frantz Fanon was born on the Caribbean Island, Martinique, in 1925, African consciousness was the prevailing feeling among the writers, artists, and thinkers in the African world. In the United States, the Universal Negro Improvement Association (UNIA) – the Garvey Movement – had reached the height of its popularity and public acceptance. This movement and its leader, Marcus Garvey, had raised Black people's consciousness of Africa to a new level. Another movement, called the Harlem Renaissance, complemented the Garvey Movement while the writers and artists expressed their feelings toward Africa in poems, essays, paintings, and monograms. In his poem, "Heritage," the poet Countee Cullen asked the question, "What is Africa to me?" Other writers expanded the question by asking, "What is Africa to the Africans?" and, "What is Africa to the world?" The answer to these questions is the literary essence of African consciousness.

There is a need to examine the concepts of African consciousness and its influence on different African peoples living outside of Africa. Black people who reside outside of the continent of Africa have responded to this concept, emotionally, culturally, and politically, depending on the nature of their alienation. Black Americans are the most alienated African people in all the world. This circumstance is reflected in their response to the writings of Frantz Fanon and their reactions to the Garvey Movement and the Nation of Islam when it was under the leadership of Elijah Muhammad and Malcolm X. It is no accident that Marcus Garvey's movement for African redemption had its greatest success in the United States, among American Blacks. This movement was a failure in Garvey's home country, Jamaica. It is also no accident that the largest Muslim, or pseudo-Muslim, movement in the Western world was built here among American Blacks.

A part of Black Americans' alienation is in the name assigned to them –*Negro*. During the rise of the European slave trade in the fifteenth and sixteenth centuries, some lazy Spaniard or Portuguese changed the word "Negro," then a descriptive adjective meaning black, into a noun. This word, or designation, was forced on a people without their approval. Ethnically speaking, there is no such thing as a "Negro." For a people to feel whole and self-respecting, their name must relate to land, history and culture. The word "Negro" relates to a condition. In his book, *The Name Negro, Its Origin and Evil Use* (1960), Richard B. Moore has said: "Slaves and dogs are named by their masters, free men name themselves." A similar observation was made by another writer, Raphael p. Powell, in his book, *The Human Side of a People and the Right Name* (1937), written a generation earlier.[3] It is interesting to note that both of these observations were made by Caribbean writers. Richard B. Moore is from Barbados. Raphael P. Powell is from Jamaica. This subject introduces another aspect of the neglected intellectual history of the Caribbean Islands. The Caribbean personality, writer, artist, and thinker, in most cases, flourishes best away from home. It is doubtful if Frantz Fanon would have become one of the greatest theoreticians of struggle in the twentieth century had he stayed on the Island of Martinique. The Island of Trinidad produced three great theoreticians of Pan-Africanism, Henry Sylvester Williams (1869–1911), George Padmore (1902–1959), and C.L.R. James, who is still living and part of the struggle. These three Caribbean personalities are best known for their writings and their organizational affiliations away from their home country.[4]

It is necessary now to view Frantz Fanon in the intellectual atmosphere that produced him. He emerged in the post-World War II atmosphere, still dealing with contradictions – personal and otherwise – that were the harvest of the colonial heritage. He had fought in World War II, thinking that this was at least in part a means for the liberation of colonial people. Disappointment led to self-analysis, new conclusions, and new associations. He had first associated himself with the school of negritude and had begun to develop some of his theories of *color* struggle within the atmosphere of that school. He cannot be understood from the vantage point of that school of thought alone; it was not a cult to him, but an intellectual arena worthy of serious investigation. So much of the thought pattern that went into the making of this concept had emerged among the intellects in the French-speaking Caribbean community, led by Aime Cesaire. One cannot understand this without looking at the Caribbean community, historically, in the role that it has played in the color politics of France. These Islands, and Senegal, had a form of political upward mobility that made them exceptions in the French colonial scheme. The aspect that the French did not seem to anticipate is that the intellects from these Islands would become the severest critics of France's colonial policy.

Frantz Fanon became generally known to some Afro-American writers and thinkers at the First International Conference of Negro Writers and Artists. His paper for that conference, "Racism and Culture," gave new insight to that subject. He stated: Racism, in its vulgar, primitive and simplified form, claimed to find the material basis of the doctrine in biology, the Scriptures having proved inadequate, it would be wearisome to recall the efforts made at that time; comparative form of the skull, the number and configuration of the grooves of the encephalon, the characteristics of the cellular layers of the skin, the dimensions of the vertebrae, the microscopic appearance of the epidermis, and so forth.

> Intellectual and emotional primitivism seemed to be the obvious consequence, a fact whose existence merely had to be recognised.[5]

Fanon is saying in this article that European racism is a form of paganism and is a concept that should be alien to an enlightened people, that it grows out of the European's insecurity in power.

In the conclusion of this article, he states:

> During the course of the struggle, the dominant nation tries to circulate racist arguments again, but the elaboration of racism shows itself increasingly ineffective. There is talk of fanaticism, of primitive attitudes in the face of death, but once again the mechanism, henceforth out of action, fails to respond. Those who were formerly motionless, those who timorously obeyed the constitution, the fearful, the eternally inferiorised spring suddenly to life, and emerge in battle.
>
> The occupying power no longer understands.
>
> The end of racism begins with this sudden comprehension.
>
> The spasmodic and rigid culture of the occupying power, once liberated, is finally open to the culture of the people who have ruly become brothers. The two cultures can stand side by side and enrich each other.
>
> In conclusion, universality resides in this decision to bear the burden of the reciprocal relativism of differing cultures, provided only that the colonial status is irrevocably excluded.

At the Second Congress of Negro Writers and Artists, Fanon addressed himself to the role of culture in the struggle for African liberation. Fanon clearly understood that African people were not without culture, but because of colonialism had a misunderstood and somewhat wounded culture. He understood, as many Africans before and after him have observed, that the Africans were not then and are not now in need of a new religion, least of all the concept coming from Europe. Africans were saturated with religions that they had not used creatively, because they had accepted religion on its face value and not as a handmaiden for power.

African religions, Fanon observed, were no competition for European religions simply because African religions were religions pure and simple. Christianity as interpreted by the Europeans was the handmaiden of European world power and the rationality and the concept of superiority. The ironic weakness in African religions is in the strength of their purity; they have not been made into political instruments. In the following statement, Fanon evaluates the impact of colonialism on the African way of life. He said:

> Colonial domination, because it was total and oversimplified, made short work of displacing, in spectacular fashion, the cultural existence of the subject people. The negation of national realities, new legal relationships, introduced by the occupying power, the rejection of the natives and their customs to the fringes of colonial society, expropriation and the systematized enslavement of men and women, rendered possible this cultural obliteration.
>
> I demonstrated three years ago, at our First Congress, that under colonial conditions, cultural dynamism is fairly rapidly replaced by a substantiation of attitudes. The field of culture is then marked off by guard rails and signposts. They are so many defense mechanisms, of the most elementary types, which can be assimilated on more than one round to the instinct of preservation.[6]

Out of this observation Fanon is basically saying that to control a people, you must first control what they think about themselves and how they regard their culture and their religion. With the missionary as a handmaiden of European colonialism, war was declared on African culture and African religions. It is enough of a tragedy for colonialists to laugh at African gods. This tragedy is compounded when the African joins in the laughter. In many ways every time an African becomes a Christian in the manner prescribed by the Europeans, he or she is laughing at African gods. When a conqueror makes a people ashamed of their culture and of their religion, he needs no prison walls or chains to hold them. The chains on their minds are more than sufficient.

Before any further discussion, it should be understood that this is not an attempt to concede the creation of Christianity or Judaism to Europeans. Both of these religions had their early development in Africa. In using the term *Christianity*, this writer refers to the European interpretation of what was once an honorable African religion.

After Frantz Fanon concluded his medical studies in Paris in 1951, his stated intentions were to work in Africa a few years and return to Martinique. He addressed a letter to Leopold Senghor inquiring about a job in an African hospital. Because the letter was late in being answered, he accepted a position in Algeria, at a time when the liberation struggle was beginning. It is interesting to speculate what would have happened had the letter from Leopold Senghor arrived on time. Frantz Fanon, with Senegal as his vantage point, might have become a different kind of revolutionary theoretician. Algeria, in the midst of a revolution was an intellectual window on the world and, literally for Fanon, a finishing school. From this vantage point, Fanon looked at the rest of Africa and developed a theory of revolutionary struggle and African consciousness. Because he saw so many European-educated Africans more committed to themselves than the struggle for African liberation, he prophesized some of the African's tragedies in leadership that are occurring today. His book, *The Wretched of the Earth*, was published in the United States during the height of the civil rights struggle, and among his books it was the most read by Black Americans, and in this writer's opinion, not thoroughly understood then or now. Some of the activists read only one chapter of the book, the chapter concerning violence. Black Americans were in the midst of a nonviolent struggle, and they questioned whether nonviolence was the final weapon in the struggle. They tended to view nonviolence as a tactic and not a way of life. Blacks then and still are trying to define nationalism and Pan-Africanism. There are those Blacks who think nationalism and Pan-Africanism are negations of socialism. This writer does not belong to this school. Nationalism, Pan-Africanism, and socialism are complementary concepts that can function together without contradiction. The writer is aware of the dangers Frantz Fanon graphically outlined in the chapter, "Pitfalls of National Consciousness." The writer is also aware of the fact that some of the biggest thieves, scoundrels, and betrayers of people in modern times have disguised themselves as nationalists and socialists. What must be understood is that the nationalism of an oppressed people is decidedly different from the nationalism of a powerful oppressive nation. Fanon sees the fight against colonialism as a means of clearing the way for an a social order that would take its precedents from African culture and African needs. Because socialism is more flexible than socialists are, this point is not easy to get across. The African consciousness of a large number of civil rights activist came from the reading of Fanon. Most read Fanon too hurriedly.

In an article in the Summer 1968 issue of *Freedomways*, John Henry Jones states the following:

> In essence Fanon lays Black people on the couch in his first bok, as he concerns himself with their subjective responses to the physical and psychological genocide of the white colonizers. It therefore has the strengths and weaknesses of the discipline, as it dredges the subterranean caverns of case histories, myths, and literature. Here is a restless mentality revolving against outward oppression; a relentless exposure of his own self-delusions. His

chapters concern themselves with "The Woman of Color and The White Man;" "The Fact of Blackness;" and "The Negro and Recognition."[7]

In a collective way Fanon is speaking about African consciousness and destiny of Blacks as a race of people. The writer will conclude with an interpretation of what he understands Fanon's message to be.

If Blacks let other people steal their political, religious, and cultural heritage, what will Blacks leave to their children and their children still unborn? This criticism causes pain, but criticism of this nature is part of this writer's responsibility as a teacher and a life-long searcher for answers to this question.

To the Black writer the crisis of identity has been the most obvious, and it may be the most important. However, there has always been another crisis of major proportion; that is a crisis of a political ideology. In this crisis Blacks have always been involved in contradiction. They have not fully realized that the political ideologies, right or left, will not save them either, unless they control it. To be more precise, a people must be the instrument of their own liberation, and the instrument must be under their control. This argument is not new. It is an unresolved situation that runs through the entire political history of Black people in the United States.

The role of the Black writer is to make an assessment of a people's history in order to understand their humanity, their "nationness," and their sense of mission in the world. Black people must draw heavily on the legacy of oppression in order to end oppression everywhere.

This statement reflects the ideology of Frantz Fanon and what use Blacks can make of his work in the struggle for the total liberation of African peoples all over the world. The feeling of African consciousness that is derived from his work can be the basis for a new coming together of African peoples who may extend their political and ideological objective beyond Pan-Africanism into a concept of an African World Union that will complete the liberation of Africa and, in turn, join other peoples of good will in an effort to bring into being a new humanity for all people everywhere.

End Notes

1. John Henrik Clarke, "Black Americans: Immigrants Against Their Will," in ed. Frank J. Coppa and Thomas J. Curran, *The Immigrant Experience in America* (Boston: Twain Publishers, 1976).
2. Edwin S. Redkey, Black Exodus: *Black Nationalists and Back to Africa Movements, 1890–1910* (New Haven: Yale University Press, 1969), pp. 24–46. See also, John Henrik Clarke, ed. *Marcus Garvey and the Vision of Africa* (New York: Random House, 1974).

3. Richard E. Moore, *The Name Negro, Its Origin and Evil Use* (New York: Afro-American Publishers, Inc., 1960). Also see, Raphael P. Powell, *Human Side of a People and the Right Name* (New York: The Philemon Co., 1937). Reprinted by University Microfilms, Ann Arbor, Michigan, 1969.
4. James R. Hooker, *Henry Sylvester Williams; Imperial Pan-Africanist* (London: Rex Callings, Ltd., 1975). See also, Hooker, *Black Revolutionary: George Padmore's Path from Communism to Pan-Africanism* (New York: Praeger Paperbacks, 1970); and George Padmore, *Pan-Africanism or Communism* (New York: Doubleday and Co., 1971).
5. Frantz Fanon, "Racism and Culture," *Presence Africaine*, Paris, September, 1956, pp. 122–133.
6. "," "The Reciprocal Basis of National Culture and the Struggles for Liberation," Presence Africaine, March 26–April 1, 1978, pp. 89–96.
7. John Henry Jones, "On the Influence of Fanon," *Freedomways*, Summer, 1968, pp. 209–210.

The Passing of Patrice Lumumba

John Henrik Clarke

Reprinted from the *Journal of Human Relations* (Summer 1962): 383–393

The life of Patrice Lumumba proved that he was a product of the best and worst of Belgian colonial rule. In more favorable circumstances, he might have become one of the most astute national leaders of the twentieth century. He was cut down long before he had time to develop into the more stable leader that he was obviously capable of being. When the Congo emerged clearly in the light of modern history, he was its bright star.

His hero was Dr. Kwame Nkrumah, and the model for his state was Ghana. "In a young state," he had said, paraphrasing a similar statement made by Dr. Nkrumah, "you must have strong and visible powers."

At the beginning of his political career he was pro-Western in his outlook. "Mistakes have been made in Africa in the past, but we are ready to work with the powers which have been in Africa to create a powerful new bloc," he said at the beginning of 1960. "If this effort fails, it will be through the fault of the West."

As a reformer, he was somewhat of a republican in his approach. "Our need is to democratize all our institutions," he had said on another occasion. "We must separate the Church from the State. We must take away all power from the traditional chiefs and remove all privileges. We must adapt socialism to African realities. Amelioration of the conditions of life is the only true meaning independence can have."

His resentment of Belgian authority was unyielding in most cases. Mostly because he believed that paternalism was at the base of this authority. This by-product of colonialism never failed to stir a rage within him. On the other hand, his reaction to the Belgian Missionary attempt to enforce Christianity on the

Congo was one of indifference. He had been subjected to both Catholic and Protestant mission influence, without showing any particular affection for either. His parents were devout Catholics. Being neither an atheist nor anti-Christian, he yet considered submission to a religion to be a curb on his ambitions. Rebellion was more rewarding and less wounding to his pride. During his long and lonely rise from obscurity to the Congo's first Prime Minister, he taught himself never to completely trust power in the hands of others. This attitude is reflected in the suspicion that developed between him and the UN Forces in the Congo.

His conflicts with the other Congo politicians were due mainly to his unyielding belief in the unitary state and partly to his lack of experience in explaining, organizing and administering such a state. Nevertheless, he was the only Congolese leader with anything like a national following; a point too often overlooked. His greatest achievement in the early difficult months of Congo independence was in maintaining, with only a few defections, the solidarity of his widely disparate coalition government.

Lumumba belonged to the company of Kwame Nkrumah, Julius Nyerere in Tanganyika, Tom Mboya in Kenya, and Sékou Touré. These leaders believe that the only way to build an effective modern state, free from the shackles of narrow tribal loyalties, is to create a single, strong central government. This firm stand joined the issues in the Congo and created both the supporters and the opposition to Lumumba.

He argued his case at the Round Table Conference that gave the Congo its independence in 1960. He laid it before the electorate in June 1960, and won an indecisive victory. Finally, he tried to force it on his Federalist opponents when he took control of the first independent government. Most of Lumumba's critics considered this to be his greatest error. He tried to cast the Congo into the tight mould of Ghana rather than into the larger, more accommodating mould of Nigeria. This argument is interesting though useless now.

Patrice Lumumba's body now lies a-mouldering in some unmarked and inglorious Congo grave... both his truth and spirit go marching on, much to the discomfort of his murderers.

No other personality in African history has leaped so suddenly from death to martyrdom. In death he might have already made a greater contribution to the liberation and understanding of Africa than he could have made had he lived. In his short lifetime, the stamp of his personality was pressed firmly into the African continent. He was purely an African of the mid-twentieth century. No other place and no other set of circumstances could have charged his life and caused his death in the same unique and tragic way. In death, he cast forth a spirit that will roam the African land for many years to come.

For a long time the Congo appeared to be a peaceful island untouched by African anticolonialism. In the twelve brief years between 1946 and 1958, the Belgians began to lose what had appeared to be an impregnable position. Some important events occurred in Africa and the rest of the world, and broke up the trinity in Belgium's alleged "perfect colony." A change of political direction in Brussels and mounting nationalist pressure coming from within Africa helped to end the illusion that all was well and would stay well in the Congo. At last the Belgians began to have some second thoughts about their policy in the Congo. The missionary-trained evolved, the supposedly emancipated, Westernized middle class had found their voices.

Certain fundamental problems formed the core of the colonial dilemma in Africa, although Belgian colonists chose to ignore this fact. The same problems existed in the Congo as elsewhere in Africa. Freedom, self-determination, hatred of racial discrimination, and white settlement without assimilation made the Congo people feel unwanted in their own country, except as servants for white people.

It was within this order of ideas that the Belgian Socialist Party attempted to change the trend of Belgium's colonial policy and devise a more humane approach to the problems of the Congo people. The accelerated economic development in the Congo during the war and after the war had changed the structure of the Congolese community. The black population of Leopoldville rose from 46,900 to 191,000 between 1940 and 1950. By 1955, the black population of Leopoldville had reached some 300,000. The mass exodus of Congolese from rural areas and their concentration in urban centers created new problems. The detribalized workers did not return to their respective villages when the city no longer afforded them employment.

It was incumbent on the Belgian Socialist Party to define its position in relation to the Congo. As far as basic premises were concerned, the party did recognize "the primacy of native interests; and the aim of its activity will be to prepare the indigenous population gradually to take charge of its own political, economic, and social affairs, within the framework of a democratic society." Further, the Party expressed its "uncompromising opposition to any kind of racial discrimination" and advised a raise in the standard of living of the people of the Congo. Only those whites prepared to work for the realization of these aims and who constitute the administrative personnel of the indigenous population are to enjoy the support of the government. This preparation for self-government presupposes the political organization of the Congo, i.e., the initiation of the native into citizenship. With this proposal, the Belgian Socialist Party admitted that the Congolese were not accepted as citizens in their own country. This fact had been the cause of a broadening dissatisfaction among the Congolese since the early part of the twentieth century. With the relaxing of political restrictions this dissatisfaction began to manifest itself in a form of embryo nationalism. The future Congolese leaders had already begun to gather their first followers. All of the early political parties in the Congo were the outgrowth of regional and tribal associations. Patrice Lumumba was the only Congolese leader who, from the very beginning of his career, attempted to build a Congo-wide political organization.

During his short-lived career Patrice Lumumba was the first popularly elected Congolese Government Prime Minister. Like a few men before him, he became a near-legend in his own lifetime. The influence of this legend extended to the young militant nationalists far beyond the borders of the Congo, and it is still spreading.

Of all the leaders who suffered imprisonment at the hands of the Belgians before 1960, Lumumba had the largest number of followers among the Congolese masses, mainly because he had more of the qualities of character with which they liked to identify. As a speaker he was equally effective in French, Ki-Swahili or Lingola. The devotion of the rank and file of his party, *Movement National Congolais* (MNC) to Patrice Lumumba was not a unique phenomenon. What is more significant is the fact that he was able to attract the strongly expressed loyalties of a tribally-heterogeneous body of the Congolese. This made him the only national political leader. While other politicians tended to take advantage of their respective associations as the path to power, Lumumba took the broader and more nationalistic approach and involved himself in other movements only indirectly related to politics.

In 1951, he joined the *Association des Evolves de Stanleyville*, one of the most active and numerically important of all the clubs in Orientale Province. He was in the same year appointed Secretary-General of the *Association des Postiers de la Province Orientale*, a professional organization consisting mostly of postal workers. Two years later he became Vice-Chairman of an Alumni Association consisting of former mission students. In 1956 he founded the *Amicle Liberale de Stanleyville*.

Patrice Lumumba is a member of the Betetela tribe, a Mongo subgroup. He was born on July 2, 1925, in Katako-Kombe in the Sunkuru district of the Kasai Province. In growing up he only received a primary education. Very early in life he learned to push himself beyond the formal limits of his education. He made frequent contributions to local newspapers such as *Stanleyvillois* and the more widely read publications, *Voix du Conlais* and *Croix du Congo*. Unlike the vast majority of Congolese writers of the period ho placed major emphasis on the cultural heritage of their own tribes, Lumumba's early writings emphasized – within the limits of Belgian official restrictions – problems of racial, social, and economic discrimination.

On July 1, 1956, the career of Patrice Lumumba was temporarily interrupted when he was arrested on the charge of embezzling 126,000 francs ($2,200) from the post office funds. He was sentenced to serve a two-year prison term. On June 13, 1957, the sentence was commuted on appeal to eighteen months, and finally to 12 months after the Wolves of Stanleyville reimbursed the sum in question. Subsequently, Lumumba left Stanleyville and found employment in Leopoldville as the sale director of the Bracongo (polar beer) Brewery.

Leopoldville became a good vantage point for Lumumba's Congo-wide activities. He had now entered into the crucial phase of his political career. In 1958, while combining the functions of vice-chairman of a liberal friendship society, the *Circle Liberal d'Etudes et d'Agreement*, with those of the president of the *Association dis Batetela*, of Leopoldville, he joined a Christian Democratic Study Group, the *Centre d'Etudes et de Recherches Sociales*, created in 1955 by the Secretary General of the *Jeunesses Ouvieres Christiennes*, Jacques Meert. Among the more prominent members of this organization were Joseph Ileo (now Prime Minister of the Kasavubu government) and Joseph Ngalula.

Joseph Ileo was editor-in-chief of the bi-monthly *Conscience Africaine*. He had already acquired a wide reputation among Congolese when he decided, in July of 1956, to publish a nationalist inspired manifesto which contained a daring 30-year plan of emancipation for the Congo.

Both Ileo and Ngalula were anxious to broaden the bases of the Movement National Congolais, a moderate nationalist organization created in 1956. Patrice Lumumba, then regarded as one of the eminent spokesmen of liberal ideas, joined the MNC.

Once affiliated with this and other groups, Lumumba readily asserted himself and became the dominant figure. Shortly after proclaiming himself chairman of the MNC's Central Committee, he formally announced on October 10, 1958, the foundation of a "national movement" dedicated to the goal of "national liberation." His action at this moment was prompted by two important development affecting the Congo. One was the forthcoming visit of a parliamentary committee appointed by the former Minister of the Congo, Mr. Patillon, for the purpose of "conducting an inquiry concerning the administrative and political evolution of the country." Another was the creation of a *Movement Pour le Progress National Congolais* in late November 1958, by the Congolese delegates to the Brussels Exposition. Lumumba moved in and around these groups and quickly projected himself into the role of a dynamic and radical nationalist leader.

A high point in his political development came in 1958, when he was permitted to attend the Pan African Conference in Accra, Ghana. Here he became a member of the Permanent Directing Committee. Patrice Lumumba had now projected himself upon a political stage of international importance. In addition to whatever personal counsel he might have received from Ghana's Prime Minister, Nkrumah, there is little doubt that the Accra Conference was an important factor in shaping Lumumba's long-range objectives and further sensitizing him to the philosophy of Pan-Africanism.

When he returned home, the emancipation of the Congo from Belgium's tutelage assumed first priority among his activities. In March 1959, when Belgium had already announced its intention to lead the Congo "without fatal procrastination and without undue haste" toward self-government, Lumumba went to Brussels where he delivered several lectures under the auspices of *Présence Congolese*, a Belgian organization dedicated to the promotion of African culture. On this occasion, Lumumba indiscreetly turned on his host and sponsors and deplored the "bastardization and destruction of Negro-African art," and the "depersonalization of Africa." He reaffirmed his Party's determination to put an end to the "camouflaged slavery of Belgian colonization" and elect and independent government in 1961. With this act of boldness, Patrice Lumumba had set the stage for most of his future troubles and probably his future death.

After the target-date for independence had been approved by the *Movement National Congolais*, new troubles began for Lumumba and his supporters. Now that the contestants for power were close to their goal, the completion between them became fiercer. Delegates to the Luluabourg Congress, in April 1959, ran against the demands of other nationalist groups anxious to put themselves forward as the standard-bearers of independence. Several of Lumumba's earlier supporters withdrew from MNC and formed their own parties. With the date for Congo independence practically rushing upon him, Lumumba set out to rebuild the *Movement National Congolais*. He involved himself in every phase of his party's activities, organizing local sections of the MNC and recruiting new supporters.

On November 1, 1959, a few days after his wing of the MNC held its congress in Stanleyville, Lumumba was arrested for the second time and charged with having made seditious statements. He was sentenced to six months in jail. After serving nearly three months of his sentence, he was released when a delegation of officials from the MNC notified the Belgian government that they would not participate in the Brussels Roundtable Conference unless Lumumba was set free. Soon after his release, Lumumba's party was victorious in the December elections. As expected, Stanleyville proved to be the main Lumumba stronghold in the Congo. In Stanleyville his party won ninety per cent of the votes.

Lumumba's status and influence continued to rise. As a representative of Orientale Province, he was appointed to the General Executive College, an interim executive body established after the Brussels Roundtable Conference. Trouble continued to brew within the ranks of his party. Victor Nendaka, vice-chairman of the MNC, broke with Lumumba for what he termed the "extreme left wing tendencies" of the party leader. In 1960, he organized his own party. Once more Lumumba reshuffled the party personnel and strengthened his position. The MNC emerged from the next electoral struggle as the strongest in the House of Representatives, with 34 out of 137 seats. In the Provincial Assembly of Orientale, Lumumba's party held 58 out of 70 seats. In the assemblies of Kivu and Kasai Provinces, 17 out of 25 seats were secured.

Lumumba employed several techniques to mobilize his support and activate the rural masses. First there was the careful selection of party officials and propagandists at the Lodja Congress, held March 9–12, 1960. The delegates of the Bakutshu and Batetela tribes agreed that they would entrust the defense of the interests to the political party which held a dominant position in the region. Namely, that was Lumumba's party, the MNC. The party's success among the Bakutshu and Batetela tribal associations was mainly due to Lumumba's tribal origin and the anti-Belgian orientation acquired by these tribes in resisting the penetration of Western rule.

Lumumba and the MNC improved their techniques of building up functional organizations in order to unify the political actions of the MNC. These organizational networks embraced a variety of interest groups and cut across tribal lines. Through a tactical alliance with minor parties, Lumumba tried to transform the MNC into an integrating structure where both sectional and national interests would be represented. This program received its formal sanction at the extraordinary congress of the MNC, held in Luluabourg, April 3–4, 1960. This was a major landmark in the history of Lumumba's party. Once more he had proven to be the most able of all Congolese leaders.

As the Congo crossed the threshold of independence, new troubles developed within the ranks of the MNC. Communication between Lumumba and some of the leaders of the party broke down. The Congo's most vital instrument of stability, the *Force Publique*, collapsed. The number and complexities of the issues now confronting Lumumba absorbed most of the time he formerly devoted to party activities. Now that the pomp and ceremony of the Belgian's handing over power to elected Congolese leaders was over, one struggle for Lumumba was over, but a new and bitter one was beginning.

His devotion to the idea of a united Congo was now more firm. He was one of the few Congolese politicians who had any conception of the Congo as a strong centralized state. Tshombe thought first of carving himself out a state in Katanga where he could be the boss, with Belgian help. Kasavubu cherished the dream of restoring the ancient empire of Bakongo. Other Congolese politicians were still involved in their tribal ideals and hostilities.

Lumumba was neither kind nor cautious toward the Belgians during the independence ceremony. This might have been one of his greatest mistakes. He announced too many of his future plans, which included not only the uniting of the Congo but giving assistance to the nations around him (especially Angola) who were still under European rule. Whoever made the decision to kill Lumumba probably made it this very day. He had crossed the path of the unseen power manipulators who wanted to control the Congo economically even if they were willing to let Lumumba control it politically. Instead of saying, "Thanks very much for our independence. We appreciate all you Belgians have done for our country," Lumumba said in effect, "It's about time, too! And it's a pity that in a half-century you didn't see fit to build more hospitals and schools. You could have made much better use of your time."

Lastly, when the *Force Publique* revolted in the first days of July, Lumumba tried earnestly to be equal to this and other emergencies exploding around him. He faced the risks of his high position with real courage. Frantically, he moved over his large country trying to restore order. Several times he escaped death by inches. Once he was saved by a Ghanian officer. Once his car was stoned by a mob. This did not keep him from trying to restore order to his troubled country. In the middle of July when the structure of order in his country was deteriorating into chaos, Lumumba flew off for a grandiose tour of the United States, Canada, North, and West Africa. This was another one of his unfortunate mistakes. In his absence confusion became worse.

In his dealings with the United Nations, he never knew exactly what he wanted; showing no steady policy toward the UN, he confused both his friends and enemies who grew impatient with his erratic behavior. When the disintegration within his country reached dangerous proportions, he asked for military from the United Nations. Within about three days, the UN troops were on the spot. When Lumumba found that the UN troops could not be used as a private army to put down his political opponents, he became disenchanted with their presence in his country.

By now Lumumba had quarreled with nearly every leading politician in the Congo. His continued erratic action shook the confidence of the outside world and of many of the African leaders who had wished him well and hoped that he could restore order rapidly. A power struggle had erupted in the Congo. Concurrent with this struggle Belgians were working behind the scenes to reconquer the Congo economically; their Congolese puppets, bought and paid for in advance, were deeply engrossed in their self-seeking venture.

In the last weeks of his life, when he was being dragged around with a rope around his neck, while his captors yanked up his head for the benefit of newsreel cameras, he still carried himself with great dignity as well as courage. When he was beaten up on the plane which carried him to be handed over to his arch enemy, Tshombe, he did not cry out nor plead for mercy. When Tshombe's troops beat him again, in Elizabethville airport, he asked no one for help or pity. He was carried off by Tshombe's troops and their Belgian officers on a journey from which he was certain never to return alive. Lumumba's conduct in the midst of these scenes will always stand to his credit in history. These traits of independence and courage in his personality went into the making of his martyrdom – a strange and dangerous martyrdom that makes Lumumba a more effective African nationalist in death than he was in life.

Some of the people who are now most vocal in their praise of the dead Lumumba include many who in the past criticized some of his actions and speeches most savagely while he was still alive. Patrice Lumumba was pulled from power mostly by his own people, who were being manipulated by forces of change and power alien to their understanding.

In the killing of Lumumba, white neo-colonialists and their black African puppets frustrated the southward spread of independence movements. Lumumba had pledged to give assistance to the African nations to the east and south of the Congo who are still struggling to attain independence, particularly Angola. Lumumba was a true son of Africa, and in his short unhappy lifetime he was accepted as belonging to all of Africa, not just the Congo.

The important point in the Lumumba story, briefly related, is this: He proved that legitimacy of a postcolonial regime in Africa relates mainly to its legal mandate; but even more, legitimacy relates to the regime's credentials as a representative of a genuine nationalism fighting against the intrigues of neo-colonialism. This is why Lumumba was and is still being extolled this "best son of Africa," this "Lincoln of the Congo," this "Black Messiah," whose struggle was made noble by his unswerving demand for centralism against all forms of Balkanization and rendered heroic by his unyielding resistance to the forces of neo-colonialism which finally killed his body, but not his spirit. This man, who now emerges as a strange combination of statesman, sage, and martyr, wrote his name on the scroll of African history during his short and unhappy lifetime.

BIBLIOGRAPHY

Books

Congo: Background and Conflict, Alan p. Merriam. Evanston, Illinois; Northwestern University Press, 1961

Congo Disaster, Colin Legum. Baltimore, Maryland; Penguin Books, 1961

The Congo: A Brief History and Appraisal, Maurice N. Hennessey. New York; Praeger, 1961

Upsurge in Africa, Anthony Delins. (Pamphlet published by Canadian Institute of International Affairs)

Periodicals

United Nations Review, January 1961

Africa Special Report, October 26, 1956

Africa Weekly Magazine, 1959 issues

The Economist, London, July 1959

Arab Observer, July 17, 1960

New York Times Magazine, July 31, 1960; August 6, 1960; August 21, 1960; January 8, 1961; February 26, 1961

I.F. Stone's Weekly, DC, September 26, 1960; October 10, 1960

The New Statesman, London, December 10, 1960

The Nation, New York City, October 15, 1960

American Magazine, August 12, 1961

The Newsleader Magazine, August 12, 1961

Africa Special Report, June 1960; February 1961; June 1961

Drum Magazine, April 1961

African Observer, Vol. 1, No. 1; February 1961

Press Releases

Ghana Information Services, February 15 & 17, 1961 and March 1961

American Universities Field Staff Reports, 1960

Paul Robeson: The Artist as Activist and Social Thinker

John Henrik Clarke

Reprinted from *"Paul Robeson: The Artist as Activist and Social Thinker," Presence Africaïne*, No. 107 (3rd Quarter, 1978): 223–241

Paul Robeson was, indeed, more than an artist, activist and freedom fighter. The dimensions of his talent made him our Renaissance man. He was the first American artist, black or white, to realize that the role of the artist extends far beyond the stage and the concert hall. Early in his life he became conscious of the plight of his people, stubbornly surviving in a racist society. This was his window on the world. From this vantage point he saw how the plight of his people related to the rest of humanity. He realized that the artist had the power, and the responsibility, to change the society in which he lived. He learned that art and culture are weapons in a people's struggle to exist with dignity and in peace. Life offered him many options and he never chose the easiest one. For most of his life, he was a man walking against the wind. An understanding of his beginnings and how he developed artistically and politically, will reveal the nature of his mission and the importance of the legacy of participation in struggle that we have inherited from him.

He was born on April 9, 1898, at a time of great crisis for his people. When he died on January 23, 1976, his people were still in a crisis, partly of a different nature, and partly the same crisis that they had faced in the closing years of the nineteenth century when Paul Robeson was born. He was born three years after Booker T. Washington made his famous Atlanta Exposition address (1895) and two years after the Supreme Court announced a decision in the Plessy *versus* Ferguson Case, in which the concept of "separate but equal" facilities for Black

Americans became law. Of course, the separateness never produced any equalness. The time and the decision did produce some of the problems that Paul Robeson would address himself to in later years.

His early years were strengthened by binding family ties. They were not easy years. He recalled those years and reflected on their meaning in the introductory issue of the newspaper *Freedom* (November, 1950).

> "My father was a slave origin. He reached as honorable a position as a Negro could under these circumstances, but soon after I was born he lost his church and poverty was my beginning. Relatives from my father's North Carolina family took me in, a motherless orphan, while my father went to new fields to begin again in a corner grocery store. I slept four in a bed, ate the nourishing greens and cornbread."
>
> "Many times I stood on the very soil on which my father was a slave, where some of my cousins were sharecroppers and unemployed tobacco workers. I reflected upon the wealth bled from my near relatives alone, and of the very basic wealth of all this America beaten out of millions of Negro people, enslaved, freed, newly enslaved until this very day."

He grew to early manhood during the Booker T. Washington era. He made his professional debut at the Harlem YWCA in 1920, in a play, *Simon, the Cyrenian,* by Redgely Torrence. The play was about an Ethiopian who steps out of a crowd to help a tired and haggard Jesus Christ carry his cross up Calvary Hill to be crucified. His role in this play was symbolic of his commitment to just courses and to oppressed people, the world over, the rest of his life. This dimension of his life is the main focus of this article. He was not persecuted, denied a passport and attacked at Peekskill because he was a world-famous concert singer and activist.

Many of his persecutors admired him in these capacities. He was persecuted, denied a passport and attacked at Peekskill because he was an artist and activist who used his art and his personality to call for change in the society in which he lived. This was not a late development in his life. He grew to manhood observing the need for change.

Paul Robeson attended elementary and high school in Westfield and Somerville, New Jersey. He won a four-year scholarship to Rutgers College and entered in the fall of 1915. Only two other black students had attended the school since its founding in 1776. Robeson's achievements in both scholarship and athletics at Rutgers were extraordinary. He won Phi Beta Kappa honours in his junior year, was valedictorian of his graduating class, and was the debating champion in all of his four years.

Although he was initially brutalized by his own teammates when he tried out for the football team, he survived to become one of the greatest football players of all time. Walter Camp selected Roberson as his first-team All-American end for two years (1917 and 1918) and he was named on all important "censesus" All-American teams for both those years. Roberson was also a great all-round athlete, winning a total of 15 varsity letters in football, basketball, baseball and track.

In May of 1918, the Reverend Roberson died. Paul's relatives and his football coach, Foster Sanford, were especially helpful to him during the trying time immediately after his father's death. Following his graduation in 1919, Paul went to live in Harlem and entered Columbia Law School, from which he graduated in 1923. To pay his way through law school, Paul played professional football on weekends, first with Fritz Pollard on the Akron, Ohio team in 1920 and 1921, and then with Milwaukee in 1922. In 1921, he met and married Eslanda Cardozo Goode, a brilliant young woman who was the first black analytical chemist at Columbia Medical Center. Their marriage lasted forty-four years until Eslanda's death in 1965.

In the early 1920s, Paul Robeson joined the Provincetown Players in Greenwich Village. This brought him to the attention of the American playwright Eugene O'Neil who selected him for the lead in his play, *All God's Children Got Wings*. His performance in this play established his importance in the American theatre. In 1924, he was in another Eugene O'Neil play, *The Emperor Jones*. By 1925, he was known both in England and in the United States as an actor and as a concert singer. Lawrence Brown, who accompanied him during his first concert in 1925, remained with him for twenty-five years.

In the years following the First World War, Black Americans were discovering themselves, their culture and their history. Thousands of black soldiers had returned from the war in Europe to face unemployment, bad housing and lynchings. The Universal Negro Improvement Association led by Marcus Garvey, and the intellectual movement called the Harlem Literary Renaissance reached their perspective heights during this period. The years of the nineteen-twenties were proving-grounds for Paul Robeson's development as an artist and a responsible person.

Many of the roles that Robeson played in America were repeated in the theatres of London. It has been reported that his political ideas took shape after George Bernard Shaw introduced him to the concept of socialism in 1928. This may be partly true about his political ideas in a formal sense, though his social awareness started before this time. His first visit to the Soviet Union in 1934 had a more profound influence on the shaping of his political ideas and understanding. Later, he publicly expressed his belief in the principles of scientific socialism. It was his conviction that a socialist society represents an advance to a higher stage of life for all mankind. The rest of his life was a commitment to his conviction.

He spoke out against oppression wherever he saw it, and not just the oppression of his own people. He went to Spain during the Civil War in that country and sang for the Republican troops and for the members of the International Brigades. This was part of a gathering of anti-Fascist forces who were backed by Hilter and Mussolini. When Paul Robeson returned to the United States, he expressed the belief that the war in Spain represented dangers for the world far beyond that country's borders. He stated:

> "I saw the connection between the problems of all oppressed people and the necessity of the artist to participate fully."

He opposed every form of racism in his own country; he was the first American artist to refuse to sing before a segregated audience. He spoke out against lynching, segregated theaters and eating-places a generation before the beginning of what is referred to as Black Revolution. He supported all organizations that he thought were working genuinely to improve the lot of his people and mankind.

In his book, Robeson: *Labor's Forgotten Champion* (Balamp Publishing Co., Detroit, Mich., 1975), Dr. Charles H. Wright states that:

> "Robeson saw the struggle of the working classes of Spain in the same terms that he saw the struggles of the black man in the United States. He made this clear after he left Spain and embarked on a series of public appearances on behalf of the Republicans, both on the continent and in England. It was from the continent, probably the Spanish Embassy in Paris, that he issued what became known as his Manifesto Against Fascism."

The *Manifesto* reads as follows:

> "Every artist, every scientist must decide, now where he stands. He has no alternative. There are no impartial observers."
>
> "Through the destruction, in certain countries, of man's literary heritage, through the propagation of false ideas of national and racial superiority, the artist, the scientist, the writer is challenged. This struggle invades the former cloistered halls of our Universities and all her seats of learning."
>
> "The battlefront is everywhere. There is no sheltered rear. The artist elects to fight for freedom or slavery."

> "I have made my choice! I had no alternative!"
>
> "The history of the era is characterized by the degradation of my people. Despoiled of their lands, their culture destroyed, they are denied equal opportunity of the law and deprived of their rightful place in the respect of their fellows."
>
> "Not through blind faith or through coercion, but conscious of my course, I take my place with you. I stand with you in unalterable support of the lawful government of Spain, duty and regularly chosen by its sons and daughters."

In January 1938, he visited Spain with his wife, Eslanda. Plans had already been made for him to sing to the troops in the International Abraham Lincoln Brigades.

This was not his introduction to the international aspects of the fight against Fascism. The Spanish Civil War started in June 1936, the Italian-Ethiopian War had started the year before. On December 20, 1937, Robeson participated in a meeting on the Spanish Civil War at the Albert Hall in London. This and other anti-Fascist activities disenchanted the United States Department of State. This was probably the formal beginning of his harassment by that agency which would continue for another twenty years. In his writings and speeches, for most of the years of his active career, Paul Robeson was very explicit in explaining the motive and antecedents of his fight against every form of racism and oppression. At a Welcome Home Rally in Harlem on June 19, 1949, he restated his position and the nature of his commitment:

> "I have traveled many lands and I have sung and talked to many peoples. Wherever I appeared, whether in professional concert, at peace meetings, in the factories at trade union gatherings, at the mining pits, at assemblies of representative colonial students from all over the world, always the greeting came: 'Take back our affection, our love, our strength to the Negro people and to the members of the progressive movement of America.'"
>
> "It is especially moving to be here in this particular auditorium in Harlem. Way back in 1938, I came here to this very hall from a football game at the Polo Grounds between Rutgers and Syracuse. There was a basketball game between St. Christopher and Alpha. Later, I played here for St. Christopher against the Alphas, against the Spartans, and the Brooklyn YMCA, time an time again. This was a home of mine. It is still my home."
>
> "I was then, through my athletics and my University
>
> Record, trying to hold up the prestige of my people; trying in the only way I knew to ease the path for future Negro boys and girls. And I am still in there slugging, yes, at another level, and you can bet your life that I shall

> battle every step of the way until conditions around these corners change and conditions change for the Negro people al up and down this land."
>
> "The road has been long. The road has been hard. It began about as tough as I ever had it – in Princeton, New Jersey, a college town of Southern aristocrats who from Revolutionary times, transferred Georgia to New Jersey. My brothers couldn't go to high school in Princeton. They had to go to Trenton, ten miles away. That's right – Trenton, of the 'Trenton Six.'"
>
> "Almost every Negro, in Princeton lived off the college and accepted the social status that went with it. We live, for all intents and purposes, on a Southern plantation. And with no more dignity that that suggests – all the bowing and scraping to the drunken rich, all the vile names, all the Uncle Tomming to earn enough to lead miserable lives."

He could not see himself accepting any form of Jim-Crow Americanism. He said that, in many ways, he hated what America was, but he loved what it promised to be. He defended the stated higher ideals and potential of the United States while calling attention to the fact that the nation's promise to all of its people had not been kept.

> "And I defied, he said, and I defy any part of this insolent, dominating America, however powerful, to challenge my Americanism, because by word and deed I challenge this vicious system to the death."

Paul Robeson would not let his public acceptance as an actor and singer make him relax in comfort and forget the struggle for basic dignity still being waged by the rest of his people. On this point he said:

> "I refuse to let my personal success, as part of a fraction of one per cent of the Negro people, to explain away the injustices to fourteen million of my people; because with all the energy at my command, I fight for the right of the Negro people and other oppressed, labor-driving Americans to have decent homes, decent jobs, and the dignity that belongs to every human being!"
>
> "Somewhere in my childhood these feelings were planted. Perhaps when I resented being pushed off the sidewalk, when I saw my women being insulted, and especially when I saw my elder brother answer each insult with blows that sent would-be slave-masters crashing to the stone sidewalks, even though jail was his constant reward. He never said it, but he told me day after day: 'Listen to me, kid'. (He loved me very dearly.) 'Don't you ever take it, as long as you live.'"

In my opinion, the artistic and political growth of Paul Roberson had its greatest stimulant during the nineteen-thirties. Paul was always discovering something new in the human situation, and new dimensions in old things he already knew. He was, concurrently, both a student and a scholar in pursuit of lives. Africa, its people and cultures was of special interest to him. In a note, dated 1936, included in his *Selected Writings* (published by the Paul Robeson Archives, 1976) he makes this comment:

> "I am a singer and an actor. I am primarily an artist. Had I been born in Africa, I would have belonged, I hope, to that family which sings and changes the glories and legends of the tribe. I would have liked in my mature years to have been a wise elder, for I worship wisdom and knowledge of the ways of men."

His artistic strength was in his love for the history, songs and folk-culture of his people. In this way he learned to respect the cultures of all people.

In an article published in the *Royal Screen Pictorial* (London, April 1935) he said:

> I am a Negro. The origin of the Negro is African. It would, therefore, seem an easy matter for me to assume African nationality (...) At present, the younger generation of Negroes in American looks towards Africa and asks, 'What is there to interest me? What of value has Africa to offer that the Western world cannot give me?' (...) Their acknowledgement of their common origin, species, interest and attitudes binds Jew to Jew; a similar acknowledgement will bind Negro to Negro. I realize that this will not be accomplished by viewing from afar the dark rites for the witch-doctor. It may be accomplished, or at least furthered, by patient inquiry. To this end I am learning Swahili.
>
> Twi and other African dialects- which come easily to me because their rhythm is the same as that employed by the American Negro in speaking English; and when the time is ripe, I propose to investigate on the spot the possibilities of such a regeneration as I have outlined. Meanwhile, in my music, my plays, my films, I want to carry always this central idea- to be African. Multitudes of men have died for less worthy ideals; it is even more eminently worth living for.

This interest in Africa, which started during his "London years" continued throughout the rest of his life and very logically led to his participation in the development and leadership of organizations like the council on African Affairs (1937–1955) and the National Negro Congress. In an article from his *Selected Writings* that was first published in *Fighting Talk* (April 1955), Paul Robeson speaks of his discovery of Africa in this way:

"I 'discovered' Africa in London. That discovery – back in the twenties – profoundly influenced my life. Like most of Africa's children in America, I had known little about the land of our fathers. But in England, where my career as an actor and singer took me, I came to know many Africans. Some of their names are now know to the world – Azikiwe, and Nkrumah and Kenyatta, who has just been jailed for his leadership of the liberation struggles in Kenya."

"Many of these Africans were students, and I spent many hours talking with them and taking part in their activities at the West African Students' Union building. Somehow they came to think of me as one of them; they took pride in my successes and they made Mrs. Robeson and me honorary members of the Union."

"Besides these students, who were mostly of princely origin, I also came to know another class of Africans- the seamen in the ports of London, Liverpool and Cardiff. They too had their organizations and much to teach me of their lives and their various peoples."

"As an artist it was most natural that my first interest in Africa was cultural. Culture? The foreign rulers of that continent insisted there was no culture worthy of the name in Africa. But already musicians and sculptors in Europe were astir with their discovery of African art. And as I plunged, with excited interest, into my studies of Africa at the London University and elsewhere, I came to see that African culture was indeed a treasure-store for the world."

"Those who scorned the African languages as so many 'barbarous dialects' could never know, of course, of the richness of those languages, and of the great philosophy and epics of poetry that have come down through the ages in these ancient tongues. I studied these languages- as I do to this day: Yoruba, Efik, Benin, Ashanti and the others."

"I now felt as one with my African friends and became filled with a great, glowing pride in these riches, new found for me. I learned that along with the towering achievement of the cultures in ancient Greece and China there stood the culture of Africa, unseen and denied by the imperialist looters of Africa's material wealth."

"I came to see the root sources of my own people's culture, especially in our music which is still the richest and most healthy in America. Scholars had traced the influence of African music to Europe-to Spain with the Moors, to Persia and India and China, and westward to the Americans. And I came to learn of the remarkable kinship between African and Chinese culture (of which I intend to write a length some day)."

"My pride in Africa, that grew with the learning, impelled me to speak out against the scorners. I wrote articles for the New Statesman and Na-

> tion and elsewhere, championing the real but unknown glories of African culture."
>
> "I argued and discussed the subject with men like H.G. Wells, and Laski and Nehru; with students and savants."

He now saw the logic in this culture struggle and realized, as never before, that culture was an instrument that was used in their enslavement. This point was brought forcefully home to him when British Intelligence cautioned him that the British claim that it would take one thousand years to prepare Africans for self-rule, was a lie. The experience led him to conclude:

> "Yes, culture and politics were actually inseparable here as always. And it was an African who directed my interest in Africa to something he had noted in the Soviet Union. On a visit to that country he had traveled east and had seen the Yakuts, a people who had been classed as a 'backward race' by the Czars. He had been struck by the resemblance between the tribal life of the Yakuts and his own people of East Africa."
>
> "What would happen to a people like the Yakuts now that they were freed from colonial oppression and were a part of the construction of the new socialist society?"
>
> "I saw for myself when I visited the Soviet Union how the Yakuts and the Uzbeks and all the other formerly oppressed nationals were leaping ahead from tribalism to modern industrial economy, from illiteracy to the heights of knowledge. Their ancient culture blossoming in new and greater splendor. Their young men and women mastering the sciences and arts. A thousand years? No, less than 30!"

During his London years, Paul Robeson was also involved with a number of Caribbean people and organizations. These were the years of the Italian-Ethiopian War, the self-imposed exile of Haile Selassie and Marcus Garvey, and the proliferation of African and Caribbean organizations, with London headquarters, demanding the improvements in their colonial status that eventually led to the independence explosion. In an article in the *National Guardian* (December 20, 1948) entitled "Freedom in Their Own Land", Paul Robeson spoke of his impressions of the Caribbean people, after returning from a concert tour in Jamaica and Trinidad. He said:

> "I feel now as if I had drawn my first breath of fresh air in many years. Once before I felt like that. When I first entered the Soviet Union I said to myself, 'I am a human being. I don't have to worry about my color'.
>
> In the West Indies, I felt all that and something new besides. I felt

that for the first time I could see what it will be like when Negroes are free in their own land. I felt something like what a Jew must feel when first he goes to Israel, what a Chinese must feel on entering areas of his country that now are free.

Certainly my people in the islands are poor. They are desperately poor. In Kingston, Jamaica, I saw many families living in shells of old automobiles, hollowed out and turned upside down. Many are unemployed. They are economically subjected to landholders, British, American and native.

But the people are on the road to freedom. I saw Negro professionals: artist, writers, scientists, scholars. And, above all, I saw Negro workers walking erect and proud.

Once I was driving in Jamaica. My road passed a school and, as we came abreast of the building, a great crowd of school children came running out to wave at me. I stopped, got out of my car to talk with them and sing to them. Those kids were wonderful. I have stopped at similar farms in our own deep South and I have talked to Negro children everywhere in our country. Here, for the first time, I could talk to children who did not have to look over their shoulders to see if a white man was watching them talk to me.

I think that this nearness to freedom, this being on the road and so near the goal, had a great deal to do with the way they received me. It was like nothing that has ever happened to me before. If I never hear another kind word again, what I received from my people in the West Indies will be enough for me.

They crowded around my car. For hours they waited to see me. Some might be embarrassed or afraid of such crowds of people pressing all around. I am not embarrassed or afraid in the presence of people.

I was not received as an opera singer is received by his people in Italy. I was not received as Joe Louis is received by our own people. These people saw in me not a singer, or not just a singer. They called to me: 'Hello, Paul. We know you've been fighting for us.'"

In many ways his concert tours were educational tours. He had a similar experience, in New Orleans, on October 19, 1942, when he sang before a capacity audience of black and white men and women, seated without segregation, in the Booker T. Washington School auditorium. On this occasion he said:

"I had never put a correct evaluation on the dignity and courage of my people of the deep South until I began to come South myself. I had read, of course, and folks counted much of it, charged much of it to what some people would have us believe. Deep down, I think, I had imagined Negroes of the South beaten, subservient, cowed.

> But I see them now courageous and possessor of a profound and instinctive dignity, a race that has come through its trials unbroken, a race of such magnificence of spirit that there exists no power on earth that could crush them. They will bend, but they will never break.
>
> I find that I must come South again and again, again and yet again. It is only here that I achieve absolute and utter identity with my people. There is no question here of where I stand, no need to make decision. The redcap in the station, the president of your college, the man in the street-they are all one with me, part of me. And I am proud of it, utterly proud of my people."

He reaffirmed his commitment to the black struggle in the South by adding:

> "We must come South to understand in their starkest presentation the common problems that beset us everywhere. We must breathe the smoke of battle. We must taste the bitterness, see the ugliness (...) we must expose ourselves unremittingly to the source of strength that makes the Black South strong!"

In spite of the years he and his family spent abroad, he was never estranged from his own people. In his book, Here I Stand, he explained this in essence when he said:

> "I am a Negro. The house I live in is in Harlem – this city within a city, Negro Metropolis of America. And now as I write of things that are urgent in my mind and heat, I feel the press of all that is around me here where I live, at home among my people."

The 1940s, the war years, were a turning point in this career. His rendition of "Ballad for Americas" made a lot of Americans (black and white) rethink the nature of their commitment, of lack of it, in the making of a genuine democracy in this country. The song stated the certainty that "our marching song to a land of freedom and equality will come again". Robeson sang: "For I have always believed it and I believe it now." In this song, and in his life, he was asking that America keep its promise to all of its people.

On October 19, 1943, he became the first black actor to play the role of Othello with a white supporting cast on an American stage. He had played this role years before in London.

In 1944, Paul Robeson was awarded the Spingarn Medal by the National Association for the Advancement of Colored People (NAACP). Soon afterwards, he took the lead in a course of actions more direct and radical than the

NAACP. He led a delegation that demanded the end to radical bars in professional baseball. He called on President Truman to extend the Civil Rights of Blacks in the South. He became a founder and chairman of the Progressive Party which nominated former Vice-President Henry A. Wallace in the 1948 presidential campaign.

In the years immediately following the Second World War, Paul Robeson called attention to the unfinished fight for the basic dignity of all people. The following excerpt was extracted from a speech he made in Detroit, Michigan, on the tenth anniversary of the National Negro Congress:

> "These are times of peril in the history of the Negro people and of the American nation.
>
> Fresh from victorious battles, in which we soundly defeated the military forces of German, Italian and Japanese Fascism, driving to oppress and enslave the peoples of the whole world, we are now faced with an even more sinister threat to the peace and security and freedom of all our peoples. This time the danger lies in the resurgent imperialist and pro-Fascist forces of our own country, powerfully organized gentlemen of great wealth, who are determined now, to attempt what Hitler, Mussolini and Tojo tried to do and failed. And the elected political leadership of the United States is serving as the spearhead of this new drive toward imperialist war in the world and the ruthless destruction of our freedom and security here at home."
>
> "I understand full well the meaning of these times for my country and my people. The triumph of imperialist reaction in America, now, would bring death and mass destruction to our own and all other countries of the world. It would engulf our hard-won democratic liberties in the onrush of native Fascism. And it would push the Negro people backward into a modern and highly scientific form of oppression, far worse than our slave forefathers ever knew."
>
> "I also understand full well the important role which my people can and must play in helping to save America and the peoples of all the world from annihilation and enslavement. Precisely as Negro patriots helped turn back the red-coats at Bunker Hill, just as the struggles of over 200,000 Negro soldiers and four million slaves turned the tide of victory for the Union forces in the Civil War, just as Negro people have thrown their power on the side of progress in every other great crisis in the history of our country-so, now, we must mobilize our full strength, in firm unity with all the other progressive forces of our country and the world, to set American imperialist reaction back on its heels."

On this occasion he further stated:

> "I have been a member of the National Negro Congress since its inception. I have taken great pride in its struggles to unite the progressive forces of the Negro people and of organized labor in common struggle. And I know that I now talk to an assembly of approximately one thouseand delegates, the overwhelming majority of whom are the elected representatives of millions of trade unionists throughout our country.
>
> Here is the concrete expression of one of the most salutary developments in the political history of America-the unity of the Negro people and the progressive forces of labor of which they are an increasingly active part."

The troubles of the post-war years, mainly the lack of civil rights for his people, made him step up his political activity. At the World Peace Congress in Paris in 1949, he stated that:

> "It is unthinkable that American Negroes will go to war on behalf of those who have oppressed us for generations against a country (the Soviet Union) which, in one generation, has raised our people to the full dignity of mankind."

His words, often exaggerated out of context, turned every Right-wing extremist organization in America against him. Their anger reached a sad and destructive climax during two of his concerts in Peekskill, New York, in the summer of 1949.

His interest in Africa, that had started early in his life, continued through his affiliations with "The Council on African Affairs" and the column that he wrote regularly for the newspaper *Freedom.*

His association with organized labor was almost as long and consistent as his association with the concert stage. In a speech, "Forge Negro-Labor Unity for Peace and Jobs," delivered in Chicago, before nine hundred delegates to the National Labor Conference for Negro Rights, in June 1950, his association and commitment to the laboring class was restated in the following manner:

> "No meeting held in America at the mid-century turning point in world history holds more significant promise for the bright future toward which humanity strives than this National Labor Conference for Negro Rights. For here are gathered together the basic forces – the Negro sons and daughters of labor and their white brothers and sisters – whose increasingly active intervention in national and world affairs is an essential requirement if we are to have a peaceful and democratic solution of the burning issues of our times.

> Again we must recall the state of the world in which we live, and especially the America in which we live. Our history as Americans, black and white, has been a long battle, so often unsuccessful, for the most basic rights of citizenship, for the most simple standards of living, the avoidance of starvation-for survival.
>
> I have been up and down the land time and again, thanks in the main to your trade unionist gathered here tonight. You helped to arouse American communities to give an answer to Peekskill, to protect the right of freedom of speech and assembly. And I have seen; and daily see, the unemployment, the poverty, the plight of our children, our youth, the backbreaking labor of our women- and too long, too long have my people wept and mourned. We're tired of this denial of a decent existence. We demand some approximation of the American democracy we have helped to build."

He ended his speech with this reminder:

> "As the black worker takes his place upon the stage of history-not for a bit part, but to play his full role with dignity in the very center of the action-a new day dawns in human affairs. The determination for the Negro workers, supported by the whole Negro people, and joined with the mass of progressive white working men and women, can save the labor movement (...) This alliance can beat back the attacks against the living standards and the very lives of the Negro people. It can stop the drive toward Fascism. It can halt the chariot of war in its tracks.
>
> And it can help to bring to pass in America and in the world the dream our fathers dreamed-of a land that's free, of a people growing in friendship, in love, in cooperation and peace.
>
> This is history's challenge to you. I know you will not fail."

In 1950, Paul Robeson's passport was revoked by the State Department, though he was not charged with any crime. President Truman had signed an executive order forbidding Paul Robeson to set foot outside the continental limits of the United States. "Committees to Restore Paul Robeson's Passport" were organized in the United States and in other countries around the world. The fight to restore his passport lasted eight years.

For Paul Robeson, these were not lost or inactive years; they were not years when he was forgotten or without appreciation though, in some circles, his supporters "dwindled down to a precious few" He was fully involved, during these years, American Labor Movement, the Peace Movements and the National Council of American-Soviet Friendship.

From its inception in November 1950 to the last issue (July–August 1955),

Robeson wrote a regular column for *Freedom*. After his passport was restored in 1958, he went to Europe for an extended concert tour. In 1963 he returned to the United States with his wife Eslanda who died two years later. After her death, he gave up his home in Harlem and moved to Philadelphia to spend his last years with his sister, Mrs. Marion Forsythe.

Next to W.E.B. DuBois, Paul Robeson was the best example of an intellect who was active in his people's freedom struggle. Through this struggle, both men committed themselves to improve the lot of all mankind. Robeson's thoughts in this matter is summed up in the following quote from his book, *Here I Stand:*

> "I learned that the essential character of a nation is determined not by the upper classes, but by the common people, and that the common people of all nations are truly brothers in the great family of mankind (...) And even as I grew to feel more Negro in spirit, or 'African' as I put it then, I also came to feel a sense of oneness with the white working people whom I came to know and love."

At the time of his death, on January 23, 1976, a new generation was discovering Paul Robeson for the first time. An older generation was regretting that it had not made the best use of the strengths and hope that he had given to them. The writer, L. Clayton Jones, made his comment in the *Amsterdam News*, after his death:

> "One watches with restrained anger as a nation of hypocrites grudgingly acknowledges the passing of a twentieth century phenomenon, Paul Robeson, All-American Athlete, Shakespearean Actor, Basso Profundo, Linguist, Scholar, Lawyer, Activist. He was all these things and more."

In December 1977, and "Ad Hoc Committee to End the Crimes Against Paul Robeson" was formed to protest the inaccurate portrayal of Paul Robeson in a new play by Philip Hayes Dean. Their statement reads, in part:

> "The essence of Paul Robeson is inseparable from his ideas- those most profoundly held artistic, philosophical into the lifelong commitments for which he paid so dear and from which he never waivered down to his final public statement in 1975.
>
> In life, Paul Robeson sustained the greatest effort in the history of this nation to silence a single artist. He defied physical and psychological harassment and abuse without once retreating from these principles and the positions to which he dedicated his life. We believe that it is no less a continuation of the same crime to restore him, now that he is safely dead,

to the pantheon of respectability on the terms of those who sought to destroy him.

Robeson is the archetype of the Black American who uncompromisingly insists on total liberation. His example and his fate strike to the very heart of American racism.

For the nation to confront him honestly would mean that it confronts itself – to begin at last the process of reclamation of the national soul."

Chapter 4

Africana Historiography

The University of Sankore at Timbuctoo: A Neglected Achievement in Black Intellectual History

John Henrik Clarke

Reprinted from *The Western Journal of Black Studies*, Vol. 1, No. 2, 1977

In the Mali Republic, in West Africa today, the ruins of some of the buildings that once housed the University of Sankore, and the Grand Mosque of Timbuctoo, can still be seen. Therefore, this subject is both topical and historical. Most Black Americans are just beginning to hear about the University of Sankore and the grandeur of the Songhay Empire during Africa's third and last Golden Age.[1] Western historians have either ignored this period in African history or attributed it to the influence of the Arabs and the Berbers.

The intellectual history of Africa has not been written. It is a history that is long, strong, and rich, and the holocaust of the slave trade did not destroy it. Contrary to misconceptions that still prevail, in spite of historical evidence that can dispel them, the Africans were producers of literature and art, and a philosophical way of life, long before their contact with the Western world.

Before the destruction of the Empire of Songhay, by the Moroccans and Europeans mercenary soldiers, at the end of the sixteenth century, the Africans in the Western Sudan (inner West Africa) had been bringing into being great empires and cultures for over a thousand years, the most notable empires were Ghana and Mali. The Songhay Empire, and the University of Sankore, at Timbuctoo, was in existence over a hundred years after the slave trade had already been started along the west coast of Africa.

During the period in West African history – from the early part of the fourteenth century to the time of Moorish invasion in 1591 – the city of Timbuctoo and the University of Sankore in the Songhay Empire were the intellectual centers of Africa. Black scholars were enjoying a renaissance that was known and respected throughout most of Africa and in parts of Europe. At this period in African history, the University of Sankore was the educational capital of the Western Sudan.[2] In his book *Timbuctoo the Mysterious,* Felix DuBois gives us the following description of this period:

> The scholars of Timbuctoo yielded in nothing, to the saints in their sojourns in the foreign universities of Fez, Tunis, and Cairo. They astounded the most learned men of Islam by their education. That the Negroes were on a level with the Arabian Savants is proved by the fact that they were installed as professors in Morocco and Egypt. In contrast to this, we find that the Arabs were not always equal to the requirements of Sankore.[3]

I will speak of only one of the great Black scholars referred to in the book by Felix DuBois.

Ahmed Baba was the last chancellor of the University of Sankore. He was one of the greatest African scholars of the late sixteenth century. His life is a brilliant example of the range and depth of West African intellectual activity before the colonial era. Ahmed Baba was the author of more than forty books; nearly every one of these books had a different theme. He was in Timbuctoo when it was invaded by the Moroccans in 1591, and he was one of the first citizens to protest this occupation of his beloved hometown. Ahmed Baba, along with other scholars, was imprisoned and eventually exiled to Morocco. During his expatriation from Timbuctoo, his collection of 1600 books, one of the richest libraries of his day, was lost.

Now, West Africa entered a sad period of decline. During the Moorish occupation wreck and ruin became the order of the day. When the Europeans arrived in this part of Africa and saw these conditions, they assumed that nothing of order and value had ever existed in these countries.

Western scholarship, in most cases has ignored the great wealth of information on intellectual life in the Western Sudan. The following details on the subject were extracted from the pamphlet,[4] "Literacy and Scholarship in Muslim West Africa in the Pre-Colonial Period," by John O. Hunwick (1974).

In sixteenth-century Timbuctoo, during the relatively settled and prosperous period of the Askias of Songhay, there was an important concentration of scholars around the famous Sankore Mosque and University. There were many celebrated families of scholars in Timbuctoo and throughout the Songhay Empire. Ahmed Baba came out of such a family. This family, and others, produced numerous scholars during the fourteenth and fifteenth centuries, and an illustrious dynasty of judges. In his book Professor Hunwick tells us that:

> The scholars of Timbuctoo were not wholly wrapped up in their theoretical studies and the preservation and handling of knowledge, important as this was... many went on pilgrimage to Mecca and while there took the opportunity to hold discussions with, or acquire knowledge from scholars from other parts of the Muslim world. On the way home, some stopped in Egypt and studied under the leading scholars in Cairo. Some also visited other African towns in the course of their travels such as Kano, Karsina, Takedota and Walata, studying if they found teachers and teaching if they found pupils.

In the book *Timbuctoo the Mysterious* the writer Felix DuBois tells us:[5]

> Timbuctoo was not merely the great intellectual nucleus of the Sudan, but also one of the great scientific centers of Islam itself.

The University of Sankore had established relationships with similar institutions in Cairo, Cardova, Fez, and Damascus. The collection of ancient manuscripts found in the library at Sankore leaves us in no doubt upon this point. These manuscripts give us the opportunity to reconstruct the life of the intellectual community at Timbuctoo and to see how this community related to the Muslim world of its day. According to Felix DuBois:

> An entire class of the population was devoted to the study of letters, being called fakirs or sheiks by the old manuscripts, and marabuts (holy men) of the Sudanese of today... these pious and cultured families of Timbuctoo lived within the precincts of the mosque of Sankore... they were held in high esteem by both dignitaries and people. The Songhay kings pensioned the most celebrated, and they received many gifts, especially in the month of Ramadan.

The great scholar Ahmed Baba, belonged to one of these families. When the Moroccan expeditionary force, composed largely of Andalusian renegades and other white mercenaries, occupied Timbuctoo in 1591, an attempt to revolt led to the deportation of the leading scholars, including Ahmed Baba.[6]

The story of Ahmed Baba is part of the story of the Songhay during the years after the death of the great ruler that is known in African history as "Askia the Great." After the death of Askia, in 1528, the Songhay Empire began to lose its strength and its control over its vast territory. When the Songhay Empire collapsed after the capture of Timbuctoo and Gao by the Moroccans in 1591, the whole of the Western Sudan was devastated by the invading troops. The Sultan of Morocco, El-Mansur, had sent a large army with European fire across the Sahara to attack the once-powerful empire of Songhay. The army did not reach Timbuctoo until 1591. The prosperous city of Timbuctoo was plundered by the army of freebooters. A state of anarchy prevailed. The greatest Sudanese scholar of that day, Ahmed Baba, was among those exiled.

Timbuctoo provides the most terrible example of the struggles of the West African states and towns as they strove to preserve what was once their Golden Age. The Arabs, Berbers, and Tuaregs from the North showed them no mercy… it had previously been sacked by the Tuaregs as early as 1433, and they had occupied it for 30 years. Between 1591 and 1593, the Tuaregs had already taken advantage of the situation to plunder Timbuctoo once more. One result of the plundering of Timbuctoo was the destruction of the great University of Sankore and the exiling of its leading teachers and scholars.

The following information on this sad period in West African History has been extracted from the book *Timbuctoo the Mysterious*, by Felix DuBois:

> However regrettable this exile may be from its consequences to the Sudan, it does not lack great historical interest. It is the touchstone which enables us to tet the Eulogies concerning the Sudanese science and learning contained in the native documents, for we now see the scholars of Sankore confronted by the highest developments of Arabian civilization. How will they stand the ordeal? The test proves entirely to their advantage.
>
> Among the exiles was a learned doctor, Ahmed Baba by name, born in 1556 at Arawan, of Sehnadjan. In spite of his youth, he enjoyed a considerable reputation in Timbuctoo at the time of the Moorish conquest, and his brethren gave him the title of "The Unique Pearl of his Time." His renown increased in Morocco and became universal, spreading from Marrakesh to Bougie, Tunis and even to Tripoli. The Arabs of the north called this African "very learned and very magnanimous," and his gaolers found him "a fount of erudition." At the request of Moorish scholars the doors of his prison were opened a year after his arrival (1596). All the believers were greatly pleased with his release, and he was conducted in triumph from his prison to the principal mosque of Marrakesh. A great many of the learned men urged him to open a course of instruction. His first thought was to refuse, but overcome by their persistence, he accepted a post in the Mosque of the Kerifs and taught rhetoric, law and theology. An extraordinary number of pupils attended his lectures, and questions of the greatest importance were submitted to him by the magistracy, his decision always being treated as final. With a modesty worthy of his learning, he said concerning these decisions:

> "I carefully examined from every point of view the questions asked me, and having little confidence in my own judgement I entreated the assistance of God, and the Lord graciously enlightened me." The ancient histories of Morocco relate many other interesting details, and the author of the *Bedzl el Nouasaha* reports the following utterance of Ahmed Baba: "Of all my friends, I had the fewest books, and yet when your soldiers despoiled me they took 1600 volumes." The Nozhei el Hadj gives the following instance of the courage and pride of the African Sheik: "After he was set at liberty Ahmed Baba presented himself at the palace of El Mansour, and the sultan gave audience to him from behind a curtain. 'God has declared in the Koran,' said the sheik, 'that no human being can communicate with Him hidden behind a veil. It is your wish to speak to me, come forth from behind the curtain.' When El Mansour raised the curtain and approached him, Ahmed Baba continued, 'What need had you to sack my house, steal my books, and put me into chains to bring me to Morocco? By means of those chains I fell from my camel and broke my leg.' 'We wished to establish unity in the Mussulman world,' replied the sultan, 'and since you were one of the most distinguished representatives of Islam in your country, we expected your submission to be followed by that of your fellow-citizens.' 'If that is so, why did you not seek to establish this unity amongst the Turks of Tiemcen and other places nearer to you?' 'Because the Prophet says, Leave the Turks in peace so long as they do not interfere with thee.' 'That was true at one time,' responded Ahmed Baba, 'but since then Iba Abbas has said, Leave not the Turks in peace even though they should not interfere with thee.' El Mansour, being unable to reply to this, put an end to the audience."

Although apparently free, Ahmed Baba was detained in Morocco for twelve years; the sultan had only released him on that condition, fearing the effect of his influence on his fellow-citizens. It was not until after the death of El Mansour that permission was obtained from the son for the learned man to return to the Sudan. Ahmed Baba then set out for the country to which he had so ardently desired to return, and of which he never spoke without tears in his eyes. The following verses were written by him in his exile:

> "O thou who goest to Gao, turn aside from thy path to breathe my name in Timbuctoo. Bear thither the greeting of an exile who sighs for the soil on which his friends and family reside. Console my near and dear ones for the deaths of the Lords, who have been entombed."

The principal marabuts of Marrakesh formed him a guard of honour at his departure, and, at the moment of farewell, one of them seized Ahmed Baba by the hand and saluted him with the following sura from the holy book: "Certainly he who has made the Koran for thee shall lead thee back to the point of departure" – a customary address to a traveller in wishing him a safe return. On hearing these words, the sheik abruptly withdrew his hand exclaiming, "May God never bring me back to this meeting, nor make return to this country."

He reached Timbuctoo in safety, and died in 1627. A man of great learning and a prolific writer, the names of twenty of his books have been handed down to us. Except for an astronomical treatise, written in verse and some commentaries on the holy texts, his books are chiefly elucidations of the law and the sciences he professed, and prove that he was above everything a jurist. Two of his books alone possess general interest; they have been preserved, happily... One is entitled the Miraz, and is a little book upon the different West African peoples, written by Ahmed Baba in exile, with a view to making the Sudanese populations known to the Moors. The other is *El Ihtihadj*, a large biographical dictionary of the Mussulman doctors of the Malekite sect; in it Ahmed Baba carried on the famous work of Ibn Ferhoun, and made it a continuation of the latter's *Dihadje*. The learned biographer added it to the lives of all the scholars whom Ibn Ferhoun had not mentioned. Ahmed Baba completed his book in 1596, and it had such a great success in both Northern and West Africa that the author was obliged to publish a popular edition containing the principal biographies only.

It is partly owing to the *Ihtihadj* that it has been possible to reconstruct the intellectual past of Timbuctoo, and for this reason the name of Ahmed Baba deserves to be held in pious memory by our savants, as it is by those of the Arabian countries of Northern Africa. To this day his name represents to the letter every effort made by the Sudan to attain the intellectual level of the Mussulman world; so much so, in fact, that any Sudanese work of unknown parentage is attributed to him.

The family of Ahmed Baba is not yet extinct... One of his great-great-grandchildren, Ahmadou Baba Boubakar, was kadi, and enjoyed a considerable reputation for learning; the other, Oumaro Baba, lived by making copies of books, which he executed in a very beautiful handwriting. The family religiously preserves a chair which had belonged to their glorious progenitor, to whom it had been presented by his liberator, the Sultan El Zidan. A curious family tradition is connected with this venerated piece of furniture. On the occasion of the marriage of a member of the family, the bridegroom is permitted to seat himself in this chair on the day of his nuptials. It is hoped, they told me, that some of the great qualities of the illustrious sheik will fall upon the husband and his descendants.

The sixteenth century, which we saw and so disastrously for the marabuts, formed the apogee of Timbuctoo's scientific and literary grandeur. The wholesale arrest and exportation of her scholars proved a fatal blow to the University of Sankore. The decline of learning, as of everything else, set in with the Moorish occupation, and yet the greatest work of all the literature of the Sudan was produced in the first days of its twilight, namely, that *Tarik and Sudan* (the history of the Sudan) which we have so often had occasion to mention.

Ahmed Baba lived in the part of inner West Africa that is now the Republic of Mali. The story of this great Black scholar has been handed down from one generation to another.[7]

There is no way to separate the name of Ahmed Baba from the University of Sankore, at Timbuctoo, during its last days before the Moroccan invasion. The destruction of this great institution, and the wreck and ruin of the Western Sudan, is one of the great tragedies in African history.[8]

End Notes

1. "Africa in Early World History," by John Henrik Clarke, *Ebony Magazine*, August, 1976. Also see: "Africa: The Passing of the Golden Age," by John Henrik Clarke, *The National Scene*, August–September, 1975, Vol. IV, No. 4.
2. "The Origin and Growth of Afro-American Literature," by John Henrik Clarke, *Journal of Human Relations*, Vol. 16, No. 3, 1968.
3. *Timbuctoo the Mysterious*, by Felix DuBois, Longmans, Green and Co., New York, 1896, pp. 352–353. Reprinted Negro Universities Press, Greenwood Publishing Col, Westport, Conn., 1969.
4. "Literacy and Scholarship in Muslim West Africa in the Pre-Colonial Period," by John O. Hunwick, an "Occasional Paper" Publication, the Institute of African Studies, University of Nigeria, Nsukka, Nigeria, West Africa, 1974.
5. *Timbuctoo the Mysterious*, by DuBois, pp. 275–281.
6. "Literacy and Scholarship in Muslim West Africa," 29–34.
7. "Ahmed Baba, A Scholar of Old Africa," by John Henrik Clarke, *Black Books Bulletin*, Chicago, IL, Vol. 2, No. 1, 1974. Also see: "Time of Troubles," by John Henrik Clarke, in the *Horizon History of Africa*, ed. by Alvin M. Josephy, American Heritage Publishing Co., New York, 1971, pp. 355–358.
8. A large portion of the information for this article was drawn from the new research on the life of Ahmed Baba by John O. Hunwick, who is presently Chairman of the History Department, University of Ghana. The following works by Professor Hunwick are recommended: "Ahmed Baba and the Moroccan Invasion of the

Sudan, 1591," Journal of the Historical Society of Nigeria. ii, 3 (1962), pp. 311–328; "Further Light on Ahmed Baba Al-Timbukti," Centre of Arabic Documentation, Institute of African Studies, University of of Ibadan, Nigeria, West Africa; "Religion and State in the Songhay Empire, 1464–1591," in Islam in Tropical Africa, ed. by I.M. Lewis, Oxford University Press, New York, NY, 1966, pp. 296–317.

9. Other references on Sankore and Ahmed Baba:

North African Prelude, by Galbraith Welch, Morrow and Co., New York, 1949, pp. 352–353.

Africa Before They Came, by Galbraith Welch, Morrow and Co., New York, 1949, pp. 271–278.

Travels and Discoveries in North and in Central Africa, by Henry Barth, Harper and Brothers, New York, 1859, Vol. 3.

Realm of the Evening Star, A History of Morocco and the Lands of the Moors, by Eleanor Hoffmann, Chilton Books, Philadelphia and New York, 1965, pp. 125–145.

Black Africa, from Pre-History to the Eve of the Colonial Area, by Russell Warren Howe, Walker and Co., New York, 1965, p. 63.

Africa in History, by Basil Davidson, Macmillan and Co., New York, 1968, p. 173.

"Africa the Wonder and the Glory," by Anna Melissa Graves, originally printed in 1942 as "Foreword" to her book *Benvenuto Cellini Had No Prejudice against Bronze*, Letters from West Africans, Waverly Press, Baltimore, MD, 1966, pp. 37–40.

The Golden Trade of the Moors, by E. W. Bovell, Second Edition, Oxford University Press (paperback), New York, 1970, pp. 66, 89, 186–7.

Introduction to African Civilizations, by John G. Jackson, University Books, Secaucus, NJ, 1970, pp. 21, 217, 300–1.

Discovering our African Heritage, by Basil Davidson, Ginn and Co., Boston, Mass., 1971. pp. 101, 102.

A Tropical Dependency, by Lady Lungard, Frank Cass and Co., Ltd., London, 1964, pp. 156, 204.

History of West Africa, Volume One, edited by J.F. Ada Adjayi and Michael Crowder, Longman, London, 1971.

An Introduction to African Civilizations, with Main Currents in Ethiopian History, by Willis N. Huggins, Avon House, Publishers, New York, 1937. Reprinted 1969 by Negro University Press, a Division of Greenwood Publishing Corp., New York, NY, pp. 111–112.

The Growth of Racism in the West

John Henrik Clarke

Reprinted from *Black World*, Vol. 19, No. 12, October 1970, pp. 4–10

Early in this century, the elder scholar among Afro-Americans, Dr. W.E.B. DuBois, said: "The problem of the twentieth century is the problem of the color line." Unfortunately, his prophecy was correct. In spite of all the talk and the sociology – good and bad – we have not made much progress in resolving this issue. We have talked about it extensively without really dealing with it. To deal with it we will have to identify and explain its genesis. To explain its genesis, we will have to ask ourselves some hard questions and we will have to be boldly honest with our answers. Some of the hard questions are: How did racism start in the first place and for whose benefit was it created? Who benefits from it now? Why do we lack the strength, or the nerve, to destroy it? I maintain that the racism that haunts the world of our day was created for a specific reason, and that reason was to justify the expansion of Europe, starting in the fifteenth and sixteenth centuries. This forces us to deal with both the genesis and the present application of racism.

The great human drama now being called "The Black Revolution in the USA" has deep historical roots, and it cannot be fully understood until it has been seen in this context. In his book, *Capitalism and Slavery*, Eric Williams places the origin of this revolution in historical perspective and calls attention to its early development:

> When, in 1492, Columbus, representing the Spanish monarchy, discovered the New World, he set in train the long and bitter international rivalry over colonial possessions for which, after four and a half centuries, no solution has yet been found. Portugal, which had initiated the movement of international

> expansion, claimed the new territories on the ground that they fell within the scope of a papal bull of 1455 authorizing her to reduce to servitude all infidel people. The two powers (Spain and Portugal), to avoid controversy, sought arbitration and, as Catholics, turned to the Pope – a natural and logical step in an age when the universal claims of the Papacy were still unchallenged by individuals and governments. After carefully sifting the rival claims, the Pope issued, in 1493, a series of papal bulls which established a line of demarcation between the colonial possessions of the states. The East went to Portugal and the West went to Spain.

Though the announcement of the fact came much later, the European "Scramble for Africa," and subsequently Asia and North America, started with this act. The labor and raw materials of Africa, Asia, South America and the West Indies financed the European Industrial Revolution.

In the year 1457, the Council of Cardinals met in Holland and sanctioned, as a righteous and progressive idea, the enslavement of black Africans for the purpose of their conversion to Christianity, and to be exploited in the labor market as chattel property.

This devilish scheme speedily gained the sanctimonious blessing of the Pope and became a standard policy of the Roman Catholic Church, and later of the Protestant churches, enduring for three centuries. And thus the ghastly traffic in human misery was given the cloak of respectability and anointed with the oil of Pontifical righteousness in Jesus's name. And so, the slave trade began, inaugurating an era that stands out as the most gruesome and macabre example of man's disregard for the humanity of man.

There is no way to understand the African slave trade without understanding slavery as an institution. It is almost as old as human societies. Every people has at some time or other been slaves! In fact, Europeans enslaved other Europeans for a much longer time than they enslaved Africans. Yet this slavery did not give birth to racism.

Slavery was a permanent feature of the ancient world, in Egypt, Kush, Greece, and Rome. The African slave period is best known to us because it is the most recent – and the best documented. These documents on slavery have often done more to confuse the issue than to explain the subject. Most people write about slavery in a manner that makes the victim feel guilty. There is probably more dishonesty related to the interpretation of this subject than any other subject known to man.

The present demand for Black Power and black history has made publishers realize that books on this subject are now a profitable enterprise. In the rush to capture this new market, a number of hurriedly written books on the slave trade have been published. None of the new "authorities" on the subject seem to see the African slave trade as the incubator of modern racism that it was.

The African slave trade – like African history in general – is often written about and rarely ever understood. I think this misunderstanding grows out of the fact that we nearly always start the study of the African slave trade in the wrong place.

The story of the African slave trade is essentially the story of the consequences of the second rise of Europe. In the years between the passing of the Roman Empire in the eighth century and the partial unification of Europe, through the framework of the Catholic Church in the fifteenth century, Europeans were engaged mainly in the internal matters within their own continent. With the opening up of the New World, after the expulsion of the Moors from Spain during the latter part of the fifteenth century, the Europeans started to expand beyond their homeland, into the broader world. They were searching for new markets and new lands to exploit. The African slave trade was created to accommodate this new expansion.

The Europeans, mainly the Portuguese who came to the West Coast of Africa in the fifteenth century, were not at first looking for slaves. The search for gold and other treasures lured them to Africa. They did not have to fight their way onto the continent. They came as guests and were treated as guests. Finally, when they grew strong enough, they turned on their hosts and decided to stay as conquerors.

The basis for the future European industrial revolution had already been established. They had already created an embryo technology – principally the gun. In the centuries that followed, they used this weapon and other advantages – mainly a larger fleet of ships and mercenary sailors and soldiers – to take over most of the world. In so doing, they destroyed a large number of nations and civilizations that were older than Europe.

In order to justify this destruction, a monster that still haunt our lives was created: racism. The slave trade and the colonial system that followed were, figuratively, the mother and father of this catastrophe.

The opening up of the New World opened up more than new territory. It opened up a new era in human relations, mostly bad. The Europeans, being "Christians," had to find a way to live with their consciences after the formal starting of the slave trade. The African made the original mistake of asking the Europeans to settle some of their family disputes. Unfortunately, the Europeans many times conquered both branches of the family.

The Europeans were no strangers to Africa, and this really wasn't their first meeting. But in order to justify the slave trade, they had to forget, or pretend to forget, all that they had previously known about Africa. They had to forget that a lot of the early culture of Europe has an African base. They also had to forget that there were periods when Africans and Europeans lived in comparative harmony and Europeans married into African royalty and saw no difference in one royal personage and the other. Therefore, Europeans had to forget that the Africans had a history and a heritage that could command respect.

In the opening up of the territory called the New World, two competing slave systems were set in motion, and each of these systems served as some form of racism. The dehumanization of the African had started in European textbooks, geographies, and travel books. In South America and the Caribbean area, the plantation owners generally bought slaves in large lots and kept the lots together principally because they thought they could work them better that way – and they were right. In the United States, however, when the most vicious form of racism was manifested, the slavery system operated more like a brokerage system. A plantation owner would very often buy 10 slaves and re-sell five of them before the end of the week. This meant the immediate breaking up of the cultural continuity, linguistic continuity, and all things that held the African together in Africa, therefore creating a family dislocation from which the black American has not recovered to this day. This dislocation was a form of racism.

The mentality, the rationales, and the various ways of justifying the slave trade had already started in Europe with Europeans attempting to justify the enslavement of other Europeans. This is a neglected aspect of history that is rarely ever taken into consideration. There was at first a concerted effort to obtain European labor to open up the vast regions of the New World. It is often forgotten that, in what became the United States, white enslavement started before black enslavement.

In an article, "White Servitude in the United States," *Ebony Magazine*, November 1969, the Afro-American historian Lerone Bennett, Jr. gives the following information about this period:

> When someone removes the cataracts of whiteness from our eyes, and when we look with unclouded vision on the bloody shadows of the American past, we will recognize for the first time that the Afro-American, who was often second in freedom, was also second in slavery.
>
> Indeed, it will be revealed that the Afro-American was third in slavery. For he inherited his chains, in a manner of speaking, from the pioneer bondsmen, who were red and white.

The story of this succession, of how the red bondsmen and of how the white men created a system of white servitude which lasted in America for more than two hundred years, the story of how this system was created and why, of how white men and white women and white children were bought and sold like cattle and transported across the seas in foul "slave" ships, the story of how all this happened, of how the white planter reduced white people to temporary and lifetime servitude before stretching out his hands to Ethiopia, has never been told before in all its dimensions. As a matter of fact, the traditional embalmers of American experience seem to find servitude enormously embarrassing, and prefer to dwell at length on black bondage in America. But this maneuver distorts both black bondage and the American experience. For white bondage and red bondage are the missing legs on the triangle of American servitude. And this triangle defines the initial American experience as an experiment in compulsion.

Both red and white bondage were integral parts of this experiment, but white bondage was particularly important. In the first place, white bondage lasted for more than two centuries and involved a majority of the white immigrants to the American colonies. It has been estimated that at least two out of every three white colonists worked for a term of years in the fields or kitchens as semi-slaves. A second point of immense importance is the fact that white servitude was the historic foundation upon which the system of black slavery was constructed.

In other words, white servitude was the historic proving ground for the mechanisms of control and subordination used in Afro-American slavery. The plantation pass system, the fugitive slave law, the use of the overseer and the house servant and the Uncle Tom, the forced separation of parents and children on the auction block and the sexual exploitation of servant women, the whipping post, the slave chains, the branding iron; all these mechanisms were tried out and perfected first on white men and white women. Masters also developed a theory of internal white racism and used the traditional Sambo and minstrel stereotypes to characterize white servants who were said to be good natured and faithful but biologically inferior and subject to laziness, immorality, and crime. And all of this would seem to suggest that nothing substantial can be said about the mechanisms of black bondage in America except against the background and within the perspective of the system of white bondage in America.

How did the system develop? And why?

Mr. Bennett's statement is indicative of the new insight into the slave system. African slave labor and the raw material taken from their countries were important features in the development of the European industrial revolution.

American abolitionists, black and white, were fighting against a form of racism that had begun to crystallize itself in the embryo of the colonies' educational systems, filtering down from the attitude prevailing in the churches. During the period of the founding fathers, the black Americans heard promises about liberty and justice and thought that these promises were meant for them. Once more they were engaging in illusions. The black American wasn't brought to this country to be given democracy, and the American promise really wasn't made to him. That was the basis of his dilemma during the formative period of this country, and it is the basis of his dilemma right now. This country was born in racism and it has evolved in racism.

Finally, in the early years of the nineteenth century, the system of chattel slavery gave way to the colonial system, after the British abolished slavery – at least on paper – in 1807. This was not the end racism as it affected Africans and other nonwhite people throughout the world; it was only a radical change in how it would be manifested. The Europeans would now change the system of capturing Africans and other nonwhite people and enslaving them thousands of miles away from their homes. They would now enslave them on the spot, within their own countries, and use them as markets for new goods coming out of the developing European industrial revolution and out of their countries and their labors to produce grist for new European mills. So the industrial rise of the West has as its base a form of racism. Racism helped to lay the base of the present economic system we now call capitalism.

Theoretical racism, in the main, is of nineteenth century origin in America and in Europe. And yet, the nineteenth century was a century of the greatest resistance against racism. It was during that century when Africans the world over began to search for a definition of themselves. The concept of African redemption is of nineteenth century origin. The theoretical basis of the Black Power concept started in 1829, with the publication of David Walker's appeal. The great Black ministers of the nineteenth century, such as Henry Highland Garnet, Samuel Ringgold Ward, and Prince Hall, who founded the black Masons, were all using Christianity in a struggle against racism. Near the end of the nineteenth century, the great intellectual giant, Dr. W.E.B. DuBois, took up this fight and ably carried it to the middle of the twentieth century. He is the father of the present struggle against racism and for African redemption. Men like Marcus Garvey, though they differed with W.E.B. DuBois, would draw in part on his intellectual conclusions on this subject.

There is now an international struggle on the part of people of African descent against racism and for a more honest look at their history. On university campuses and in international conferences, they are demanding that their history be looked at from a black perspective or from an Afrocentric point of view. This has taken the struggle against racism to the world's campuses, where the theoretical basis of racism started. This has helped to create new battle lines and a lot of fear and frustration on the part of white scholars. They still do not recognize that removing the racism that they created is the healthiest thing that present day Black scholars can contribute to the world; that in the cry for Black Power and black history, Black people are saying a very powerful, complex, yet simple thing: "I am a man." The struggle of racism all along has been a struggle to regain the essential manhood lost after the European expansion into the broader world and the attempt to justify the slave trade. This struggle has been brought to where we are now, standing on the "black and beautiful" plateau. From this position Black people will go into another state, much higher and more meaningful for mankind. I think they will make a contribution toward the reclamation of the humanity of man. First, they will have to realize that in the kind of world we live in, being black and beautiful means very little unless we are also black and powerful. There is no way to succeed in the struggle against racism without power. That is a part of our new reality and our new mission.

African-American Historians and the Reclaiming of African History*

John Henrik Clarke

Reprinted from, Molefi Kete Asante and Karimu Welsh Asante, Editors, *African Culture: The Rhythms of Unity*, Trenton, New Jersey: African World, 1990

The Africans who came to the United States as slaves started their attempt to reclaim their lost African heritage soon after they arrived in this country. They were searching for the lost identity that the slave-system had destroyed. Concurrent with the black man's search for an identity in America has been his search for an identity in the world which means, in essence, his identity as a human being with a history, before and after slavery, that can command respect.[1]

The Afro-American connection with Africa is not new. In fact, this connection was never completely broken. "Africa-consciousness", in varying degrees, good and bad, has always been part of the psyche of the African people, in forced exile in South America, the Caribbean Islands and in the United States. There has always been a conflict within the Black American's "Africa-consciousness". This conflict was created early and was extended beyond all reasonable proportions by the mass media of the 20th century, such as jungle movies, elementary textbooks on geography and history and travel books written to glorify all distorted images have created both a rejection of Africa and a deep longing for the Africa of our imagination which was our home and the first home of what man has referred to as a civilization.[2]

Contrary to a still prevailing opinion, most of the literate Africans in forced exile have always had a positive image of Africa. They have rejected the image of Africa as a backward and barbarous land. To the extent that the information was available, the early black writers and thinkers made every attempt to locate

Africa on the map of human geography. They soon discovered that Africa and her people had a history older than the history of their oppressors. They also learned how and why the Europeans came to Africa in the first place, and the circumstances, in Africa and in Europe, that set the slave-trade in motion. They learned why the "Christian" Church had to read the Africans out of respectful commentary on human history. While the pretence was that Africans were being civilized and Christianized, this was really the beginning of what Walter Rodney has called "the under-development of Africa", he points out, "*after surveying the developed areas of the continent in the 15th century, and those within Europe at the same time, find the difference between the two in no way to African's discredit.*"[3]

He quotes a Dutch account of Benin City in West Africa to prove that, at first, the Europeans compared African cities and cultures favorably to their own.

> "The town seems to be very great. When you enter into it, you go into a great broad street, not paved, which seems to be seven or eight times broader than the Warmoes Street in Amsterdam (...)
>
> "The King's palace is a collection of buildings which occupy as much space as the two of Harlem, and which is enclosed with walls. There are numerous apartments for the Prince's ministers and fine galleries, most of which are as big as those of the Exchange at Amsterdam. They are supported by wooden pillars encased with cooper, where their victories are depicted, and which are carefully kept very clean.
>
> "The town is composed of 30 main street, very straight and two hundred and twenty feet wide, apart from an infinity of small intersecting streets. The houses are close to one another, arranged in good order. These people are in no way inferior to the Dutch as regards cleanliness; they wash and scrub their houses so well that they are polished and shining like a looking-glass."[4]

In his essay, "The African Roots of the War", written for the Atlantic Monthly in May 1915, the great Afro-American scholar, W.E.B. DuBois, decries the fact that:

> "There are those who would write world history and leave out this most marvelous of continents. Particularly today, most men assume that Africa lies far afield from the center of our burning social problems and especially from our present problem of world war.
>
> "Yet, in a very real sense, Africa is a prime cause of this terrible overturning of civilization (...) In Africa are the hidden roots, not simply of war today, but of the menace of war tomorrow.

"Always Africa is giving us something new or some metempsychosis of a world-old thing. On its black bosom arose one of the earliest, if not the earliest, of self-protecting civilizations, and grew so mightily that it still furnishes superlatives to thinking and speaking men. Out of its darker and more remote forest vastnesses came, if we may credit many recent scientist, the first welding of iron, and we know that agriculture and trade flourished there when Europe was a wilderness.

"Nearly every human empire that has arisen in the world, material and spiritual, has found some of its greatest crises on this continent of Africa, form Greece to Great Britain. As Mommsen says: 'It was through Africa that Christianity became the religion of the world'. In Africa, the last flood of Germanic invasions spent itself within hearing of the last gasp of Byzantium, and it was again in Africa that Islam came to play its great role of conqueror and civilizer"[5]

In the re-establishment of the connection with Africa and in the search for a more enlightened image of that continent and its people, the early black writers in the United States soon learned that Africa was an important factor in world history and that, in the great human drama of the rise and fall of nations, Africans had played every role from saint to buffoon.

These writers, preachers and self-educated men of affairs referred to themselves mainly as Africans: not "Coloreds" or "Negroes" or "Blacks", but as African! Nearly all their as an African people. This small group of black freedmen and escaped slaves began to develop during the latter half of the 18th century. By the end of that century, their presence was being felt as petitioners, anti-slavery speakers and pamphleteers. Their writings and their place in history is well recorded in a recent book by Dorothy Porter, in Early Negro Writing 1760-1837, by Dorothy Porter, giving the following information.[6]

The first literary talent of Afro-Americans began to develop in the years between 1760 and 1837, concurrent with mutual benefit organizations expressing their social consciousness. In most cases, these organizations bore African names and their leaders referred to Africa as their homeland. Mrs. Porter tells us that:

"This early disposition to associate together for mutual improvement provided a training ground for the half-educated as well as for the educated and ambitions among the sons of Africa in the United States. The very titles of these organizations suggest that they were directed in the main to the improvement of the social and political status of Blacks."

The Free African Society was organized by the Black Methodist in 1787. This

Society, under the leadership of Richard Allen and Absalom Jones, brought into being the independent Black Church in the United States: the African Methodist Episcopal Church. The early black churches were more than religious organizations. They performed the services of social agencies, publishers, community centers and, occasionally, hiding places for escaped slaves. The first historical protest and literary writings of the black freedmen in the New England States found an outlet in the church or organizations affiliated with the church. In the *Essay on Freedom with Observations on the Origins of Slavery*, written by a member of the Sons of Africa Society that was formed in 1798, the writer outlines some of the difficulties Blacks were encountering in seeking freedom, and expresses appreciation to the people of the city of Salem, Massachusetts, for showing signs of its "approbation of the Africans' freedom". These pamphlets, broadsheets and monographs would continue to appear throughout the first half of the 19th century and their writers would help to establish the early black press in the United States. Some of these writers became editors of such papers as *Freedom's Journal, The North and The Anglo-African Magazine.*

The spiritual and cultural return to Africa is reflected in the names of early black institutions, especially in the churches. Professor St. Clair Drake draws this picture of the black church during its formative years.

> "Black people under slavery turned to the Bible to 'prove' that black people, Ethiopians, were so powerful and respected when white men in Europe were barbarians. Ethiopia came to symbolize all of Africa and throughout the 19th century the redemption of Africa became one important focus of meaningful activity for leaders among New World Negroes. 'Ethiopianism' became an energizing myth in both the New World and in Africa itself for those pre-political movements that arose while the powerless were gathering their strength for realistic and rewarding political activity. Its force is now almost spent, but 'Ethiopianism' left an enduring legacy to the people who fought for Black Power in the 20th century, and some of its development needs to be understood"[7]

In the closing years of the 19th century, the Africans in the Caribbean Islands, South America and in the United States continued to object to the distorted pictures of Africans given in elementary textbooks, geographies, travel-books and histories. As far back as 1881, the renowned Dr. Edward Wilmot Blyden, on the occasion of his inauguration as President of Liberia College, sounded the note that called for a new approach to the teaching of African history and culture. Dr. Blyden is the best known of the Caribbean scholars who returned to Africa.

Of his many books, Christianity, Islam and the Negro Race, first published in 1837, is an enduring classic.[8]

In the United States, W.E.B. DuBois continued some of the work of Dr. Blyden and carried it into the 20th century. The unity and liberation of all Africa was the main mission of the life of DuBois. He did not pursue this mission in isolation. He sought allies wherever he could find them. His interest in Africa began early in life, during his student days at Harvard University. As a result of this interest, he wrote his first major work, The Suppression of the African Slave-Trade to the United States (1896). This interest was continued in two other works, *The Souls of Black Folk* (1903) and the *Gift of Black Folk* (1903) and *The Gift of Black Folk* (1924). During his editorship of the *Crisis Magazine* (1910–1934), he introduced Africa as a subject of concern for Black Americans. His book, *The Negro* (published in the same year. In this essay, he had dared to deal with the imperialist origins of the First World War, and Africa in general.

After World War I, new men and movements rose to challenge the old social order and ask for a new one. The best know movement of this period was the Universal Negro Improvement Association (UNIA). The best-known personality was its dynamic founder, Marcus Garvey. Concurrent with the rise of the Garvey movement, a literary awakening called The Harlem Renaissance brought more attention to the world's most way, was an African-consciousness movement, accentuated by consider a return to their motherland.[9]

Among black writers, artists and thinkers like W.E.B. DuBois, James Weldon Johnson, J.A. Rogers, Arthur A. Schomburg and William Leo Hansberry, the period of the Harlem Renaissance was a time of African rediscovery. In their writings, these scholars affirmed that Africans were great story-tellers long before their first appearance in Jamestown, Virginia in 1619. The rich and colorful history, art and folklore of West Africa, the ancestral home of most Afro-Americans, present evidence of this, and more.

Contrary to a misconception which still prevails, the Africans were familiar with literature and art for many years before their contact with the Western World. Before the breaking up of the social structure of the West African States of Ghana, Melle and Songhay, and the internal strife and chaos that made the slave-trade possible, the forefathers of the Africans who eventually became slaves in the United States lived in a society where University life was fairly common and scholars were beheld with reverence.

There were, in this ancestry, rulers who expanded their kingdoms into empires, great and magnificent armies whose physical dimensions dwarfed entire nations into submission generals who advanced the techniques of military science, scholars whose vision of life showed foresight and wisdom, and priests who told of gods that were strong and kind. To understand fully any aspect of Afro-American life, one must realize that the Black American is not without a cultural past, though he was many generations removed from it before his achievements in American literature and art commanded any appreciable attention. I have been referring to the African origin of Afro-American literature and history. This preface is essential to every meaningful discussion of the role of the Afro-American in every major aspect of American life, past and present. Before getting into the body of this article, I want to make it clear that the African people did not come to the United States culturally empty handed.

I will elaborate very briefly on my statement to the effect that "*the forefathers of the Africans who eventually became slaves in the United States once lived in a society where University life was fairly common and scholars were beheld with reverence.*" During the period in West African history ranging from the early part of the 14th century to the time of the Moroccan invasion in 1591., the City of Timbuctoo and its University of Sankore (in the Songhay Empire) were the intellectual centers of Africa. Black scholars were enjoying a renaissance that was known and respected throughout most of Africa and in parts of Europe. At this period in African history, the University of Sankore was the educational capital of the Western Sudan. In Lady Lugard's 'A Tropical Dependency,' there is a fitting description of ancient Timbuctoo:

> "The scholars of Timbuctoo yielded in nothing to the saints in their sojourns in the foreign Universities of Fez,Tunis and Cariro. They astounded the most learned men of Islam by their erudition. That these Negroes were on a level with the Arabian savants is proved by the fact that they were installed as professors in Morocco and Egypt. In contrast to this, we find that the Arabs were not always equal to the requirements of Sankore".

I will speak of only one of the great black scholars referred to in this book. Ahmed Baba was the last Chancellor of the University of Sankore. He was one of the greatest African scholars of the late 16th century. His life is a brilliant example of the range and depth of West African intellectual activity before the colonial era. Ahmed Baba was the author of more than 40 books; nearly everyone the first citizens to protest against this occupation of his beloved home town. Ahmed Baba, along with other scholars, was imprisoned and eventually exiled to Morocco. During his expatriation from Timbuctoo his collection of 1,600 books, one of the richest libraries of his day, was lost.

Now, West Africa entered a sad period of decline. During the Moroccan occupation, wreck and ruin became the order of the day. When the Europeans arrived in this part of Africa and saw these conditions they assumed that nothing of order and value had ever existed in these countries. This mistaken impression, too often repeated, has influenced the interpretation of African and Afro-American life in history for over 400 years.[10]

The essence of the African-consciousness of the writers who were a part of the Harlem Renaissance is contained in a book edited by Alain Locke of Howard University. In essays like "The Mind of the Negro Reaches Out" by W.E.B. DuBois, "The Legacy of the Ancestral Arts" by Alain Locke and "The Negro Digs Up His Past" by Arthur A. Schomburg, a creative concern for Africa is shown.[11] When this book was published in 1925, the Association for the Study of Negro Life and History, under the leadership of its founder, Carter G. Woodson, was ending the first decade of its existence. In 1926, he founded what we now know was "Afro-American" or "Black History Week".

The terms Black or Afro-American History Week, taken at face value and without serious thought, appears to be incongruous. At the time, the question did arise: why is there a need for a "Black History Week" when there is no similar week for the other minority groups in the United States? The history of the United States in total consists of the collective histories of minority groups. What we call "American civilization" is no more than the sum of their contributions. The Afro-Americans are the least integrated and the most neglected of these groups in the historical interpretation of the American experience. This neglect has made "Black History Week" a necessity.

Most of the large ethnic groups in the United States have had, and still have, their historical associations. Some of these associations predate the founding of the Association for the Study of Negro Life and History (1915). Dr. Charles H. Wesley tells us that "*historical societies were organized in the United States with the special purpose in view of preserving and maintaining the heritage of the American nation.*"[12] In 1944 there were a total of 904 ethnic historical societies in the United States and Canada, an increase of 46% over the 583 listed in 1936. Among these societies were those representing groups whose origins were German, Irish, French, Jewish, Dutch, Spanish, Russians, Norwegian, Swedis, Swiss and Finnish. The leaders of these historical societies were of the opinion that the history of the United States could not be written from the point of view of "adaptation and assimilation" but that the (...) cultural riches brought to the Western world, in what has been termed the elements composing the national whole, must be studied and appraised before a complete understanding of American history and American civilization is possible."

In "Racial and Historical Societies and the American Tradition," included in his book, Neglected History (1962), the Afro-American historian Charles H. Wesley, describes the work of ethnic historical societies in this manner:

> "They must gather up precious records and interpret them. Both in language and in that subtle understanding which they have absorbed by natural circumstances of the way of life of their own folk, they possess keys to unlock doors that bar the way to a full comprehension of the social history of America"

Within the framework of these historical societies, many ethnic groups (black as well as white) engaged in those endeavors that would keep alive their beliefs in themselves and their past as part of their hopes for the future. For Black Americans Carter G. Woodson led the way and used what was then called "Negro History Week" to call attention to his peoples' contribution to every aspect of world history. Dr. Woodson (then Director of the Association for the Study of Negro Life and History) conceived this special week as a time when public attention should be focused on the achievements of American's citizens of African descent. Initially, the observance was widely supported by schools, churches and clubs among Black Americans. Gradually, the movement found support among other ethnic groups and institutions in America and abroad.

The acceptance of the facts of Black History and the black historian as a legitimate part of the academic community, did not come easily. Slavery ended and left its false images of black people intact. In an article, the noted Afro-American historian, Dr. Benjamin Quarles, says:

> "The Founding Fathers, revered by historians for over a century and a half, did not conceive of the Negro as part of the body politic. Theoretically, these men believed in freedom for everyone, but actually they found it hard to imagine a society where Negroes were of equal status to Whites. Thomas Jefferson, third President of the United States, who was far more liberal than the run of his contemporaries, was nevertheless certain that' the two races, equally free, cannot live n the same government.'[13]

Early white American historians did not accord African people anywhere a respectful place in their commentaries on the history of man. In the closing years of the 19th century, black historians began to look at their people's history from their vantage point and point of view. "As early as 1883, this desire to bring to public attention the untapped material on the Negro prompted George Washington Williams to publish his two-volume History of the Negro Race in America."

The first formally trained Afro-American historian was W.E.B. DuBois, whose doctoral dissertation (published in 1896) The Suppression of the African Slave Trade to the United States 1638–1870, became the first title to be published in the Harvard Historical Studies Collection. It was with Woodson, another Harvard Ph.D., that African world history took a great leap forward and found a defender who could document his claims. He was convinced that unless something were done to rescue the black man from history's oversight, he would become "a negligible factor in the thought of the world." In 1915, he founded the Association for the Study of Negro Life and History. During the preceding 20 years, an American Negro Academy had been founded in Washington and a Negro Society for Historical Research had appeared in New York. These organizations were short-lived because they lacked a historian of Woodson's ability, who was also a leader of men and an organizational administrator.

Carter G. Woodson was born of former slaves, Annie and James Woodson, in 1875 at New Canton, Virginia. He suffered all the hardships of poverty while growing up. Only a five-month district school was available to him and he was unable to attend it on a regular basis. He studied at home while working on the family's farm. Already he had established a lifetime habit of studying at home. In his early years, he was mostly self-taught. He mastered all the fundamentals of common school subjects by the time he was seventeen, then went to Huntington, West Virginia, where he worked in the coal mines. He later entered Douglass High School and earned a teaching certificate in less than two years; he pursued further education at Berea College in Kentucky where he received the Litt. B. degree. He continued his education at the University of Chicago, where he was awarded the BA and MA degrees. His travels in Europe and Asia and graduate studies at the Sorbonne in Paris enriched his cultural background and prepared him for graduate work at Harvard University, where he was awarded the Ph.D. in 1912. after Harvard he had an extensive career as an educator: principal of Douglass High School, teacher of languages and history in high schools of Washington, DC, dean of the School of Liberal Arts, Howard University, and supervisor of schools in the Philippines., This varied experience made Carter G. Woodson see the need for a special time each year to call attention to his people's contribution to the history and culture of this country and the world. Thus, Black History Week.

After serving many years as a teacher in public schools, Woodson became convinced that the role of his people in American history and in the history of other cultures was being either ignored or misrepresented. The Association for the Study of Negro Life and history was founded to conduct research into the history of African people all over the world. The next year he began publication of the *Journal of Negro History*, which has never missed an issue.

A chronicle of Woodson's far-reaching activities must include the organization in 1921 of the Associated Publishers, Inc., which had as one of its purposes the publication of books on African people not usually accepted by most publishers; the establishment of Negro History Week in 1926; the initial subsidizing of research on Black history; and the writing of many articles and books on Afro-American and American life and history.

Woodson believed that there was no such thing as "Negro history." He said what was called "Negro history" was only a missing segment of world history. He devoted the greater portion of his life to restoring this segment. He also realized that once this segment was integrated into school textbooks and taught with respect and understanding, there would no longer be a need for a Negro History Week.[14]

In the U.S. Civil War blacks fought bravely and died in great numbers for their own freedom. The idea that the black man played an insignificant role while white men fought and died to set him free is not supported by official records. Material related to the Black Americans are available in official Civil War records, but unfortunately are completely omitted in most school textbooks.

Africa came into the Mediterranean world mainly through Greece, which had been under African influence; and then Africa was cut off from the melting pot by turmoil among the Europeans and the religious conquests incident to the rise of Islam. Africa prior to these events had developed its history and civilization, indigenous to its people and lands. Africa came back into the general picture of history through the penetration of North Africa, West Africa, and the Sudan by the Arabs. European and American slave traders next ravaged the continent. The imperialist colonizers and missionaries finally entered the scene and prevailed until the recent reemergence of independent African nations.

Africans are, of course, closely connected to the history of both North and South America. The Afro-American's role in the social, economic, and political development of the American states is an important foundation upon which to build racial understanding, especially in areas in which false generalizations and stereotypes have been developed to separate peoples rather than to unite them.

The spiritual and intellectual journey to Africa was continued by many black scholars other than Carter G. Woodson. At Howard University, Williams Leo Hansberry, considered to be the greatest Africanist to emerge from the Black American community, trained a generation of students to learn and respect African history. His articles, monographs, and conference papers on the subject appeared in leading journals throughout the world.

In the period of the Italian-Ethiopian War, the streets of Harlem were an open forum, presided over by master speakers like Arthur Reed and his protégé, Ira Kemp. Young Carlos Cooks, founder of the Garvey-oriented African Pioneer Movement, was on the scene, also bringing a nightly message to his street fellows. Part of every message was about Africa.

The Blyden Society, the Ethiopian World Federation, and other organizations attracted a number of African supporters, some of them students like Nkrumah. The American black press improved its coverage of news about Africa. In reporting on the Italian-Ethiopian War, this press was fortunate in having in its service at least two reporters who had been well schooled in African history in general. The reporters were J.A. Rogers, a historian and journalist, and Dr. Willis N. Huggins, historian, teacher and community activist. In his dispatches from Ethiopia, Rogers gave an astute analysis of the war to the *Pittsburgh Courier*, He was the only reporter on the scene who was looking at the Italian-Ethiopian conflict from a black point of view. He also commented on the political intrigues in Europe that led to this conflict. Later, in a small book, The Real Facts About Ethiopia, he digested his reports and produced the most revealing document about the Italian-Ethiopian War that has so far appeared in print. Huggins, a high school history teacher and founder of the Blyden Society for the Study of African History, went to Geneva and reported on the League of Nations' meeting concerning the war for the *Chicago Defender*. He had already written two books on Africa: *A Guide to Studies in African History* and *Introduction to African Civilizations*.

In the collective talent of Rogers and Huggins, the Afro-American press was fortunate enough to have observers who could see through the subterfuge and pretences of the European Powers and their frantic schemes to keep their African colonies. Both saw behind and beyond the headlines and foretold the future repercussions of Ethiopia's betrayal. Their reports were a high-water mark in black American journalism.

A revolution in thinking about Africa occurred after World War Two. The revolution was most widespread among black Americans who are the most estranged and alienated African people in all the world.

In 1947, J.A. Rogers published his most outstanding work, *World's Great Men of Color*, in two volumes. This is the enduring masterpiece in African World biography. Before his death in 1966, at the age of 85, he had devoted at least 50 years of his existence researching the lives of great African personalities and the roles they had played in the development of nations, civilizations and culture.[15]

In 1958, the American Society of African Culture produced the book, *Africa As Seen by American Negroes*. The editors had creatively compiled some of the best essays that black American scholars had written on Africa during the preceding 10 years.[16]

In 1964, *Ebony Magazine* published a series of articles on the ancient and medieval history of Africa by Hansberry. This was the most extensive series of this nature ever to appear in a black publication. The articles were extracted from a projected four-volume history of Africa that he had been writing for nearly a generation. Unfortunately, this larger work was not finished before he died in 1965. However, two of his books (edited by Professor Joseph E. Harris, Head of the History Department of Howard University) were published in 1974 and 1977: *Pillars in Ethiopian History* and *Africa and Africans as Seen by African Writers*.

During the Civil Rights Movement (called the "American Black Revolution"), interest in Africa led to a massive demand for Black Studies, mostly by black students at predominantly white Universities. A number of books by black American scholars helped to place Africa in proper historical focus during this period. In my opinion, some of the most important of these are: *The African Presence in Asia* by Joseph E. Harris (1971); *Introduction to African Civilization* by John G. Jackson (1974); *The Destruction of Black Civilization: Great Issues of a Race From 45 BC to 2000 AD* by Chancellor Williams and three books by Yosef Ben-Jochannan, *Black Man of the Nile* (1970) and *African Origins of the Major Western Religions* (1971).

Afro-American and Afro-Caribbean scholars, from the early part of the 19th century to the present, have made a personal mission of the effort to reclaim African history. They have repudiated the often repeated charge that Africans have no history. They found that we cannot place African humanity and history in proper perspective until we deal with the distortions of African history. The hard fact is that what we call "world history," in most cases, is only the history of Europe and its relationships to non-European people. The Western academic community, in general, is not yet willing to acknowledge that the world did not wait in darkness for European people to bring the light. The history of Africa was already old when Europe was born.

END NOTES

1. John Henrik Clarke, *In the Absence of a Curriculum: Creative Approaches to the Teaching of African and African American History* (New York: Hunter College, Department of Black and Puerto Rican Studies, 1978), p. 3.
2. John Henrik Clarke, "The Afro-American Image of Africa," *Black World* (February 1974), p. 4.
3. Walter Rodney, *How Europe Underdeveloped Africa* (London: Bogle-L'Ouverture Publications, 1972), p. 69.
4. Ibid.
5. W.E.B. DuBois, *The African Roots of War* (1915) in W.E.B. DuBois,' A Reader, ed. Meyer Weinberg (New York: Harper and the Row, 1970), pp. 360-71.
6. Dorothy Porter, Early Negro Writing, 1760-1837 (Boston: Beacon Press, 1971) pp. 1-86.
7. Ibid., pp. 1-2.
8. St. Clair Drake, *The Redemption of African and Black Religion* (Chicago: Third World Press, 1971), pp. 11-15.
9. Edward Wilmot Blyden, Christianity, Islam and the Negro Race (1887; rpt. Edinburgh: University of Edinburgh Press, 1967).
10. John Henrik Clarke, ed., *Marcus Garvey and the Vision of Africa* (New York: Random House, 1973), pp. 173-97.
11. Lady Lugard, A Tropical Dependency (London: Nisbet Ltd., 1906), p. 216.
12. John Henrik Clarke, "*The Origin and Growth*," pp. 632-33.
13. Alain Locke, ed., *The New Negro* (1925; rpt. New York: Atheneum Publishers, 1969).
14. Charles H. Wesley, "Racial Historical Societies and the American Tradition," in *Neglected History: Essays in Negro American History* (Wilberforce, Ohio: Central State College Press, 1965), pp. 9-22.
15. Ibid., p. 9.
16. Ibid., p. 11.
17. Ibid.
18. Benjamin Quarles, "What the Historian Owes the Negro," *Saturday Review*, 3 September 1966, pp. 10-13.
19. Ibid., p.12.
20. Carter G. Woodson, *The Negro in Our History* (Washington, DC: Associated Publishers, 1922); Negro Makers of History (Washington, DC): Associated Publishers, 1928); *The Mis-Education of the Negro* (Washington, DC: Associated Publisher, 1933); *The Story of the Negro Retold* (Washington, DC: Associated Publishers, 1935); *The African Background Outlined* (Washington, DC: Associated Publishers); and *African Heroes and Heroines* (Washington, DC: Associated Publishers, 1939).

21. Willis N. Huggins, and John Jackson, *A Guide to Studies in African History* (Chicago: privately published, 1934): and Willis Huggins and John Jackson, Introduction to African Civilizations (Chicago: privately published 1937).
22. Valerie Standoval, "The Brand of History: A Historiographic Account of the work of J.A. Rogers," *Schomburg Center for Research in Black Culture Journal* (Spring 1978), pp. 11-17.
23. American Society of African Culture, *Africans as Seen* by American Negroes (Paris: Presence Africaine, 1958).
24. William Leo Hansberry, *Pillars in Ethiopian History*, ed. Joseph E. Harris (Washington, DC: Howard University Press, 1974); and *Africa and Africans as Seen* by classical Writers, ed. Joseph E. Harris (Washington, DC: Howard University Press, 1977)
25. Joseph E. Harris, *The African Presence in Asia* (Washington, DC: Howard University Press, 1971); John G. Jackson, *Introduction to African Civilization* (Secaucus, NJ: Citadel, 1974): Chancellor Williams, *The Destruction of Black Civilization: Great Issues of a Race from 4500 BC to 2000 AD* (Chicago: Third World Press, 1974): Yosef Ben-Jochannan, *Black Man of the Nile* (New York: Alkebu-lan Books, 1970), *Africa: Mother of Western Civilization* (New York, Alkebu-lan Books, 1970), and *African Origins of the Major Western Religions* (New York: Alkebu-lan Books, 1971).

The Origin and Growth of Afro-American Literature

John Henrik Clarke

Reprinted from *African Intellectual Heritage*,
Molefi Kete Asante and Abu S. Abarry, Editors,
Philadelphia: Temple University Press, 1996.

Africans were great story tellers long before their first appearance in Jamestown, Virginia, in 1619. The rich and colorful history, art and folklore of West Africa, the ancestral home of most Afro-Americans, present evidence of this, and more.

Contrary to a misconception which still prevails, the Africans were familiar with literature and art for many years before their contact with the Western world. Before the breaking up of the social structure of the West African states of Ghana, Melle (Mali), and Songhay, and the internal strife and chaos that made the slave trade possible, the forefathers of the Africans who eventually became slaves in the United States lived in a society where university life was fairly common and scholars were beheld with reverence.

There were in this ancestry rulers who expanded their kingdoms into empires, great and magnificent armies whose physical dimensions dwarfed entire nations into submission, generals who advanced the technique of military science, scholars whose vision of life showed foresight and wisdom, and priests who told of gods that were strong and kind. To understand fully any aspect of Afro-American life, one must realize that the black American is not without a cultural past, though he was many generations removed from it before his achievements in American literature and art commanded any appreciable attention.

I have been referring to the African Origin of Afro-American literature and history. This preface is essential to every meaningful discussion of the role of the Afro-American in every major aspect of American life, past and present. Before getting into the main body of this talk, I want to make it clear that the Black Race did not come to the United States culturally empty-handed.

I will elaborate very briefly on my statements to the effect that "the forefathers of the Africans who eventually became slaves in the United States once lived in a society where university life was fairly common and scholars were beheld with reverence."

During the period in West African history – from the early part of the fourteenth century to the time of the Moorish invasion in 1591 – the City of Timbuktu, with the University of Sankore in the Songhay Empire, was the intellectual center of Africa. Black scholars were enjoying a renaissance that was known and respected throughout most of Africa and in parts of Europe. At this period in African history, the University of Sankore, at Timbuktu, was the educational capital of the Western Sudan. In his book *Timbuktu the Mysterious*, Felix DuBois gives us the following description of this period:

> The scholars of Timbuktu yielded in nothing, to the saints in their sojourns in the foreign universities of Fez, Tunis and Cairo. They astounded the most learned men of Islam by their erudition. That these Negroes were on a level with the Arabian Savants is proved by the fact that they were installed as professors in Morocco and Egypt. In contrast to this, we find that the Arabs were not always equal to the requirements of Sankore.

I will speak of only one of the great black scholars referred to in the book by Felix DuBois.

Ahmed Baba was the last chancellor of the University of Sankore. He was one of the greatest African scholars of the late sixteenth century. His life is a brilliant example of the range and depth of West African intellectual activity before the colonial era. Ahmed Baba was the author of more than 40 books; nearly every one of these books had a deferent theme. He was in Timbuktu when it was invaded by the Moroccans in 1592, and he was one of the first citizens to protest this occupation of his beloved home town. Ahmed Baba, along with other scholars, was imprisoned and eventually exiled to Morocco. During his expatriation from Timbuktu, his collection of 1,600 books, one of the richest libraries of his day, was lost.

Now, West Africa entered a sad period of decline. During the Moorish occupation, wreck and ruin became the order of the day. When the Europeans arrived in this part of Africa and saw these conditions, they assumed that nothing of order and value had ever existed in theses countries. This mistaken impression, too often repeated, has influenced the interpretation of African and Afro-American life in history for over 400 years.

Negroes played an important part in American life, history and culture long before 1619. Our relationship to this country is as old as the country itself.

Africans came to the new world as explorers. They participated in the exploratory expeditions of Balboa, the discoverer of the Pacific, and Cortes, the conqueror of Mexico. An African explorer helped to open up New Mexico and Arizona and prepared the way for settlement of the Southwest. Africans also accompanied French Jesuit missionaries on their early travels through North America.

In the United States, the art and literature of the Negro people has had an economic origin. Much that is original in black America folklore, or singular in "Negro spirituals" and blues, can be traced to the economic institution of slavery and its influence upon the Negro's soul.

After the initial poetical debut of Jupiter Hammon and Phillis Wheatley, the main literary expression of the Negro was the slave narrative. One of the earliest of these narratives came from the pen of Gustavas Vassa, an African from Nigeria. This was a time of great pamphleteering in the United States. The free Africans in the North, and those who had escaped from slavery in the South, made their ark upon this time and awakened the conscience of the nation. Their lack of formal educational attainments gave their narratives a strong and rough-hewed truth, more arresting than scholarship.

Gustavas Vassa established his reputation with an autobiography, first printed in England. Vassa, born in 1745, was kidnapped by slavers when he was 11 years old and taken to America. He was placed in service on a plantation in Virginia. Eventually, he was able to purchase his freedom. He left the United States, made his home in England and became active in the British anti-slavery movement. In 1790, he presented a petition to Parliament to abolish the slave trade. His autobiography, The Interesting Narrative of the Life of Gustavas Vassa, was an immediate success and had to be published in five editions.

At the time when slave ships were still transporting Africans to the New World, two 18th century Negroes were writing and publishing works of poetry. The first of these was Jupiter Hammon, a slave in Queens Village, Long Island. In 1760, Hammon published An Evening Thought: Salvation by Christ with Penitential Cries... In all probability, this was the first poem published by an American Negro. His most remarkable work, "An Address to the Negroes of New York," was published in 1787. Jupiter Hammon died in 1800.

Phillis Wheatley (1753–1784), like Hammon, was influenced by the religious forces of the Wesley-Whitefield revival. Unlike Hammon, however, she was a writer of unusual talent. Though born in Africa, she acquired in an incredibly short time both the literary culture and the religion of her New England masters. Her writings reflect little of her race and much of the age in which she lived. She was a New England poet of the third quarter of the 18th century, and her poems reflected the poetic conventions of the Boston Puritans with whom she lived. Her fame continued long after her death in 1784 and she became one of the best known poets of New England.

Another important body of literature came out of this period. It is the literature of petition, written by free black men in the North, who were free in name only. Some of the early petitioners for justice were Caribbean-Americans who saw their plight and the plight of the Afro-Americans as one and the same.

In 18th century America, two of the most outstanding fighters for liberty and justice were the West Indians, Prince Hall and John B. Russwurm. When Prince Hall came to the United States, the nation was in turmoil. The colonies were ablaze with indignation. Britain, with a series of revenue acts, had stoked the fires of colonial discontent. In Virginia, Patrick Henry was speaking of liberty or death. The cry, "No Taxation Without Representation," played on the nerve strings of the nation. Prince Hall, then a delicate-looking teenager, often walked through the turbulent streets of Boston, an observer unobserved.

A few months before these hectic scenes, he had arrived in the United States from his home in Barbados, where he was born about 1748, the son of an Englishman and a free African woman. He was, in theory, a free man, but he knew that neither in Boston nor in Barbados were persons of African descent free in fact. At once, he questioned the sincerity of the vocal white patriots of Boston. It never seemed to have occurred to them that the announced principles motivating their action (were) stronger argument in favor of destroying the stem of slavery. The colonists held in servitude more than a half million human beings, some of them white; yet they engaged in the contradiction of going to war to support the theory that all men were created equal.

When Prince Hall arrived in Boston, that city was the center of the American slave trade. Most of the major leaders of the revolutionary movement, in fact, were slaveholders or investors in slave-supported businesses. Hall, like many other Americans, wondered what did these men mean by freedom?

The condition of the free black men, as Prince hall found them, was not an enviable one. Emancipation brought neither freedom nor relief from the stigma of color. They were still included with slaves, indentured servants, and Indians in the slave codes. Discriminatory laws severely circumscribed their freedom of movement.

By 1765, Prince Hall saw little change in the condition of the blacks, and though a freeman, at least in theory, he saw his people debased as though they were slaves still in bondage. These things drove him to prepare himself for leadership among his people. So, through diligence and frugality, he became a property owner, thus establishing himself in the eyes of white people as well as the blacks.

But the ownership of property was not enough. He still had to endure sneers and insults. He went to school at night, and later became a Methodist preacher. His church became the forum for his people's grievances. Ten years after his arrival in Boston, he was the accepted leader of the black community.

In 1788, Hall petitioned the Massachusetts Legislature, protesting the kidnaping of free Negroes. This was a time when American patriots were engaged in a constitutional struggle for freedom. They had proclaimed the inherent rights of all mankind to life, liberty, and the pursuit of happiness. Hall dared to remind them that the black men in the United States were human beings and as such were entitled to freedom and respect for their human personality.

Prejudice made Hall the father of African secret societies in the United States. He is the father of what is now known as Negro Masonry. Hall first sought initiation into the white Masonic Lodge in Boston, but was turned down because of his color. He then applied to the Army Lodge of an Irish Regiment. His petition was favorably received. On March 6, 1775, Hall and fourteen other black Americans were initiated in Lodge Number 441. When, on March 17, the British were forced to evacuate Boston, the Army Lodge gave Prince Hall and his colleagues a license to meet and function as a Lodge. Thus, on July 3, 1776, African Lodge No. 1 came into being. This was the first Lodge in Masonry established in America for men of African descent.

The founding of the African Lodge was one of Prince Hall's greatest achievements. It afforded the Africans in the New England area a greater sense of security, and contributed to a new spirit of unity among them. Hall's interest did not end with the Lodge. He was deeply concerned with improving the lot of his people in other ways. He sought to have schools established for the children of the free Africans in Massachusetts. Of prime importance is the fact that Prince Hall worked to secure respect for the personality of his people and also played a significant roll in the downfall of the Massachusetts slave trade. He helped to prepare the groundwork for the freedom fighters of the 19th and

20th centuries, whose continuing efforts have brought the Black American closer to the goal of full citizenship.

The literature of petition was continued by men like David Walker whose Appeal, an indictment of slavery, was published in 1829. Dynamic ministers like Samuel Ringgold Ward and Henry Highland Garnet joined the ranks of the petitioners at the time a journalist literature was being born.

Frederick Douglass the noblest of American black men of the 19th century, was the leader of the journalist group. He established the newspaper North Star and, later, the magazine Douglass Monthly. John B. Russwurm and Samuel Cornish founded the newspaper Freedom's Journal in 1827.

In 1829, a third poet, George Moses Horton, published his book, The Hope of Liberty. In his second volume, Naked Genius (1865), he expressed his anti-slavery convictions more clearly. George Moses Horton was the first slave poet to openly protest his status.

Throughout the early part of the 19th century, the slave narrative became a new form of American literary expression.

The best known of these slave narratives came from the pen of Frederick Douglass, the foremost Negro in the anti-slavery movement. His first bok was The Narrative of the Life of Frederick Douglass (1845). Ten years later, an improved and enlarged edition, My Bondage and My Freedom, was published. His third autobiography, Life and Times of Frederick Douglass, was published in 1881 and enlarged in 1892. Douglass fought for civil rights and against lynching and the Ku Klux Klan. No abuse of justice escaped his attention and his wrath.

It was not until 1887 that an Afro-American writer emerged who was fully a master of the short story as a literary form. This writer was Charles W. Chesnutt. Chesnutt, an Ohioan by birth, became a teacher in North Carolina while still in his middle teens. He studied the traditions and superstitions of the people that he taught and later made this material into the ingredient of his best short stories. In August 1887, his short story, "The Goophered Grapevine," appeared in The Atlantic Monthly. This was the beginning of a series of stories which were later brought together in his first book, The Conjure Woman (1899). "The Wife of His Youth" also appeared in the Atlantic (July 1898) and gave the title to his second volume, The Wife of His Youth and Other Stories of the Color Line (1899). Three more stories appeared later: "Baxter's Procrustes" in the Atlantic (June 1904), and "The Doll" and "Mr. Taylor's Funeral" in The Crisis magazine (April 1912 and April–May 1915).

Chesnutt's novel did not measure up to the standards he had set with his short stories, though they were all competently written. In 1928 he was awarded the Springarn Medal for his "pioneer work as a literary artist depicting the life and struggle of Americans of Negro descent."

Paul Laurence Dunbar, a contemporary of Charles W. Chesnutt, made his reputation as a poet before extending his talent to short stories. Both Dunbar and Chesnutt very often used the same subject matter in their stories. Chesnutt was by far the better writer, and his style and attitude differed radically from Dunbar's.

Dunbar's pleasant folk tales of tradition-bound plantation black folk were more acceptable to a large white reading audience with preconceived ideas of "Negro characteristics." In all fairness, it must be said that Dunbar did not cater to this audience in all of his stories. In such stories as "The Tragedy at Three Forks," "The Lynching of Jube Benson," and "The Ordeal at Mt. Hope," he showed a deep concern and understanding of the more serious and troublesome aspects of Afro-American life. Collections of his stories are: Folks from Dixie (1898), The Strength of Gideon (1900), In Old Plantation Days (1903), and The Heart of Happy Hollow (1904). Only one of his novels, The Sport of the Gods (1902), is mainly concerned with Afro-American characters.

Chesnutt and Dunbar, in their day, reached a larger general reading audience than any of the black writers who came before them. The period of the slave narratives had passed. Yet the black writer was still an oddity and a stepchild in the eyes of most critics. This attitude continued in a lessening degree throughout one of the richest and most productive periods in Afro-American writing in the United States – the period called "the Negro Renaissance." The community of Harlem was the center and spiritual godfather and midwife for this renaissance. The cultural emancipation of the Afro-American that began before the first World War was now in full force. The black writer discovered a new voice within himself and liked the sound of it. The white writers who had been interpreting our life with an air of authority and a preponderance of error looked at last to the black writer for their next cue. In short story collections like Jean Toomer's Cane (1923) and Langston Hughes' The Ways of White Folks (1934) heretofore untreated aspects of Afro-American life were presented in an interesting manner that was unreal to some readers because it was new and so contrary to the stereotypes they had grown accustomed to.

In her book Mules and Men (1935), Zora Neal Hurston presented a collection of folk tales and sketches that showed the close relationship between humor and tragedy in Afro-American life. In doing this, she also fulfilled the first requirement of all books – to entertain and guide the reader through an interesting experience that is worth the time and attention it takes to absorb it. In other stories like The Gilded Six Bits, Drenched in Light, and Spank another side of Miss Hurston's talent was shown.

In the midst of the renaissance, two strong voices from the West Indies were heard. Claude McKay, in his books Ginger Town (1932) and Banana Bottom (1933), wrote of life in his Jamaican homeland in a manner that debunked the travelogue exoticism usually attributed to Negro life in the Caribbean area. Before the publication of these books, Harlem and its inhabitants had already been the subject matter for a group of remarkable short stories by McKay and the inspiration for his book, Home to Harlem, still the most famous novel ever written about that community.

In 1926, Eric Walrond, a native of British Guiana, explored and presented another side of West Indian life in his book, Tropic Death, a near classic. In these ten naturalistic stories, Eric Walrond concerns himself mostly with labor and living conditions in the Panama Canal Zone where a diversity of people and ways of life meet and clash, while each tries to survive at the expense of the other. Clear perception and strength of style enabled Mr. Walrond to balance form and content in such a manner that the message was never intruded upon the unfolding stories.

Rudolph Fisher, another bright star of the Harlem literary Renaissance, was first a brilliant young doctor. The new light touch he brought to his stories of Afro-American life did not mar the serious aspect that was always present. The message in his comic realism was more profound because he was skillful enough to weave it into the design of his stories without destroying any of their entertainment value. His stories "Blades of Steel," "The City of Refuge," and "The Promised Land" were published in The Atlantic Monthly. "High Yaller" appeared in The Crisis magazine during the hey-day of that publication, and was later reprinted in the O'Brien anthology, Best Short Stories of 1934. Unfortunately, he died before all of his bright promise was fulfilled.

The Harlem literary renaissance was studded with many names. Those already mentioned are only a few of the most outstanding. During the period of this literary flowering among black writers, Harlem became the Mecca, the stimulating Holy City, drawing pilgrims from all over the country and from some places abroad. Talented authors, playwrights, painters, and sculptors came forth eagerly showing their wares.

Three men, W. E. B. DuBois, James Weldon Johnson, and Alain Locke, cast a guiding influence over this movement without becoming a part of the social climbing and pseudointellectual aspect of it. W. E. B. DuBois, by continuously challenging the old concepts and misinterpretations of Afro-American life, gave enlightened new directions to a whole generation. As editor of The Crisis, he introduced many new black writers and extended his helpful and disciplined hand when it was needed. Following the death of Booker T. Washington and the decline of the Booker T. Washington school of thought, he became the new spiritual father of the new black intelligentsia.

James Weldon Johnson moved from Florida to New York. His diversity of talent established his reputation long before the beginning of the "New Negro literary movement." Later, as a participant in and historian of the movement, he helped to appraise and preserve the best that came out of it. In his books, Autobiography of an Ex-Colored Man (1912), The Book of American Negro Poetry (1932), Black Manhattan(1930), and Along This Way, an autobiography (1933), James Weldon Johnson showed clearly that Negro writers have made a distinct contribution to the literature of the United States. His own creative talent made him one of the most able of these contributors.

Alain Locke is the writer who devoted the most time to the interpretation of the "New Negro literary movement" and to Afro-American literature in general. In 1925, he expanded the special Harlem issue of the magazine Survey Graphic (which he edited) into the anthology, The New Negro. This book is a milestone and a guide to Afro-American thought, literature, and art in the middle twenties. The objective of the volume "to register the transformation of the inner and outer life of the Negro in America that had so significantly taken place in the last few preceding years," was ably achieved. For many years, Mr. Locke's annual appraisal of books by and about Negroes, published in Opportunity magazine, was an eagerly awaited literary event.

Early in the Harlem literary renaissance period, the black ghetto became an attraction for a varied assortment of white celebrities and just plain thrill-seeking white people lost from their moorings. Some were insipid rebels, defying the mores of their upbringing by associating with Negroes on a socially equal level. Some were too rich to work, not educated enough to teach, and not holy enough to preach. Others were searching for the mythological "noble savage" – the "exotic Negro."

These professional exotics were generally college educated Negroes who had become estranged from their families and the environment of their upbringing. They talked at length about the great books within them waiting to be written. Their white sponsors continued to subsidize them while they "developed their latent talent." Of course the "great books" of these camp followers never got written and, eventually, their white sponsors realized that they were never going to write – not even a good letter. Ironically, these sophisticates made a definite contribution to the period of the "New Negro literary renaissance." In socially inclined company, they proved that a black American could behave with as much attention to the details of social protocol as the best bred and richest white person in the country. They could balance a cocktail glass with expertness. Behind their pretense of being writers they were really actors – and rather good ones. They were generally better informed than their white sponsors and could easily participate in a discussion of the writings of Marcel Proust in one minute, and the music of Ludwig van Beethoven the next. As social parasites, they conducted themselves with a smoothness approaching an artistic accomplishment. Unknown to them, their conduct had done much to eliminate one of the major prevailing stereotypes of Afro-American life and manners.

Concurrently with the unfolding of this mildly funny comedy, the greatest productive period in Afro-American literature continued. The more serious and talented black writers were actually writing their books and getting them published.

Opportunity magazine, then edited by Charles Johnson, and The Crisis, edited by W. E. B. DuBois, were major outlets for the new black writers.

Opportunity short story contests provided a proving ground for a number of competent black writers. Among the prize winners were Cecil Blue, John F. Matheus, Eugene Gordon, and Marita Bonner.

Writers like Walter White, Jessie Fauset, Wallace Thurman, Nella Larsen, George S. Schuyler, Sterling A. Brown, and Arna Bontemps had already made their debut and were accepted into the circle of the matured.

The stock market collapse of 1929 marked the beginning of the depression and the end of the period known as "The Negro Renaissance." The "exotic Negro," professional and otherwise, became less exotic now that a hungry look was upon his face. The numerous white sponsors and well-wishers who had begun to flock to Harlem ten years before no longer had time or money to explore and marvel over Harlem life. Many Harlem residents lived and died in Harlem during this period without once hearing of the famous literary movement that had flourished and declined within their midst. It was not a mass movement. It was a fad, partly produced in Harlem and partly imposed on Harlem. Most of the writers associated with it would have written just as well at any other time.

In the intervening years between the end of "The Negro Renaissance" and the emergence of Richard Wright, black writers of genuine talent continued to produce books of good caliber. The lack of sponsorship and pampering had made them take serious stock of themselves and their intentions. The Crisis, organ of the National Association for the Advancement of Colored People, and Opportunity, organ of the National Urban League, continued to furnish a publishing outlet for new black writers. The general magazines published stories by black writers intermittently, seemingly on a quota basis.

During this period writers like Ralph Ellison, Henry B. Jones, Marian Minus, Ted Poston, Lawrence D. Reddick, and Grace W. Thompkins published their first short stories.

In 1936 Richard Wright's first short story to receive any appreciable attention, "Big Boy Leaves Home," appeared in the anthology, The New Caravan. "The Ethics of Living Jim Crow: An Autobiographical Sketch" was published in American Stuff, anthology of the Federal Writers' Project, the next year. In 1938, when his first book, Uncle Tom's Children, won a $500 prize contest conducted by Story Magazine, his talent received national attention. With the publication of his phenomenally successful novel, Native Son, in 1940, a new era in Afro-American literature had begun. Here, at last, was a black writer who undeniably wrote considerably better than many of his white contemporaries. As a short story craftsman, he was the most accomplished black writer since Charles W. Chesnutt.

After the emergence of Richard Wright, the period of indulgence for Negro writers was over. Hereafter, black writers had to stand or fall by the same standards and judgments used to evaluate the work of white writers. The era of the patronized and pampered black writer had at last come to an end. The closing of this era may, in the final analysis, be the greatest contribution Richard Wright made to the status of Negro writers and to Negro literature.

When the United States entered the second World War, the active Negro writers, like most other writers in the country, turned their talents to some activity in relation to the war.

The first short stories of Ann Petry began to appear in The Crisis. The Negro Caravan, the best anthology of Negro literature since Alain Locke edited The New Negro sixteen years before, had already appeared with much new material. Chester B. Himes, a dependable writer during the depression period, managed to turn out a number of remarkable short stories while working in shipyards and war industries in California. In 1944, he received a Rosenwald Fellowship to complete his first novel, If He Hollers Let Him Go. In 1945, Frank Yerby won an O. Henry Memorial Award for his excellent short story, "Health Card," which had been published in Harper's magazine a year before.

A new crop of postwar black writers was emerging. In their stories they treated new aspects of Afro-American life or brought new insights to the old aspects. Principally, they were good story tellers, aside from any message they wanted to get across to their readers. The weepy sociological propaganda stories (so prevalent during the depression era) had had their day with the Negro writer and all others. There would still be protest stories, but the protest would now have to meet the standards of living literature.

Opportunity and The Crisis, once the proving ground for so many new black writers, were no longer performing that much needed service. The best of the new writers found acceptance in the general magazines. Among these are James Baldwin, Lloyd Brown, Arthur P. Davis, Owen Dodson, Lance Jeffers, John O. Killens, Robert H. Lucas, Albert Murray, George E. Norford, Carl R. Offord, John H. Robinson, Jr., John Caswell Smith, Jr., and Mary E. Vroman.

With the rise of nationalism and independent states in Africa, and the rapid change of the status of the Negro in the United States, the material used by black writers and their treatment of it did, of necessity, reflect a breaking away from the old mooring.

Among black writers the period of the late 1940s was the period of Richard Wright. The period of the 1960s was the period of James Baldwin.

The now flourishing literary talent of James Baldwin had no easy birth, and he did not emerge overnight, as some of his new discoverers would have you believe. For years this talent was in incubation in the ghetto of Harlem, before he went to Europe a decade ago (1959) in an attempt to discover the United States and how he and his people relate to it. The book in which that discovery is portrayed, The Fire Next Time, is a continuation of his search for place and definition.

Baldwin, more than any other writer of our times, has succeeded in restoring the personal essay to its place as a form of creative literature. From his narrow vantage point of personal grievance, he has opened a "window on the world." He plays the role traditionally assigned to thinkers concerned with the improvement of human conditions – that of alarmist. He calls national attention to things in the society that need to be corrected and things that need to be celebrated.

When Richard Wright died in Paris in 1960, a new generation of black writers, partly influenced by him, was beginning to explore, as Ralph Ellison said, "the full range of American Negro humanity." In the short stories and novels of such writers as Frank London Brown, William Melvin Kelly, LeRoi Jones, Paule Marshall, Rosa Guy, and Ernest J. Gaines, both a new dimension and a new direction in writing are seen. They have questioned and challenged all previous interpretations of Afro-American life. In doing this, they have created the basis for a new American literature.

The black writer and his people are now standing at the crossroads of history. This is the black writer's special vantage point, and this is what makes the task and the mission of the black writer distinctly different from that of the white writer. The black writer, concerned with creating a work of art in a segregated society, has a double task. First: he has to explain the society to himself and create his art while opposing that society. Second: he cannot be honest with himself or his people without lending his support, at least verbally, to the making of a new society that respects the dignity of men.

The black writer must realize that his people are now entering the last phase of a transitional period between slavery and freedom; it is time for the black writer to draw upon the universal values in his people's experience, just as Sean O'Casey and Sholem Aleichem drew upon the universal values in the experiences of the Irish and the Jews. In the next phase of Afro-American writing, a literature of celebration must be created – not a celebration of oppression, but a celebration of survival in spite of it.

Chapter 5

Narratives

Third Class on the Blue Train to Kumasi

John Henrik Clarke

Reprinted from *Phylon,* Vol. 23, Third Quarter (Fall 1962): pp. 294–301

The night before my departure for Kumasi most of the families in the apartment compound, in Jamestown, the Ga community of Accra, Ghana, had ventured to my small room and wished me "safe journey." Soon after I arrived to live among them, they readily adopted me and became concerned about all of my activities during my "African Mission." Someone jokingly forewarned me against the Ashantis of Kumasi. Many years ago they were the traditional enemies of the Ga people. Their disputes and wars and how they were eventually settled are now a part of the history and legends of these two proud African tribes.

My Ga friend and host, James A. Kotey, packed my handbag with tender care and thoroughness. In many ways he was more "civilized" than I, because he was more adaptable to the hereness and nowness of every occasion.

On the morning of my departure, Mr. Tamakloe, the community business man, dispatched one of his helpers to the station ahead of me to pick up my ticket. The old ladies who sat all day on the veranda of the house and the children bade me "goodbye" after I assured them that I would be returning to Accra in four days.

Mr. Tamakloe was still amazed over my preference to travel third class. Most visitors to his country do not travel on African trains, third class or otherwise. The ticket to Kumasi, about two hundred miles into the interior of Ghana by railroad route, cost seven shillings and seven pence – a little more than one dollar in American money. The travel time from Accra to Kumasi had been announced as being seven hours. On a continent where most people take an informal attitude about punctuality, I had been emphatically told that the blue Train from Accra to Kumasi would depart and arrive at its destination on time.

Mr. Tamakloe had arranged for me to stay at the home of Mr. Stanley C. Lokko, Senior Prison Superintendent at Kumasi. Mr. Lokko is a member of the Ga tribe who formerly lived in the community of Jamestown in Accra.

We arrived at the station at five minutes to seven. Most of the passengers had already boarded the train. A contagious circus atmosphere prevailed in the station and extended far beyond it. Market women, petty traders, friends and relatives of the passengers fiercely endeavored to make themselves heard. One of the Station Master's assistants blew a whistle and announced the time of the train's departure.

Mr. Tamakloe's helper took my bag and led me on the train, which was now almost full. The first two cars in the third-class section of the train have leather cushioned seats. All of these seats had been taken before I arrived. I found a seat near a window in one of the cars with hard board seats. I gave Mr. Tamakloe's helper a shilling for handling my bags. He seemed embarrassed about accepting it. In spite of the sharp buying and selling ability of the Ga people, they do not like to be paid for service rendered to a friend.

In the few minutes left before departure Mr. Tamakloe found a traveling companion for me. One of his friends, a Mr. Codjoe, was going to Kumasi. I asked Mr. Codjoe the meaning of his name. In answering my inquiry he taught me the first in a series of lessons on the history and customs of the Akan people.

The engineer blew the whistle of the panting train. The tempo of the many conversations was shattered. For a fleeting moment the noise diminished almost to a hush. The Station Master's assistant also blew his whistle repeatedly and turned completely around several times, making sure he was heard. Why? I will never know. The happy faces of the friends and relatives of the passengers were wishing them "safe journey." No doubt, at this moment the circus atmosphere in the station had reached its highest point of excitement. Over the heads of the crowd, I could barely see the waving hands of Mr. Tamakloe and his helper. It was exactly seven o'clock as the train pulled away from the station. The celebrated Blue Train to Kumasi departed on time.

We passed the new Kwame Nkrumah station, recently finished and waiting for its official opening. About two hundred yards to the right of the station the fountains in Kwame Nkrumah Circle, on Kwame Nkrumah Boulevard, sprayed streams of water toward the sky.

My appointed traveling companion, Mr. Codjoe, was a civil servant on vacation. He was a small man, neat and handsome. Like most Africans he wore his dark complexion with unobtrusive pride – a trait the people of African descent living in the Western world lost long ago. The lesson he was teaching me about the history and customs of the Akan people continued.

His name, Codjoe, meant male child born on Monday. Had he been born on Tuesday, his name would have been Kwabina, Wednesday Kwaku, Thursday Yaw, Friday Kofi, Saturday Kwame. (So the Prime Minister of Ghana was born on Saturday.) Kwesi is the name for a male child born on Sunday.

The coastal city of Accra was behind us now. The train moved toward Kumasi. The first stop was at Achimota Station, near the famous college that was inspired and developed by the great African, James E.K. Aggrey. Leaving Achimota Station, the train moved into the forest area. The faces of the passengers no longer reflected the buoyant excitement of the departure. Children left their mothers' care and made a playground in the aisles between the seats. In the crosscurrents of conversation the languages spoken were mostly Ga, Twi and Ewe. I could distinguish the sound of one from the other without understanding any of them. Figuratively, the conversation in English between Mr. Codjoe and me was an island of speech surrounded by a large alien sea.

The maximum speed of this train, on its good days, is thirty-five miles per hour. This was not one of its good days. The large toy engine plunged ahead on the narrow tracks past more forest, then a cluster of small fields. Occasionally an African farmer straightened up and waved at the passengers. The farmer was nearly always a woman working in an odd-shaped patch of land with a short hoe. We rode through several villages. In this country, as in most of Africa, the effects of rapid transition are altering the face of the land and the people. The traditional huts are being replaced by cement-block houses. This country has large quantities of high-grade hard wood. Why this wood is rarely ever used in building houses, I do not know.

Mr. Codjoe interrupted his teaching and looked toward the front of the train. The head of the engine was bending into a city. The city was Kotoku, our second stop. Some of the passengers got off here. A small group of men looking like government officials boarded the second-class car. Market women, petty traders and other sellers of everything from baby nippers to full dress suits, swarmed over the train. I tried in vain to get the attention of the fruit sellers.

The train was in motion, pulling away from the station before the army of salesmen lowered the crescendos of their chatter and moved their baskets and bundles away from the tracks. Inside the car some of the children had left their playground in the aisles between the seats and were being fed by their mothers. A beautifully dressed woman – with her feet as bare as they were when she came into the world – stretched out on her seat and went to sleep. Two of the market women who had got on at the last stop were still walking through the cars selling sweet cakes. A male food seller, was also selling the same items as the women and there was no apparent conflict between them.

Beyond the city the train entered the forest area again and increased its speed to what Mr. Codjoe said was thirty miles an hour, seemingly to refute my premature assumption that this was not one of the train's good days. Mr. Codjoe continued to explain the history and customs of the Akan people of Ghana. The present lesson was about the land tenure system among the Akans and the significance of the earth Goddess Asase Efua. Asase means earth or ground; Efua means originating or born on Friday and female.

We reached our third stop, the city of Nsawam, before the lesson was concluded. The market women at this station were selling a more substantial quality of food, mostly fish, beef and rice, and fried plantains. A bare-breasted woman, well dressed from the waist down, came to the train to greet a friend.

The train left Nsawam and crossed the bridge of a small river called Densu. The last part of the city was built away from the railroad tracks. The steeple of what seemed to be an old church was seen in the foreground.

In one corner of the car a lady was nursing her child and eating sweet cakes. Another lady had gathered up part of her loose-fitting garment and made a shield for her face while she slept. After the nursing baby finished its meal, the mother opened up a can of sardines that she had bought at the last was stop. Now that the baby was fed and peaceful, she leisurely enjoyed her meal of sardines and bread.

I bought some sweet cakes that were not very sweet or very good. As we moved once more through deep forest country, the engineer slowed the speed of the train, seemingly in meditation and in respect for the grandeur of nature's handiwork in the tall, singing forest. The lady passenger who had covered her face with her garment while sleeping was now watching the world from the window of the train. The well-dressed lady with no shoes finished her nap and assisted another passenger in calming a crying child.

Mr. Codjoe concluded a lesson on the early history of the Akan people, calling my attention to a coco tree and a local vegetable called coco yams. The train came out of the deep forest country and moved across a green valley that ended before we reached the city of Kofariqua, our fourth stop. Kofariqua is the capital of the Eastern Region and the headquarters of the Regional Commissioner.

The station was larger than the one at Accra, and cleaner. Small boys competed with each other, selling Ghana newspapers to the passengers. The sugar cane sellers were doing a brisk business. I bought a piece, mostly because eating sugar cane is a habit I used to have during my childhood days in the state of Georgia. The men in the second-class car, who looked like government officials, got off here. They were waving at some of the passengers as the train moved on to Tafo, the fifth stop.

The station at Tafo was only a shed. We stopped here for about two minutes. Some of the sleeping babies had awakened and were being breast fed. I was eating sugar cane, as were some of the other passengers. We passed through a village where coco kernels were drying in the sun. The next town was Nhawkaw, the sixth stop. We arrived at Nhawkaw as Mr. Codjoe was explaining the ceremony of marriage and the components of the family structure in the social community of the Akan people. The town and its tin-roofed houses were soon behind us.

We moved deeper into the part of the country that is heavily populated by the Akan people. Who are the Akan people? What is the significance of the role they have played in the old and new history of Ghana?

According to the eminent Ghanaian scholar, Joseph B. Danquah, greatest living authority on the Akan people, the Akan, as a distinct social community, formed part of the great migration of people who were dislodged by the Moslem conquest of the Western Sudan in the tenth and eleventh centuries. They gravitated southward and settled in the territory later called the Gold Coast.

The original home and empire of the Akan people was known as Ghana, and was located on the bend of the Niger River. This country fell to the Moslems, under the leadership of Abu Bekr of the Sasso Empire, in 1076 AD

The Akan of Ghana are classified in three major groups, Nta, Ntu, and Nxe. The Nta stock embraces the Gonja, Later (Guan), Etsi Fetu, Affutu, Obutu, Awutu, Asebu, Ante (Ahanta) and allied tribes in the east and south of Ghana. The Fante (Fa-Nte) came in the second wave of the great migration. Their first habitation was near Techiman in Ashanti. Eventually they moved their capital to Mankessim. The Portuguese came into this territory as traders in 1481. At that time the Fantes were still paying homage to the ruler of Walata as their superior king. Walata was the successor of the ancient Empire of Ghana. The third Nta stock, the Asante (Asa-Nte) was the last and most powerful of the waves of Akan people to come from the north. Many centuries later, after the Asante (called Ashanti by the Europeans) had formed a great federation, they built the capital of modern Ashanti, Kumasi. The Ashantis became the most powerful of all the Akan people and the central power of Akan dynastic rulers.

Their power grew and remained intact until the British entered Kumasi toward the end of the seventeenth century.

Historically speaking, Europeans have been preying upon the west coast of Africa for over five hundred years. The Portuguese came in the fifteenth century and built Elmina Castle. The Dutch, Swedes, Danes and English came afterwards. The Swedes established themselves at Cape Coast and the Danes built Christianborg Castle at Accra. By 1662 the British had gained the upper hand in the Gold Coast slave trade. After the withdrawal of the Dutch, the British monopoly over the West African slave trade prevailed until it was abolished in 1807.

In 1896, Kwaku Dua III, King Prempeh of Ashanti, was seized and exiled by the British. Ashanti was declared a "Protectorate" of the British in 1901, after its great woman warrior, Yaa Assantewa, Queen-ruler of Ejisu, had been defeated in the last Ashanti uprising (called the Yaa Asantewa war) in 1900. King Prempeh was permitted to return home in 1925, after taking an oath of allegiance to the British. The nearly thirty years of exile had not broken his spirit. The Ashanti Confederacy was restored in 1935 and once more it became the paramount centralized Akan government in the whole of the country then called the Gold Coast.

The culture of the three Nta races of the Gold Coast was spoken of as Akan, meaning 'the first,' possibly 'first in culture.' The land inhabited by the Akan people, before the disruption of their social community by the Moslem conquest, was known as Akana or Akane, called Ghana by the Arabs and Guinea by the Europeans. At the beginning of their modern history, the main feature of Akan political life had been a democratic form of kingship which the warrior kings of Asante stock imposed upon all the tribes and lands around them. These were the people that I had set out to visit.

The train passed through another town and slowed its speed without stopping. A flock of vultures sat on a dilapidated house at the edge of the town and stared vacantly at the passengers. Except for Mr. Codjoe and me, and the ladies with small babies, most of the passengers were asleep. We had now been riding on the Blue Train to Kumasi for nearly four hours. The group of chatting women who had gotten off at the last stop had taken away most of our amusement.

The train came out of another stretch of forest and passed the Kwahu Mountain Range. At the last stop Mr. Codjoe had bought a bunch of ten bananas for tuppence. I ate some of them after I had finished my sweet cakes. The long mountain range disappeared and the train moved through another cluster of farms. Mr. Codjoe explained the names and uses of the vegetation growing along the tracks. I can neither pronounce nor remember the names.

Before we reached the seventh stop, Wahu-Prasu – "city on the Pra River" – the mountain range came back into view. The Pra River was once the dividing line between warring tribes. Osei Tutu, first great King of Ashanti, was ambushed and killed in 1731 while crossing this river at a place called Coromartee, and his body was never recovered. A royal entourage of three hundred persons, including sixty wives of the king and the nobles of his court, was also killed. This great tragedy occurred on Saturday. In commemoration of the sad event, Osei Tutu's people initiated their most sacred oath – Coromartee Memento (Coromartee Saturday) – known as "The Great Oath of the Dreadful Day." This oath is considered so solemn and binding that it is rarely mentioned by name. On the few occasions when it is mentioned, it is spoken of in fearful whispers.

Mr. Codjoe unfolded lesson after lesson in the history, religion, and folklore of the Akan people as the rattling Blue Train took us closer to our destination, Kumasi. A Mohammedan passenger put down his rug and said his midday prayers, after which a beggar who had boarded the train at Wahu-Prasu chanted for pennies in the same aisles.

Mr. Codjoe paused hastily in his teaching as the train was approaching the city of Konongo, the eighth stop. He stared expectantly out of the window and was rewarded as the train screeched to a halt. His wife, who was visiting friends in Konongo, came to the train to greet him. As he leaned out of the window, their hands touched and they talked a full minute in the language of their tribe before Mr. Codjoe introduced me. His wife was a beautiful Ashanti girl, obviously much younger than he, dressed in expensive hand-loomed Ashanti cloth. Her two female companions looked over her shoulders and speculated about me, showing by their expressions that they were amused.

By then, the food sellers had invaded the station in full force. Mr. and Mrs. Codjoe had to raise thier voices to a shout in order to hear each other. Mr. Codjoe was giving his wife some money as the heavy, strained panting of the train engine started its forward thrust. The food sellers scrambled from the train while hurriedly returning change to their customers.

Outside of Konongo, Mr. Codjoe called my attention to a gold mine. A new conductor, the third since Accra, came through the cars and picked up all of the tickets. Why so many? I do not know. It was now 12:55 PM Across the aisles from the forever hungry baby was being fed again. The engineer was bringing the train back to its maximum speed, about thirty miles per hour. After the feeding, the mother gave the child a sponge bath. No one, except me, was surprised at seeing a baby being bathed on a train. On my last trip to the private place (toilet), I had noticed a lady at the far end of the car with a small crate of chickens near her seat. Yes, chickens on the Blue Train!

The baby, a girl child, now redressed and seemingly happy, was handed over to another lady passenger while its mother refreshed herself.

Mr. Codjoe finished teaching me the last lesson on the history and customs of the Akan people at 1:40 PM I had been a passenger on the Blue Train to Kumasi since 6:55 AM The love affair I originally had with the hard seats, and this mode of travel was over.

The well-dressed lady who gave the impression of having no shoes took her belongings down from the rack and displayed a pair of African sandals before she put them on. All of the lady passengers with small children had placed them in the cloth cradles on their backs. Nearly every passenger on the train was standing, anticipating the moment of thier departure. We were on the outskirts of Kumasi.

The time was now one minute after 2 PM According to my advance information, Kumasi is a city of about eighty thousand people. On the left side of the train the buildings of the Kumasi College of Technology could be seen. The train curved toward the station. Soon, and with breathtaking suddenness, Kumasi was in full view, a city built on a group of sloping hills, beautiful, as are most beautiful cities, in spite of the incidence of squalor and ugliness. As the train reached the station and slowed to a halt, I looked at my watch and discovered that the celebrated Blue Train from Accra to Kumasi, highly publicized for its consistency in arriving at its destination on time, had arrived four minutes late.

In the station, bedlam reigned unabated. The passengers for the Blue Train's trip back to Accra were already waiting and showing no patience. The arriving passengers called out to friends and relatives and took their own time leaving the train.

In the midst of this scene, I thanked Mr. Codjoe for his teaching and his kindness, gathered up my notes and my belongings and searched over the thickening mob of people, in hope of being able to identify the face of Mr. Stanley C. Lokko, who was to be my host during my stay in Kumasi. I alighted from the train and inquired about him. Without knowing it, I was standing near his car. Mr. Lokko and his son, Ferdinand, had gone to the first class cars to wait for me, believing or assuming that an American visitor to thier country would not travel any other way.

A tall man wearing the uniform of a prison guard greeted me and departed; soon he brought Mr. Lokko back to the car where I was waiting. He was a fine example of Ga manhood, solid, black and handsome, with a proud soldierly swagger in his walk. His smile, thoroughly genuine, said: "You are welcome." He wore the uniform of his office, Senior Prison Superintendent in this Ashanti town. With absolute confidence I moved toward his outstretched hand.

The Morning Train to Ibadan

John Henrik Clarke

Reprinted from *Journal of Negro Education,* Vol. 31, Fall 1962, pp. 527–30

Lagos is far from being my favorite African city. Its cosmopolitan air and the incongruous mixture of African and European ways of life left me singularly unimpressed. In spite of my feelings about it, I must admit Lagos is not a city without attractions. Lagos is a colorful city with a dual personality – one foot in the 19th century and the other one stepping, with awkward rapidity toward the 20th.

> I left the hotel, absurdly called "The Palace," with a feeling of relief that was closely related to happiness. The Palace was absolutely the worst hotel that I have ever encountered in all of my years of travel. The spell of early morning was still upon the city and I had more than enough time at my disposal. I decided to walk the mile and a half to the Lagos Train Terminus. The cab drivers, already on the street in full force, offered their services and accepted my refusal with bad humor, as though I was an escaping thief.
>
> The road to the stretched through one of the worst slums I have ever seen; crossed a long bridge over a lagoon, intruding upon the landscape in the heart of the city with touches of magical beauty.

At the station I showed my ticket and watched the expression on the clerk's face as he weighed my hand bag and viewed the ticket again, frowning in disbelief. He was surprised to see an American traveling third class. I have been in Africa over two months now, traveling in mostly out of the way places that most tourists never see. This is as it should be because I am not a tourist. My life-long interest in Africa brought me here to my ancestral home to see and try to understand, at least part of the temperament and importance of this emergent continent and its people who will, no doubt, influence the future of mankind.

In the station there were separate eating facilities for third class travelers. This duplication made no sense to me and seemed rather silly. This is a new station built under British supervision. British city planning in Africa always leaves much to be desired. I purchased a cup of tea and a sweet bun before boarding the morning train to Ibadan. Some of the cars were almost full a half hour before the time of departure. I walked through the train until I found a seat near a window. Chatting Nigerian women wearing multi-colored dresses and large bandana-like head pieces give the train a circus atmosphere. Nearly all of the women had children. More passengers with odd-shaped luggage and some carrying their belongings in bags and boxes soon filled up the train. Friends and relatives of the passengers stood inside and on the platform, giving out last minute instructions and advice, sometimes in serious tones, as if the passengers were about to depart for the moon. At exactly eight o'clock the train started its journey to Ibadan.

A beggar came on pleading for the price of his morning meal. Leaving Lagos, we passed through Yaba, a residential suburb where most of the better class Africans and a few Europeans live. Shops, theatres, and small hotels were scattered through the settlement.

At Ebute Mutta, the first stop, the beggar left the train and three more got on. After one more sub-station stop we were out of Lagos. When we left the third stop, Mushin, the countryside began to unfold. Shacks and huts punctuated the blankets of green foliage stretching before us further than the eye could see.

From my accumulated provisions I made a large sardine sandwich and I was still I the process of consuming it when we reached Agece, the fourth stop. Two conductors moved rapidly to the back of the train, talking in excited tones. They were hurrying to the first and second class cars where some kind of commotion was attracting the attention of the people waiting to board the train. I called out in vain to a chatting market woman who was selling boiled guinea fowl eggs, two for three pence. The train pulled away as she noticed me and tried to reach the window where I was sitting.

A beggar boarded the train at this stop, carrying a sign saying he was deaf and dumb. He wore the attire of a Mohammedan – a poorly kept Mohammedan. His long white robe was dirty and torn in several places. For a hat he wore a red fez. He looked to be of Hausa extraction, though he was much shorter than most of the Hausa people that I have seen.

At 9:15, we stopped at Kajawya. The market women along the tracks offered nothing for sale that I had enough nerve to eat.. As the train was leaving Kajawya I noticed the "deaf and dumb" beggar standing by the tracks laughing and talking to a group of similarly dressed men.

The train moved through a thick forest area. The stray cinders from the engine had spoiled my bargain basement suit. Still another beggar came through the train wearing a sign announcing that he too was "deaf and dumb." The soliciting methods of this beggar were much more intriguing than those of the last one. He was calling attention to his sign with a tin rattle that made a sad, haunting kind of music. He was also more imaginative and more energetic than the last beggar. He turned completely around several times, almost aggressive in acting out his plight. Even without this ceremony his manner of dress was colorful enough to get him all the attention he needed. A pang of depression and disappointment touched my spirit when he left at the next stop.

There was no lull in the excitement. More third class passengers were boarding the train. A lady came into the car carrying a large straw sleeping mat on her head, one child in the cloth cradle on her back and a bundle on one arm. Other passengers were equally burdened, some were carrying cooking facilities.

In spite of my fascination for third class travel, I still have some prejudice against it that is being rapidly dispelled by scenes like this. Third class accommodation makes it possible for a lot of people, with very little money, and an excessive amount of luggage, to travel at a fare that they can afford. But for third class accommodations, most people in Africa who fit into this category would not be able to travel by train at all.

The lady with the straw sleeping mat put down the first load of her belongings and brought in a tin pan that was much larger than most American wash tubs. Her little girl came over to me, greeted me warmly in the Yoruba language and climbed into my lap. I answered her with a smile as she continued to talk. When she finally discovered that I did not know her language her small face lost some of the bright glow of friendship and plainly showed its bewilderment. The child waited with admirable patience while her mother found a place for her many belongings and found time to take her. Her mother was noticeably pregnant.

As the train started to move forward the chatter of the newly arrived passengers, acquainting themselves with the others, rose to crescendos of clashing sounds and created, for me at least, a strange kind of confused jubilation. From the window I saw the green countryside unfolding its primeval splendor. About a half hour later we stopped by a thick forest. I sat in the window speculating about the names of the diverse species of trees scattered along the tracks. The train stood panting, as if anticipating the journey that lay ahead... seemingly wondering as I was wondering, why this stop was made. We were nowhere near a station. No one got on or off. My American mind expects a reason for everything. The Nigerian passengers were still filling the car with criss-cross conversations.

The child of the lady with the straw mats and all the other bulky paraphernalia had fallen asleep. The train started jerkily, awakening the child who looked up at her mother for one surprised moment and closed her eyes again. Still no one, except me, seemed to care why the train had stopped in the first place.

I left my seat and walked through the third class cars until I reached the one marked: CANTEEN. This was the closest approximation to an American dining car I could find. A cup of tea cost me three pence. The scant choice of food was not impressive. I arrived back at my seat as the train was making another stop, for no reason that I could understand. Up ahead of us I saw a city built on the side of a hill. It looked new. The shiny tin-roofed houses looked as if they had been freshly painted. The city was Aro.

The market women at this station did not have any attractive items for sale... mostly sugar cane and agidi. Agidi consists mainly of maize (corn) meal. It is one of the most important items in the West African diet. My favorite market women, the fruit sellers, arrived a few seconds before the train pulled away. I bought a bunch of eight bananas for three pence.

A few miles away from Aro we reached a large city called Aby. Some passengers left at Aby. For less than one minute the aisles were uncongested. Soon, more colorfully dressed people came aboard. Some were carrying straw mats. Where are they taking those mats? A lady pushed a large dishpan under my seat. A child was tied to her back and another one was growing in her abdomen. On the platform near the window where I was sitting an argument was in process. A white-robed man was in the middle of a cluster of people, standing stonily silent as their uninhibited wrath was poured upon him. All of his tormentors were dressed in smocks of different colors. This made the completely white robe of the assailed man stand out with contrasting sharpness. His face bore a particularly passive expression. He seemed neither for nor against his assailants. He stood and listened as though listening was a penitence, totally unrelated to guilt.

Every seat in the car was occupied now. Market women invaded the train along with the new passengers. Movement in the aisles became a problem – a rather hectic one. The local argument outside of the train continued, heated and confusing. The lady with the large pots and pans prepared some food for her child. The child was beautiful. To me she seemed overdressed. I could be absolutely wrong because I am not sure what being overdressed consists of in this or any other part of Africa.

As the train started its forward thrust the argument on the platform ended abruptly. The white-robed man got into the third class car behind us. The group of men wearing the colorful smocks who had been addressing him in heated tones, were looking toward the train now. Their faces uniformly showed a flush of satisfaction, as if they had won some kind of victory. Probably just being heard was all they wanted or needed.

The lady with the many pots and pans had one full of agidi wrapped in banana leaves. She took one ball of agidi from the pan and gave it to the child who made no attempt to eat it. She held the food in her hand and watched me as though I was likely to take it from her. A group of men carrying briefcases and flaunting airs of officialdom walked through the train.

At the next stop some of the passengers with the straw mats left. A new passenger came into the car carrying what seemed to be a large catfish. One of the "deaf and dumb" beggars ended his tour at this station and was met by friends. He took off his sign and stood by the tracks, laughing and talking as other friends came up to greet him. Hereafter it is going to be difficult for me to believe that anybody in Nigeria is really deaf and dumb.

The little girl seated opposite me took off her headpiece, unfolded it, covered herself and went to sleep. The train moved through a valley. At another stop a stout Nigerian woman boarded the train carrying a large basket of bark and some earthenware pots and dishes. She leaned out of the window and gave instructions to three people standing outside as we got underway again. The station was only a large platform with no cover. A small herd of goats was grazing near the tracks. They looked up for a moment as the heavy straining noise of the engine was becoming incongruous in the midst of this pastoral scene. The new passenger found a seat, mad a new friend or rediscovered an old one.

The little girl who had been sleeping under her headpiece got up and opened one of the pots of food. She prepared a meal for herself, using banana leaves for a plate. Her mother gave her one glance of approval and continued a conversation with another passenger across the aisle. At 12:40 the train made another one of its unheralded stops. We were near a village of small farms. Finally the train resumed its journey, jarring the little girl's food in its banana-leaf plate. The man with the big catfish had hung his property above his seat. No one, except me bothered to stare at this sight. The train moved over a long stretch of straight track. For the first time it reached a speed that might have been thirty-five miles an hour.

The little girl finished her meal, threw the banana-leaf plate out of the window and rediscovered my presence. For a moment I thought she was going to stare me through my seat. She was not hostile. She was intensely curious. I think she had realized I was, at least, not a local African and there was something out of the ordinary about my presence in a third class car on the morning train to Ibadan.

We reached a village of red clay houses with tin roofs. A train to Lagos, full of passengers, was waiting on the side tracks. I saw a few drops of rain. The rain made me more conscious of wanting and needing a bath. The cinders from the engine, flying through the open window, had ruined my cheap suit. I must remind myself to never again wear a light colored bargain basement suit on an African train.

Another stop was made at 2:05 PM. The stout woman with the basket of bark and the earthenware pots and dishes got off, while handing her belongings adroitly and continuing a conversation with her friends. Fifteen minutes later, the train was pulling into Ibadan. The conductor walked through the cars, announcing: "Ibadan! We are now in Ibadan!"

The man with the large catfish brushed against me on his way to the door. The conductor continued to give out his needless message until he came to me. His observation of me was slow and thorough.

"American?" he asked.

"Yes."

"Ever been to Ibadan before?"

"No."

His expression became a mixture of pride and condescension. His next message was also needless.

"You are now in the largest city in West Africa," he said.

Journey to the Sierra Maestra

John Henrik Clarke

Reprinted from *Freedomways*, Spring 1961, pp. 32–35

When our delegation arrived in Havana last summer, the pilgrimage to Oriente Province and the Sierra Maestra had already started. The nucleus of this delegation was composed of writers and artists who had been contributors to the special issue (July 4th) of the newspaper/supplement *Lunes De Revolucion*. Robert F. Williams, a member of this delegation, was returning to Cuba for a second visit. Before we left New York City, he had told me that no experience in his lifetime had impressed him more profoundly than the Cuban Revolution. Extending his explanation, he said:

> "I am returning to Cuba because I wanted to see this social miracle again. It is unbelievable to a Southerner – particularly a Southern Negro. The inspiring truth of the Cuban Revolution is more than I can absorb in the course of one visit. This government follows the true teachings of Christian humanitarianism. The Cuban problem is related to the underprivileged people of the world. The enemies of Cuba are using the same tactics as the people of Tennessee and other southern states use against my people in their struggle against economic pressure."

When the delegation left Havana for the Sierra Maestra on the evening of July 25th, the inspiring truth of the Cuban Revolution had touched me with the same kind of profoundness. As a Negro writer concerned with the plight of other Negroes throughout the world, I am particularly interested in the administrative and cultural aspects of the Cuban Revolution, as it applies to the blending of people of diverse cultural backgrounds. In the United States, this is the promise that was never kept.

On the eve of our departure for the Sierra Maestra, I was obsessed by a far greater interest. I wanted to see some of rural Cuba and observe the program of land reform. My reasons were deep and selfish. I was born in the state of Alabama in the southern part of the United States. My family were landless peasants – sharecroppers. My father dreamed of being a land owner all his life. The dream died with him. This American Negro farmer, who loved land with a feeling akin to holiness, never owned so much as one inch of land. For me the Cuban Revolution will stand or fall on the basis of what is done to improve the lives of people in Cuba whose hopes and dreams are similar to those of my father. My all too brief study of agrarian reform in Cuba has stimulated me to believe that some of the same methods can be made applicable to certain parts of the United States where there are still sharecroppers. More specific, I think of agrarian reform in relation to the newly emergent nations of Africa. In these nations, the possibilities of friendship and trade with Cuba are a bright prospect for the future. Though an American Negro, I have been a devout African nationalist most of my life.

As my delegation walked into the happy bedlam of the Central Terminus in Havana and waited to tenter the train to the Sierra Maestra, I was thinking intensely of my late father, an Alabama sharecropper who never owned an inch of land, of the landless Cuban farmers now being given land, and of the dispossessed African farmers whose land has been taken over by European settlers. At this moment I knew that nothing I would see or hear in Cuba would interest me more than agrarian reform.

In the Terminus in Havana pageants of delegations and patriotic groups were singing the praise of Fidel Castro and the Cuban Revolution while marching to their trains. Finally we were settled in our seats and the journey to the Sierra Maestra began. Dr. Cardero and her husband, the writer Julian Mayfield, were seated in front of me. Both of them spoke Spanish and were most generous in translating for me the conversations in the train.

The last car on the train was full of writers, photographers and journalists from the leading news services of the world. Francoise Sagan, the young and world famous French author, was among the writers. She represented the Parisian weekly newspaper, "*L'Express.*"

A group of young Cubans passed through the train happily shouting: Cuba Si! Yankee No! In traveling and talking to many people in Cuba, I have found no real animosity against the people of the United States. Their anger is directed against the present policy of the United States government and the distorted concepts of the Cuban Revolution now appearing in the American press.

The train stopped at Matanzas where a large patriotic demonstration greeted us. From the joyful noise outside of the windows it seemed as if the entire population of the town had assembled to salute the delegations journeying to the July 26th celebration in the Sierra Maestra. The composition of the demonstrators inspired me more than the band-playing, the flag-waving and the revolutionary songs. In this demonstration Cubans of every color from blond white to jet black were participating in absolute equality and with the same show of enthusiasm.

The sight of Robert F. Williams waving from a window of the train accelerated the demonstration. His forthright endorsement of the Cuban Revolution during his last visit had made him an accepted friend of the Cuban people. Amid the crescendo of greetings the train began to move again. A thought came to my mind and refused to leave. In all the countries in which I have traveled on this hemisphere, I have never been made to feel more welcome.

After a short stop at Colon, the train made a much longer stop at Santa Clara, where the delegations were greeted by another demonstration. A group of officers and soldiers boarded the train and made us welcome in the name of the town and its people. The delegations flocked to the windows, identifying themselves with hastily made signs. The Mexican delegation had a sign that stretched across the entire length of the car. Dr. Cardero had assembled a Puerto Rican delegation, who were shouting their approval of the Cuban Revolution. In the midst of this joyful pandemonium of sight and sound, it was difficult to hear a clear word spoken. A Cuban Negro, Isrial Mazorra Palacio, gave me his address and instructed me to tell the people of the United States that the people of Cuba are happy. The soldiers left the train and joined the demonstrators on both sides of the tracks. The journey to the Sierra Maestra continued.

Our Cuban hosts passed through the train distributing food for the third time. The food was well prepared and tasty, but more than we could eat. Some of the lights in the cars were tuned off as the train full of delegations moved through the night.

The sun rose on the green fields and hills of Cuba. Most of us had been awakened by the singing of the Mexican delegation. We were served coffee and tomato juice. By seven o'clock on the morning of July 26th we arrived at the city of Marti, named after the great benefactor of Cuba. We passed through many towns and villages in rural Cuba before we arrived at Yara, in Oriente Province. From Yara we climbed into what seemed to be a sugar cane train that took us to

Las Mercedes. Changing transportation again we boarded a truck to the plateau near the reviewing stand.

Here on this plateau were the largest concentrations of people that I have ever witnessed. A surging sea of people had gathered to pledge their allegiance to Fidel Castro and the program of the Cuban Revolution. Delegations from many parts of the world crowded the speakers' platform as others passed in review. The leader of our delegation, Robert F. Williams, and the interpreter for the group, Olga Findley, led us through several clusters of people until we reached the outstretched and welcoming hand of Premier Fidel Castro. He greeted Robert F. Williams first and expressed his pleasure at seeing him in Cuba again. One of the ladies in our delegation was complaining of thirst. When Fidel Castro overheard this, he halted his greeting long enough to bring her a glass of water. This very human gesture of consideration, coming from a busy revolutionist now engrossed in rebuilding his nation, told me more about the character of Fidel Castro then the small mountain of newspaper articles that I have already read about him.

The inspiring climax of the evening came with Fidel Castro's speech, lasting two hours and twenty minutes. In spite of the length of this speech and its far reaching importance, it can be summed up briefly:

> "Fidel Castro pledged to give Cuba back to the Cuban people. The people gratefully accepted the gift and pledged to defend it with their lives."

Chapter 6

Pan Africanism

Africana Studies: A Decade of Change, Challenge and Conflict

John Henrik Clarke

Reprinted from James E. Turner, Editor,
The Next Decade: Theoretical and Research Issues in Africana Studies,
Ithaca, New York: Africana Studies and Research Center, Cornell University, 1984

Nearly a generation ago, in "The Negro Writer and His Relationship to His Roots," the speech that opened the first conference of Black American Writers to be held in this country, Saunders Redding said:

> I do not feel in the least controversial or argumentative about the announced subject. Indeed I have touched upon it so often in one way or another that I long ago exhausted my store of arguments, and if I now revert to a kind of expressionistic way of talking, my excuse for it is patent.[1]

The subject of my paper was already old, with me, before this decade, and before the Black Studies explosion. The serious study of the plight of African people all over the world, in all ages, conditions, and geographical settings, has been the main part of my life's work. It is the all-consuming passion of my existence. It is something I do, just as breathing is something I do.

In his speech, Professor Redding said that his was the kind of subject which, if he talked directly on it for more than twenty minutes, he would have to talk at least a year. He assured his audience that he would not talk directly on the subject and, of course, that he would not talk a year; that his treatment would be more suggestive than exhaustive. The rereading of his paper has influenced my approach to Africana Studies. I prefer the phrase "Africana Studies" to "Black Studies." Black is an honorable word and I am glad to see so many people lose their fear of using it, but it has its limitations. Black, or Blackness, tells you how you look without telling you who you are, whereas Africa, or Africana, relates you to land, history, and culture. No people are spiritually and culturally secure until it answers only to a name of its own choosing, a name that instantaneously relates that people to the past, present, and future. As the Caribbean writer, Richard B. Moore has said in his book *The Name "Negro": Its Origin and Evil Use*, "Slaves and dogs are named by their masters. Free men name themselves."[2] In his book, Moore also expresses something that is increasingly rare in the present academic climate – a conviction based on research and reason. "Human relations," he writes, "can not be peaceful, satisfactory, and happy until placed on the basis of mutual self-respect. The proper name for people has thus become, in this period of crucial change and rapid reformation on a world scale, a vital factor in determining basic attitudes involving how, and even whether, people will continue to live together on this shrinking planet."

One of the many crises in what is called Black Studies is a crisis in semantics. What exactly do we mean by Black Studies?[3]

I have called Black Studies a dilemma at the crossroads of history. This dilemma has long historical roots and we cannot understand it if we regard it as only a current event. Indeed, the dilemma dates from the rise of Europe in the fifteenth century. Looking back, we see that entire peoples have to be read out of the respectful commentary of history in order to justify the slave trade and the colonial system that followed.[4] Europeans and white people, in general, benefited from this distortion of world history, and it is clear that they know more about history than they are prepared to admit. They had to know a great deal in order to distort history so effectively, and then use this distortion as an element of world control. They knew that history is a two-edged sword that can be used both as an instrument of liberation and as a weapon of enslavement. And I might add, they knew then and they know now that history, like a gun, is neutral – it will serve anyone who uses it effectively.

To understand, then, what brought this dilemma into being, we return, at least briefly, to the fifteenth and sixteenth centuries, the period of the second rise of Europe. All the world was changed to accommodate this event, which was followed by the European conquest of most of mankind. This conquest was achieved by the astute use of two political instruments – the Bible and the gun. In addition to colonizing the world, the Europeans colonized information about the world – the writing of world history. They were so successful that today not a single book with the title "World History" is an honest history of the world and all of its people. World history lost its broad definition and became a rationale for European conquest and control, and a means for the glorification of European people at the expense of other people and nations whose colonizations were old before Europe was born.

The first European attack was on African culture. The next move was to deny that this culture ever existed. A look at African culture, especially in West Africa, will show what Africana Studies Programs are about, or should be about.[5]

There is now a need for a global approach to Africana Studies, one that embraces the Africans in Africa, in North and South America, and in the Caribbean Islands, as well as the millions of Africans in Asia and the Pacific Islands who are just discovering that they are African people. Because history is both topical and ancient, and cannot be separated, there is no way to talk about Africana Studies without looking again at the roots of world history and the interplay among the histories of various peoples. The Black historian, who knows his people's history and its relationship to the history of the world, should start with the bold assertions that Africa is the basis of world history, and that African people are the mothers and fathers of mankind. Black scholars, the world over, must be courageous enough to make this assertion and prepare themselves to prove it academically.

This is the basis of the Black scholar's dilemma and the root of the crisis over definition and direction. The special role that history assigns to the scholar eludes most of us: the role is simple, therefore it is complex. In most societies the scholar is not required to labor in the fields, to draw the water, or to bring wood for the fires. Then what is the scholar required to do? What is his or her special mission? The scholar is the clock watcher of history and the keeper of the compass that must be used to locate his or her people on the map of human geography: where they have been and what they have been, where they are and what they are. Most important, the scholar should be able to prophesy where his people still must go and what they still must be.

The scholar should be ale to find the special clock that tells his people their historical, cultural, and political time of day. Part of our tragedy is that we have been, figuratively speaking, telling time by our oppressor's clock. By his clock it could be midnight in December because he is losing control of the world. Because we are reemerging, with hope flowing before us like a river, it is a morning in spring on our special historical clock.

If we look honestly at the Black writer in crisis, we must see that Black writers collectively are an integral part of all those Black people who have been in a continuous crisis ever since their forced exile from Africa to what was later called the New World. It is logical that a people who live in continuous crisis should produce a literature of crisis and this, in essence, is what Black literature has been from the beginning and what it remains today. There is no place that Black writers can hide from this crisis; they take it with them wherever they go. Indeed, they are bound to it most profoundly even on those sad occasions when some of them try to pretend that they have escaped it. In spite of these pretenders who think that they are writers first and Black people second, most Black writers feel their responsibility to Black people.[6]

More than any other writers in the world, Black writers live in the midst of their material and cannot escape from it. Estranged in the Western world, where even after five hundred years of exile fro Africa their people are neither guests nor citizens, their life is a repeated contradiction; and so is the literature about their life. It is a literature that is simultaneously negative and positive. It is negative because it is a literature about alienation; it is positive because it is a literature about heroic struggle and survival in spite of alienation.

Black writers are, concurrently, the most fortunate and the most unfortunate writers of this age. They are fortunate because the most important thing that is happening in this age is happening to their people. They are unfortunate because, in most cases, they do not understand the nature and historical importance of this happening. The reverberation of their people's struggle has pushed the oppressor's originality, if indeed he ever had any, to the limits of its logic, has worn its source out, and has forced him to lose control of the world. Part of the crisis of Black writers is to explain this world to themselves and to their people – a task that cannot be accomplished without a historical frame of reference.

This is an extraordinary situation so let us use our imagination to create an extraordinary way of looking at it. Let us take this crisis out of the framework of history and sociology for the moment and instead regard it as a drama with many dimensions and with long historical roots. The drama is not pure: part comedy and part tragedy, it is sometimes also a satire and there are even elements of farce. It is a mystery play about the greatest crimes ever contrived by the mind of man. The recurring theme of this drama is rape – the rape of a continent and its people. This rape set in motion an act of protracted genocide that lasted for five hundred years and that has not completely exhausted itself today. The aftermath of this crime is the basis of the Black world drama and the crisis that no Black writer can avoid.

With this said we can now, figuratively, put the players on stage. In the unfolding of this great human drama that we call the "Black Crisis," the characters play every role from saint to buffoon. The first scene in the play is pleasant, and there is nothing that suggests future developments. Some sailors have arrived along the coast of West Africa. The year is 1438. With their customary hospitality to strangers, the Africans have invited the sailors to dinner – a scene that will be repeated many times before it is turned into a tragedy. The Africans do not know the temperament of these strangers, nor do they sense the ambition and intent that are hidden behind their smiles. The sailors have come from the thawed-out icebox in northern Asia called Europe. The people from this violent land have begun to search for new gold, labor, and a new supply of food. They find all of these items in Africa and they do not buy or bargain for them – they take them. In the second scene of our play's first act, the dinner is over and the guests are looking around the house of their hosts. They like many of the things that they see, including the wife of the host. Suddenly all expressions change. The guests take out guns, rape the wife of the host, and enslave both of them (and I do not mean figuratively). Thus the long night begins. The curtain falls on the first act of a play that, in many ways, is still on the road.

My basic point is that all Black writers in the West, and most of them in Africa, have been reacting to the consequences of this play. As guests in the homes of non-European people, the Europeans turned on their hosts and forced them away from their homes to labor in the far reaches of the world, mainly in North and South America, the Caribbean Islands, and in the United States. The dilemma and the crisis in Black writing is how to interpret this event and its far-reaching, tragic aftermath. These consequences are the primary content of the literary heritage of Black writers – the materials from which they can never escape. Out of these materials came the slave narratives, the spirituals, and the blues.

I am talking about something that is both historical and topical, which helps to explain why we can understand the present by looking through the lenses of the past. We need both vantage points in order to understand the present disputes over the ideas of nationalism and Pan-Africanism. We Blacks have had these arguments before, much to our sorrow. As a people, each time we forget that our Blackness (or Africanity) is our rallying cry, our window on the world, and the basis of our first allegiance, we find ourselves in serious trouble to explain this fact I must make an admission that breaks my heart as well as yours. Throughout history we have been a politically naive people. We have never made a good alliance with another people, least of all with white people. I do not mean that we have never made alliances with other people, only that they have not been in our favor. In the future we should enter into only those alliances that we can control.[7]

Africans are the only people who permit other people to live in their home, meaning their country, for hundreds of years without declaring allegiance to their house. We have nearly always invited our future conquerors to dinner. This misplaced humanity and hospitality to strangers is at once the strongest and the weakest aspect of an African way of life. It is the strongest because it is the basis of African humanity; it is the weakest because all too many strangers have come into Africa and taken advantage of the African's generosity. People who think they can trust every stranger who enters their home are politically naive. This is an aspect of the African world situation which we have not studied or fully acknowledged as a problem, and it will remain as long as we ignore its ancient roots. When what we call Black Studies matures, we will take a global view of African people and understand how they relate to other peoples. This will be the culmination of a long intellectual struggle that started in the first half of the century.

Early in the twentieth century there emerged Black scholars who began to analyze and interpret the history and struggles of African people from an international point of view. They saw how African history related to world history, and they, more than their predecessors, were successful in locating their people on the map of human geography. A new African awareness developed with the concept of Pan-Africanism.

This atmosphere nurtured new men and movements, who gave Black scholarship the real text of its existence: DuBois' book of essays, *The Souls of Black Folks*, published in 1903. This was a different kind of scholarship, more explanatory than argumentative. In 1905, DuBois helped to bring the Niagara Movement into being. In 1909, the idea of this movement helped to create the National Association for the Advancement of Colored People (NAACP).

The need to analyze and interpret the place of African people in world history grew more critical during the first two decades of this century. In his own way, Carter G. Woodson answered that need. After serving many years as a teacher in public schools, Woodson became convinced that the role played by his people in American history and in the history of other cultures was being either ignored or misrepresented. In 1915 he founded the Association for the Study of Negro Life and History to conduct research into "the history of the Negroes all over the world." The next year he began publication of the *Journal of Negro History*, which has never missed an issue.

A chronicle of Woodson's far-reaching activities must include: the organization in 1921 of the Associated Publisher, Inc. to "make possible the publication and circulation of valuable books on the Negro not acceptable to most publishers"; the establishment of Negro History Week in 1926; the initial subsidizing of research in Black history; and the writing of many articles and books on Afro-American and American life and history.[8]

Woodson believed that there was no such thing as "Negro history," insisting that what was called Negro history was only a missing segment of world history. He devoted the greater portion of his life to restoring this segment. He also realized that once this segment was integrated into school textbooks and taught with respect and understanding, there would no longer be a need for a Negro History Week.

Woodson also argued that history cannot be restricted by the limits of race, nation, or people. Roman history is Greek as well as Roman; both the Greek and Roman are Egyptian because the entire Mediterranean was civilized from Egypt; and Egypt in turn borrowed from other parts of Africa, especially Ethiopia, and from the Orient. Africa came into the Mediterranean world mainly through Greece, which had been under African influence; and then Africa was cut off from the melting pot by the turmoil among the Europeans and the religious conquest incidental to the rise of Islam. Prior to these events, Africa had developed an indigenous history and civilization. It reentered the general picture of history through the penetration of North Africa, West Africa, and the Sudan by the Arabs, but subsequently was subjected to the ravages of the European and American slave traders. The imperialist colonizers and missionaries finally entered the scene and prevailed until the recent reemergence of independent African nations.

In sum, we can say that scholars such as DuBois and Woodson created the theoretical basis for the "Black Power" and "Black Studies" explosion, and for a reconsideration of the concept of Pan-Africanism.[9]

Up to the end of the nineteenth century, with a few exceptions, American literature was still an imitation of European literature. American literature, coming from white writers in the genuine American way, is principally a literature of the twentieth century. Before this time there was very little that was imaginative in American literature except the slave narrative and the slave autobiography, which was an improvement on the slave narrative.

During the same decades that DuBois and Woodson were laying the foundations of the future Black Studies Movement, education was a recurring theme in Black writing. In most cases the educated Black man was the pillar of the Black community. A generation later, some Black writers would see, in retrospect, how miseducated a large number of Blacks were, for they had been trained to fit into a society that had rejected them. This, in part, was the basis of the fight between Booker T. Washington and W.E.B. DuBois. A few Black scholars believed that the Afro-Americans had no African heritage to reclaim. W.E.B. DuBois and his followers opposed this view. At the start of the twentieth century, then, Afro-Americans found that two schools of thought competed for their attention in their search for new directions: the school of Booker T. Washington and the school of W.E.B. DuBois.[10]

Black Americans had entered the twentieth century searching for new directions politically, culturally and institutionally. The Black woman was very much a part of this search. Booker T. Washington's Atlanta Cotton Exposition address (1895) had set in motion a great debate among Black people about their direction and their place in the developing American social order. As new men and movements were emerging, some men, principally Bishop Henry McNeal Turner, questioned whether Black people had any future in America. The Black woman answered this question in the affirmative by pouring massive energy into building new institutions, primarily schools.

This nineteenth- and early twentieth-century reaction to oppression by the Black American community was part of the search for direction, definition, and status in the world community. At the center of this search stood W.E.B. DuBois.[11]

After being introduced to the international significance of Africa at the First Pan-African Congress in London in 1900, DuBois remained committed to the unification of Africa for the rest of his life. At the Second Pan-African Congress in Paris in 1919 (sometimes referred to as the First Congress), DuBois emerged as the movement's world leader, the capacity in which he appealed to the League of Nations and other international organizations on behalf of African people.

In his essay "My Mission," published in *Crisis Magazine* in April 1919, DuBois said: "I went to Paris during the time of the Peace Conference because the destinies of mankind for a hundred years to come were being settled by the big four, because they had the power through their armed forces, capital and propaganda machines to do so." He went on to say that thirty-two nations, people, and races had permanent headquarters in Paris. He felt it imperative for African people to make their presence known in Paris at this time.

The Second Pan-African Congress adopted eleven resolutions and submitted them to the Peace Conference then meeting at Versailles. The first two resolutions applied only to Africans, calling for a Code of Laws for the international protection of Africans and for the establishment of a permanent bureau to oversee the application of that code to their political, social, and economic welfare. The remaining resolutions applied to Africans and people of African descent living in countries outside the African continent. The question of the slave trade had been raised by the British at the Congress of Vienna and the specific question of the Belgian Congo had been raised on the international level, but the Second Congress marked the first time that the Blacks themselves had raised the international issue of the Black condition.

Referring to this congress, DuBois has said:

"I went (to Paris) with the idea of calling a 'Pan-African Congress' and trying to impress upon the members of the Peace Congress meeting at Versailles the importance of Africa to the future world. I was without credentials, but the idea took on. I tried to get a conference with President Wilson, but only got as far as Colonel House, who was sympathetic but non-commital."

The Pan-African Congress of 1921 made resolutions similar to those of the 1919 congress, but was more specific in the proposals that it presented to the new League of Nations. It called for the study of African problems and asked that an international section to project African labor be set up under jurisdiction of the Labor Bureau of the League.

After the Pan-African Congress of 1921, DuBois went to Geneva where he met with the head of the Mandates Commission and talked with Albert Thomas, head of the International Labor Organization. Through the Haitian representative to the League, the Pan-African Congress submitted a petition that asked that a "man of African descent" be appointed to the Mandates Commission as soon as a vacancy occurred. The petition also asked for the League to devote some of its attention to the plight of the millions of Black people living in countries outside of Africa who were being discriminated against. An interesting landmark in the development of Black political thought, this petition has far-reaching implications for international politics both because it asserts that the race problem is international and because it maintains that an international organization has a responsibility to concern itself with that problem within particular nations. The petition also asserts the ultimate aim of self-government for all people.

The petition thus illustrates my point that W.E.B. DuBois was never a narrow partisan. For most of his pubic life, extending over two generations, he had an international view of the problems of his people. He was a nationalist, a Pan-Africanist, and a socialist, and he saw no contradiction between these three positions; his love of his own people gave him an appreciation of all people. He was one of the pioneers in calling for a reinterpretation of the history of Africa and of African people throughout the world. A generation before the proliferation of Black Studies Programs in the United States, he said:

> Afro-American history cannot be honestly taught without some reference to its African background and the Black American's search for the meaning of that background and its relationship to their present day lives. The Africans who came to the United States as slaves started their attempts to reclaim their lost African heritage soon after they arrived in this country. They were searching for the lost identity that the slave system had developed. Concurrent with the Black man's search for an identity in America has been his search for an identity in the world, which means, in essence, his identity as a human being with a history, before and after slavery, that can command respect.

The elder statesman among Afro-Americans, DuBois addressed himself to the broader aspects of this situation on the celebration of the Second Anniversary of the Asian-African (Bandung) Conference and the rebirth of Ghana of April 30, 1957, when he said:

> From the fifteenth through the seventeenth centuries, the Africans imported to America regarded themselves as temporary settlers destined to return eventually to Africa. Their increasing revolts against the slave system, which culminated in the eighteenth century, showed a feeling of close kinship to the motherland and even well into the nineteenth century they called their organizations "African," as witness the "African Unions" of New York and Newport, and the African churches of Philadelphia and New York. In the West Indies and South America there was even closer indication of feelings of kinship with Africa and the East.

DuBois affirmed this statement in practice during the last years of his life. In the fall of 1961, he and his wife, Shirley Graham DuBois, took up residence in Ghana at the invitation of the late Kwame Nkrumah, then president of Ghana. He had gone to Ghana mainly to work on the *Encyclopedia of Africana*, a massive project that he had conceived as early as 1909. Soon after arriving in Ghana, he and his wife became Ghanaian citizens, a choice consistent with their Pan-Africanist commitment. He had helped to organize and participated in all of the Pan-African Congresses that occurred in his lifetime.

DuBois died in Accra, Ghana, on 27 August, 1963 at the age of ninety-five, on the eve of the historic March on Washington. On 9 September, the Board of Directors of the NAACP passed a resolution mourning his death and calling him "a pioneer in the struggle for human rights." The members of the Board noted that DuBois was:

> The prime inspirer, philosopher and father of the Negro Protest Movement, a founder of the NAACP, an impassioned and eloquent spokesman for equal rights, a fierce and uncompromising foe of colonialism and promoter of the Pan-African Congress, and the most eminent scholar and historian of the Black race in America and Africa… .His literary, historical and sociological contributions were so vast and all-inclusive that no serious research in the American field can be done without reference to the work of Dr. W.E.B. DuBois.

All the events that I have reviewed constitute a long preface to the change, challenge, and conflict in Africana Studies over the last decade. Beyond the search for definition and direction is the search for an ideology. Africana Studies without an ideology is a recitation of days, places personalities, and events. A people search for their past in order to understand the present and reshape the future. The search referred to here is a recurring theme in the history of African people; in particular, and of all people in general. Because our memories are short and we have not creatively converted history into an instrument of our liberation, most of us do not know that there was no ideology in our world until we created one. Therefore, our search for an ideology is a search for our lost values. We are trying to restore what the slave trade and colonialism took away. Ours is a search for a positive ideology, and ideology of liberation – an ideology that asks and answers the question: How will our people stay on this earth?

Yet at this critical moment in our history, Black intellectuals, young and old, are engaged in an ideological battle that is a sad waste of time. They are trying to resolve the proposition, "to be or not to be a socialist," despite the fact that everyone who has done any serious thinking lately realizes that some form of socialism is our only viable political alternative. Men and women of vision and intelligence with a knowledge of history, no longer debate this point. My argument is with the new motley crew calling themselves "socialists," which they are not. In most cases they are political copouts, looking for another white slave-master; failing that, they will accept a yellow master from China or a mulatto master from Cuba. They will do anything except be their own masters.

These self-proclaimed "theoreticians" act as though Black people have no ideological contributions to make to their own salvation, yet, had they done their homework they would know that the concept of socialism was old among African people before Karl Marx and even Europe was born. If the matter were left to them, they would lead us – like whores and hungry dogs – in search of the political ideological leavings of a dying people. For our salvation we should draw on the intellectual heritage of the whole world – beginning with our own intellectual heritage. If our people are cold, we should invade hell and borrow fire from the devil, but we should not become the devil's disciple. We should properly read the signs of history and remember: What we do for ourselves depends on what we know of ourselves and what we accept about ourselves.[12]

This is what the struggle in Africana Studies over the last decade has been about. This is what our revolt against white scholars in Montreal, Canada, in 1969 was about. All too many of us who were at Montreal, and who were also founding members of the African Heritage Studies Association (AHSA), seem to have forgotten the challenge we flung before white scholarship at Montreal, a challenge that we also agreed to accept for ourselves. We dreamed some big dreams that day and we promised to make them into realities. Just for the record, let's hear some of them again, taken from the "Aims and Objectives of AHSA":

Introduction

The Africa Heritage Studies Association (AHSA) is an association of scholars of African descent, dedicated to the preservation, interpretation and academic presentation of the historical and cultural heritage of African peoples both on the ancestral soil of Africa and in the diaspora in the Americas and throughout the world.

Aims and Objectives

Education

a. Reconstruction of African history and cultural studies along Afrocentric lines while effecting an intellectual union among Black scholars all over the world.
b. Acting as a clearing house of information in the establishment and evaluation of a more realistic African Program.
c. Presenting papers at seminars and symposia where any aspect of the life and culture of the African peoples are discussed.
d. Relating, interpreting and disseminating African materials for Black education at all levels and in the community at large.

International

a. To reach African countries in order to facilitate greater communication and interaction between Africans and Africans in the Americas.
b. To assume leadership in the orientation of African students in the US and orientation of Afro-Americans in Africa (establish contacts).
c. To establish an Information Committee on African and American relations whose function it will be to research and disseminate to the membership information on all aspects of American relations with respect to African peoples.

Domestic

a. To relate to those organizations that are predominantly involved in and influence the education of Black people.
b. To solicit their influence and affluence in the promotion of Black Studies and in the execution of AHSA programs and projects.
c. To arouse social consciousness and awareness of these groups.
d. To encourage their financial contribution to Black schools with programs involving the study of African peoples.

Black Students and Scholars

a. To encourage and support students who wish to major in the Study of African peoples.
b. To encourage Black students to relate to the study of the heritage of African people, and to acquire the ranges of skills for the production and development of African peoples.
c. To encourage attendance and participation including the reading of papers at meetings dealing with the study of African life and history so that the American perspective is represented.
d. To ask all Black students and scholars to rally around AHSA to build it up as a sturdy organization for the reconstruction of our history and culture.

Black Communities

a. To seek to aid Black scholars who need financial support for their community projects or academic research.
b. To edit a newsletter or journal through which AHSA activities will be known.

In Montreal we called for an Afrocentric approach to the history of African people. In the last decade most of the books written from an Afrocentric point of view have been written by African and Afro-American writers who did not belong to our group. In closing I would like to call attention to the importance of this approach to our history.

End Notes

1. Saunders Redding, "The Negro Writer and His Relationship to His Roots," in *The American Negro Writer and His Roots: Selected Papers from The First Conference of Negro Writers, March 1959*, (New York, 1960), The American Society of African Culture, pp. 1–8.
2. Richard B. Moore, "The Name 'Negro': Its Origin and Evil Use," (New York, 1960), Afroamerican Publishers, Inc. Also Raphael p. Powell, "Human Side of a People and the Right Name," (New York, 1927), The Philemon Co. Reprinted by the University Microfilms, Ann Arbor, Michigan, 1969.
3. "Black Studies, A Dilemma at the Crossroads," by John H. Clarke, Lecture prepared for the Afro-American Studies Program, Simmons College, Boston, MA, 5 April 1978.
4. "Black History and the Future," lecture by John H. Clarke, prepared for Department of Afro-American Studies, Howard University, Washington, DC, 18 February 1976.
5. "The Black American Writer in Crisis," by John H. Clarke. Lecture prepared for The National Conference of Afro-American Writers, Howard University, Washington, DC, 8–10 November 1974.
6. "Black-White Alliances: A Historical Perspective," by John H. Clarke. Institute for Positive Education, Chicago, IL, 1972.
7. A Adu Boahen, in The Horizon History of Africans of Africa (New York: 1971), p. 304–351. American Heritage Publishing Co. In the same book see also, John H. Clarke, "Africa: Time of Trouble," pp. 352–399.
8. W.E.B. DuBois, *The Souls of Black Folk*, (Greenwich, CT, 1961) Crest Books, Fawcett Publications, pp. 42–53.
9. John H. Clarke, "The Black Woman in Education: A Figure in World History," *Black Collegian Magazine*, Vol. 5, No. 2 (1974); p. 40. Also see, Dorothy Porter, "Early Negro Writers 1760–1837," (Boston, 1937), Beacon Press, p. 3.
10. John H. Clarke, "Education in the Making of the Black Urban Ghetto," in *Black Manifesto for Education*, James Haskins (New York: William Morrow and Co. Inc., 1973), pp. 16–40.
11. Sadie Iola Daniel, "Women Builders" (Washington, DC, 1969), Associated Publishers, pp. 79–167.
12. "Pan-Africanism and the Liberation of Southern Africa: A Tribute to W.E.B. DuBois," edited by John H. Clarke, for the United Nations Centre Against Apartheid, published by the African Heritage Studies Association, New York, 1978. See Introduction.

13. "The Black American's Search for and Ideology," by John H. Clarke. Lecture prepared for the Eighth Conference of the Center for African and African-American Studies, Atlanta, GA, 4–6 December 1975.

Africa: New Approaches to an Old Continent

John Henrik Clarke

Reprinted from *Freedomways*, Vol. 11, No. 3, 1971, pp. 298–306

The continent of Africa and its people are the most written about and the least understood of all places and people. This condition has prevailed for nearly five hundred years. During the rise of Europe and the expansion of the slave trade in the fifteenth and sixteenth centuries, the attitude of Europeans toward Africa changed radically. The Europeans now had to justify the slave trade and the colonial system that was to follow it. These circumstances made it necessary, from a European point of view, to read the Africans out of the respectful commentary of human history, and out of consideration as a part of humanity. This explains, at least in part, why we are now in the midst of a "black studies revolution." Black people are trying to restore some of the things that the slave trade and the colonial system took away, mainly the knowledge that African people have a history and a culture that predates the very existence of Europe. The Africans are older than their oppressors. There are a number of unusual recent books attesting to this fact. The situation is encouraging enough for it to be said, with some degree of certainty, that a renaissance of African history is now emerging. A number of very able new African and Afro-American historians are leading this renaissance.

In the book, *Introduction to African Civilization,* (1970) by John G. Jackson the old picture of Africans as a people without a history is reversed.

Mr. Jackson has not written this book on African history to tell benevolent stories about so-called savages and how the Europeans came to civilize them. Quite the contrary, in many ways he has reversed the picture and proven his point. Civilization did not start in European countries and the rest of the world did not wait in darkness for the Europeans to bring the light. In order to understand how this attitude came about, one needs to look at the sad state of what is called "World History." There is not a single book in existence with the title "World History" on it that is an honest commentary on the history of the world and its people. Most of the history books in the last five hundred years have been written to glorify Europeans at the expense of other peoples. The history of Asia has been as shamefully distorted as the history of Africa.

Most Western historians have not been willing to admit that there is an African history to be written about, and that this history pre-dates the emergence of Europe by thousands of years. It is not possible for the world to have waited in darkness for the Europeans to bring the light, because for most of the early history of man, the Europeans themselves were in darkness. When the light of culture came for the first time to the people who would later call themselves Europeans, it came from Africa and Middle Eastern Asia. Most history books tend to deny or ignore this fact. John G. Jackson has examined this fact and its dimensions with scholarly honesty. He has also examined the origins of racism and their effects on the writing of history. It is too often forgotten that when the Europeans emerged and began to extend themselves into the broader world of Africa and Asia during the fifteenth and sixteenth centuries, they went on to colonize most of mankind. Later, they would colonize world scholarship, mainly the writing of history. History was then written or rewritten to show or imply that Europeans were the only creators of what could be called a civilization. In order to accomplish this, the Europeans had to forget, or pretend to forget, all they previously knew about Africa.

In the years when the slave trade was getting effectively underway, some Europeans were claiming parts of Africa, especially Egypt as an extension of their "continent" and their "culture." These writers wrote as if the African was an interloper in his own land.

In John G. Jackson's chapter on "Ethiopia and the Origin of Civilization," the reader is literally challenged to reconsider the prevailing definition of civilization and the story of its origin. In the book *Progress and Evolution of Man in Africa*, Dr. L.S.B. Leakey states that: "In every country that one visits and where one is drawn into a conversation about Africa, the question is regularly asked by people who should know better 'But what has Africa contributed to world progress?' The critics of Africa forget that men of science today are, with few exceptions, satisfied that Africa was the birthplace of man himself, and that for many hundreds of centuries thereafter, Africa was in the forefront at all world progress."

In his book, *Egypt*, Sir E.A. Wallis Budge says: "The prehistoric nature of Egypt, both in the old and in the new Stone Ages, was African and there is every reason for saying that the earliest settlers came from the South."

He further states that: "There are many things in the manners and customs and religions of the historic Egyptians that suggest that the original home of their prehistoric ancestors was in a country in the neighborhood of Uganda and Punt." (Some historians believe that the Biblical land of Punt was in the area known on modern maps as Somalia.)

The period covered by the chapter "The Golden Age of West Africa" has a special significance for the whole world. Europe was languishing in her dark ages at a time when Western Africa was enjoying a Golden Age. In the non-European world beyond Africa, Asians built and enjoyed an age of advancement in technology before a period of internal withdrawal and isolation permitted the Europeans to move ahead of them.

It should be realized that during the Middle Ages, Oriental technology was far more advanced than European technology, and that until the thirteenth century Europe, technologically, was but a mere appendix of Asia. While the Greeks and Romans were weaving subtle philosophies, the Chinese were busy inventing gunpowder, paper, alchemy, vaccinations, plastic surgery, paint, and even the pocket handkerchief, which was unknown to the fastidious Greeks.

For more than a thousand years the Africans had been bringing into being empire after empire until the second rise of Europe, internal strife, and the slave trade turned what was an "Age of Grandeur" to the Africans into an age of tragedy and decline. Certain events in Europe and in Africa set this period of history in motion. In this respect no year was more important than 1492.

In the chapter on "The Destruction of African Culture," Mr. Jackson has dealt with some of the main reasons that African History is so misunderstood and why so many students of the subject get confused while trying to make an assessment of the available information. There has been a deliberate destruction of African culture and the records relating to that culture. This destruction started with the first invaders of Africa. It continued through the period of slavery and the colonial system. It continues today on a much higher and more dangerous level. There are now attempts on the highest academic levels to divide African history and culture within Africa in such a manner that the best of it can be claimed for the Europeans, or at the very least, Asians. That is the main purpose of the Hamitic and Semitic hypothesis in relationship to African history. It is also one of the main reasons so much attention is being paid to the Berbers and the Arabs in Africa. There is a school of thought supporting the thesis that, if the main body of African history, culture and achievement has not European origin, it must, at least, have an Asian origin.

Mr. Jackson debunks most of the standard approaches and concepts of African history in a way that will make many academic feathers fly. This is one of the best books on African history that ha appeared in recent years.

The Africans in the Greco-Roman Experience

In the book, *Blacks in Antiquity*, by Dr. Frank M. Snowden, Chairman of the Classics Department, Howard University, a little known, though very important aspect of African history is brought to light. Both the Greeks and Romans knew the Africans and knew them very well, and respectfully. The Africans who came to ancient Greece and Italy participated in an important chapter in classical history, and not as slaves. Though the Africans come from many geographical locations in Africa, the Greeks and the Romans referred to them, collectively, as Ethiopians. For his book, Dr. Snowden spent more than thirty years doing his home work and his findings are worth waiting for. Dr. Snowden examines a broad span of Greco-Roman experience – from the Homeric era to the age of Justinian. He has drawn directly upon the widely scattered literary evidence of classical and early Christian writers. There are more than 140 illustrations that show the Africans in a number of occupations, such as servant, diplomat, warrior, athlete, and performer. In the text and in the illustrations ancient Africans are seen meeting and developing relationships with two young Mediterranean nations, Greece and Rome. Another important thing about this book is that is shows how people of the ancient world, who belonged to different ethnic groups, behaved one to the other before the introduction of racism.

The anthology, *Africa in Classical Antiquity*, (1969) edited by L.A. Thompson and J. Ferguson shows how Africans related to the people of the Middle East and other Mediterranean nations during this period. Most important, it shows how Africans related to the different nations within Africa. This book seems to have been prepared for classroom use. If this is so, the book was well prepared. It includes articles by a number of African and European scholars, who write exceptionally well. These scholars extend the information beyond the period covered by Dr. Snowden's book. They write about the time when relationships between the Africans and the Romans had deteriorated and the Romans had established themselves as a North African power.

New Tools for the Teachers

Basil Davidson is one of the best-known writers in the field of African history. His books are good basic texts for the teachers of African history who wish to discard the old myths and deal with the new facts. In two recent books, *The African Genius* (1969) and *Discovering Our African Heritage* (1971), he opens up new areas of interest in African history and puts some of the old information in a more readable context. *The African Genius* is an introduction to the social and cultural history of Africa, in which he examines African cultures and how they developed. Consideration is given as to what the Africans had to endure while building these early societies, without any precedents or prior models to guide them. The basic framework of this new inquiry evolves around a set of questions that this book answers. The questions are: What did the slaves bring with them from Africa? What are the foundations for modern Africa civilizations? What can black Americans take and use from the African experience? In the answers to these questions the author shows how history, all history, relates to the hereness and nowness of our lives. In looking at African history and culture in this way, it can be seen as a current event – an instrument of people's liberation.

Discovering Our African Heritage is a good introduction to African history and it is the kind of book that can be understood by people with no prior knowledge of the subject. It is well illustrated. The suggested reading list placed after all of the major sections of the book makes it very useful for both teacher and student.

Mary Penick Motley's book *Africa, Its Empires, Nations and People* (1969) is one of the growing list of basic books on African history by Afro-American scholars and teachers. This was written in response to her students' demands for an introductory book of this kind. In answering this need Mrs. Motley has expanded the visions of Africa and made it possible for students to study this continent and its people with new insight.

Among the young African historians whose work is beginning to receive national and international attention, Professor Adu Boahen, of Ghana, is one of the best examples of the new and creative scholar. His book, *Topics in West African History* (1966, reprinted 1969), is the most useful basic text that has so far been written on this part of Africa. The book was developed from a series of lectures that were originally prepared for the Ghana Broadcasting Corporation.

In 1915, Dr. W.E.B. DuBois, the dean of Afro-American scholars, published his first book on Africa. The simple title of the book was *The Negro*. This book has been reprinted without any changes in the content. In spite of the more than fifty years that have passed since the book was first published, neither the information nor the interpretation is dated. In those early years when Dr. DuBois was discovering the significance of Africa and its relationship to world history, he had more insight into the subject than most of the present-day scholars. In his preface to the book he seemed to have anticipated the trouble that lay ahead for the scholars who wanted to bring some honest light to this much distorted subject, when he said:

> The time has not yet come for a complete history of the Negro peoples. Archeological research in Africa has just begun, and many sources of information in Arabian, Portuguese, and other tongues are not fully at our command; and, too, it must frankly be confessed, racial prejudice against darker peoples is still too strong in so-called civilized centers for judicial appraisement of the peoples of Africa. Much intensive monographic work in history and science is needed to clear mooted points and quiet the controversialist who mistakes present personal desire for scientific proof.

The advent of the Black Studies Revolution and the need for new and uncomplicated materials for the classroom teacher have generated a new interest in African people the world over. A large number of unprepared people have rushed into this field and hurriedly produced books that are a disservice to the subject. There are a number of exceptions and these exceptions should be noted. In the book, *Great Civilizations of Ancient Africa* (1971), by Lester Brooks, we have an honest layman's view of African history that is not complicated by unsupportable theses that demean the subject. Mr. Brooks is a general writer who, like most of the new people in the field, came late to African history. He has been associated with the National Urban League since 1950, as assistant public relations director, and member of the public relations committee. In writing his book Mr. Brooks made use of some of the neglected documents on African history, including the papers of the late Dr. William Leo Hansberry.

Old Africans in a New Land

Early in this century Afro-American historians, who are still generally ignored by white historians, began to speculate one the possibility that African settlements existed in what was later called the New World, long before the year 1492. This speculation led to some sound research. A recent book, *The Art of Terracotta Pottery in Pre-Columbian Central and South America* (1959), by Alexander Von Wuthenau, makes use of the best of this research and supports most of the precious assumptions about this subject.

The pre-Columbian presence of the Africans in what is called the New World has long been a subject for speculation. Any honest examination of the old and the new evidence relating to this subject will put all speculations to rest. While this paper deals mainly with the second impact of Africans on the Western hemisphere, it is important that we look, at least briefly, at this first impact in the light of the old and the new evidence.

The formal investigation into this subject was started in 1920 with the publication of Professor Leo Wiener's massive three-volume work, *Africa and the Discovery of America*. In the first volume of this work, Professor Wiener shows that American archaeology on both the Africans and the Indians is built on sand and suppositions and that the chronology of culture development for both of these peoples is totally out of order. He also shows that the Africans have had a far greater influence on American civilization than has heretofore been suspected.

The second volume of this work is a study of African religions and their influence on the culture of this hemisphere. His documents tend to prove, to an extraordinary extent, that the Indian medicine-man owes his evolution the African medicine-man.

In explaining the diaries of Christopher Columbus, Professor Wiener calls attention to the fact that this European explorer admits that he found a dark-skinned people in the Caribbean Islands trading with the Indians.

Some of the best work in this field has been done by Afro-American historians and researchers. This work can be found in the following books and articles: *The African Background Outline* (1936), by Carter G. Woodson, *Africa's Gift to America* (1959), by J.A. Rogers, "African Explorers of the New World" (1962), by Harold G. Lawrence, and "Black Men in Ancient and Medieval America" (1969) parts one and two, by Legrand H. Clegg II.

The Makers of Modertn Africa – The Movers and the Shakers

The late J.A. Rogers devoted the greater part of his life to research relating to the impact of the African personality on world history. This is another body of work by a Black historian that most of the white historians have chosen to ignore. In the last few years a number of white historians have ventured into the field, still without acknowledging that J.A. Rogers ever existed. Their interest is reflected in the following books: *The Zulu Aftermath* (1966), by J.D. Omer-Cooper, *Lords of the Atlas* (1966), by Gavin Maxwell, *Leadership in Eastern Africa*

(1968), edited by Norman R. Bennett, and *Africa South of the Sahara* (1970), by Philip D. Curtin.

One Nigerian writer and two Afro-American writers have written biographies of the African personalities in the resistance and independence movements in the following books: *Africa and Unity: The Evolution of Pan-Africanism* (1969), by Vincent Bakpetu Thompson, and *The African Reader*, books one and two (1970), by Wilfred Cartey and Martin Kilson.

BIBLIOGRAPHY

Introduction to African Civilizations. By John G. Jackson. University Books, New York. 384 pages.

Blacks in Antiquity. By Frank M. Snowden, Jr. The Belknap Press of Harvard University Press, Cambridge, Massachusetts. 364 pages.

Discovering Our African Heritage. By Basil Davidson. Ginn and Company, Boston, Massachusetts. 279 pages.

Africa, its Empires Nations and People. By Mary Penick Motley. Wayne State University Press, Detroit, Michigan. 164 pages.

The Negro We. Burghardt DuBois. Oxford University Press, London, Oxford, New York. 157 pages.

Topics in West African History. By A. Adu Boahen. Longmans, Green and Co. Ltd., London. 172 pages.

Great Civilizations of Ancient Africa. By Lester Brooks. Four Winds Press, New York. 340 pages.

The Art of Terracotta Pottery in Pre-Columbian Central and South America. By Alexander Von Wuthenau. Crown Publishers, Inc., New York. 203 pages.

Africa's Gift to America. By J.A. Rogers. Futuro Press Inc., New York. 254 pages.

The African Genius. By Basil Davidson. Atlantic Monthly Press Book, Boston, Toronto. 367 pages.

Africa in Classical Antiquity. Edited by I.A. Thompson and J. Ferguson. Ibadan University Press, Nigeria. 221 pages.

The Zulu Aftermath. By J.D. Omer-Cooper. Longmans, Green and Co., Ltd., London. 208 pages.

Lords of the Atlas. By Gavin Maxwell. E.P. Dutton & Co., Inc., New York. 318 pages.

Leadership in Eastern Africa. By Norman R. Bennett. Massachusetts University Press, Boston. 260 pages.

Africa South of the Sahara. By Philip D. Curtin. Silver Burdett Company. 112 pages.

Africa and Unity: The Evolution of Pan-Africanism. By Vincent Bakpetu Thompson. Longmans, London. 412 pages.

The Africa Reader: Colonial Africa. By Wilfred Cartey and Martin Kilson. Vintage Books, New York. 264 pages.

The Africa Reader: Independent Africa. By Wilfred Cartey and Martin Kilson. Vintage Books, New York. 428 pages.

Revolt of the Angels

John Henrik Clarke

Reprinted from *Freedomways*, Vol. 3, Summer 1963, pp. 355–60

The two Harlem piano movers who had taken the negative side of the argument were quiet now, waiting for the defender of the affirmative to gather his thoughts. He was a big man; seemingly bigger than his two friendly opponents put together. Because of this, it did not seem unfair that he had no one to assist him in imparting his point of view.

For more than an hour the three men had been standing by their large red truck, waiting between assignments. It was their custom on these occasions to test each other's knowledge of the great subjects and issues that influence the destiny of mankind. The fact that their formal knowledge of these subjects was extremely limited did not deter their discussion in the slightest.

The two small men waited and stole quick glances at their large companion. Their faces were aglow with the signs of assured victory. Finally one turned to the other and said: "We've got 'im at las', Leroy. We've taken King Solomon off of his throne. We've made another wise man bit th' dust."

The speaker's dark face looked as if age had been baked into it. He kept watching the large man who was collecting his thoughts in preparation for stating his side of the argument.

"I knew we'd tame this wise man some day," the other small man said. The note of triumph and mock haughtiness in his voice gave it a distinct play acting tone. "We've got 'im up a creek without a paddle," he went on, laughing a little. "Now, Hawkshaw, lemme see you talk your way out of this trap."

"Don't count your eggs before you buy your chickens," the big man said, straightening up as his loosely hanging stomach spilled over the rim of his belt.

"Th' thing to be resolved is whether a man who has been a drunkard most of his life can straighten himself out and become a pillar of respectability an' a credit to his community. You fellas have said this can not be done an' I disagree... I know just th' case to prove my point." He exhaled audibly with some of the pompousness of a political orator preparing for a long discourse. Then he spoke again, slowly, measuring his words very carefully at first.

"During th' last part of th' depression years there was fella here in Harlem named Luther Jackson who had been drunk so long nobody could remember how he looked when he was sober. Luther wasn't a violent man; he didn't bother nobody unless he wanted some likker and they wouldn't give it to him.

"One day when Luther was near th' end of a three week stupor, he wandered into one of Father Divine's restaurants and sat down at th' bes' table. He thought th' restaurant was a bar and the bes' table in the house meant nothing to him. Now, fellas, when I say this was th' bes' table in th' house, I mean it was th' bes' table you'd see anywhere. In those days most of Father Divine's restaurants set up a special table for Father just in case he came in an' wanted to dine in style. This special table had snow white linen, th' bes' of silverware, crystal glasses, th' kind you only see in the homes of millionaires, and a fresh bowl of flowers. A picture of Father Divine was in front of th' flowers with a message under it sayin', 'Thank you Father.' It was some kind of deadly sin for anybody but Father Divine and his invited guests to set at this table.

"A big fat angel saw Luther at th' table an' strutted out of th' kitchen blowin' like a mad bull.

"'Peace, brother,' she said real loud, 'This is Father Divine's table, get up an' get out of here.'

"'I want some likker,' Luther says, 'an' I want some more t' wash it down.'

"'Peace, brother,' the angel says, puffin' an' trying to keep her temper from exploding. 'This is Father Divine's table, get up an' get out of here.'

"'I won't go till you give me some likker,' Luther says, 'an' I don't care whose table this is.'

"Th' angel threw her hands in th' air and looked at th' ceilin' like she expected something over her head to come down an' help her. 'Peace, Father,' she says, 'Remove this evil man from your premises.'

"'I want some likker!' Luther shouted at her an' slammed his hand on th' table, knocking down some of the fine silverware. 'A drinkin' man is in th' house. Go away old woman an' send me a bartender.'

"This made th' angel madder than ever. She went back to th' kitchen holdin' her head like she was scared it was goin' t' fly off.

"'Where's th' bartender in this place?' Luther asked an' stood up lookin' 'round like he was just fixin' to mop up th' place with his madness.

"Th' big angel was standing in th' kitchen door, shoutin', 'Father Divine don't allow no alcohol drinkers in here. No obscenities! No adulteries!'

"Luther slammed his hand on th' table again an' knocked down some more of th' fine silverware. This made th' angel so angry she couldn't speak. She just stood in th' door of th' kitchen swellin' up like a big toad frog.

"'Gimme some likker and let me get gutta here,' Luther says.

"Then th' angel hollered out all of a sudden and frightened Luther so much he almost jumped over the table.

"'Peace Father!' th' angel was sayin'. 'Give me console, Father, you are wonderful.'

"Father or someone else must have given her console an' some new strength to go with it, because she threw a pot at Luther's head like he was a long lost husband who deserted her with a house full of hungry young 'uns.

"The pot bounced off of Luther's head an' he hollered like a wild bull. 'What's goin' on in this place?' Luther was sayin'. 'Where's th' bartender?'

"'Father Divine don't 'low no alcohol drinkers in here,' th' angel was sayin' again, 'No obscenities! No adulteries!' Before she finished sayin' this she threw another pot at Luther's head.

"Luther ducked and stood up in a chair as a skillet missed his head by an inch. Then he stepped into the middle of th' table. He had knocked down th' flowers and some of th' fine silverware. Now th' angel was hollerin' like judgement day was at hand. You see, fellas, Luther was standin' on Father Divine's picture. She ran out of pots an' began t' throw big spoons and ladles.

"'Peace Father, give me strength,' she hollered, 'give me th' strength to move this Satan from your premises.'

"Then she jumped toward Luther like a tiger an' knocked 'im off th' table with a rollin' pin. As Luther fell, he turned th' table over. All of the snow white table linen was on th' floor. Th' silverware was scattered around th' table and some of it was in Luther's pockets. Most of th' millionaire crystal glasses were broken.

"The fat angel kept screamin', 'Peace! Peace! Peace!' until some more angels joined up with her. They came at Luther with fire in their eyes. They beat him until he got up, then they beat him down again. Still more angels came and joined the war on Luther – black ones, white ones, lean ones, fat ones, an' all th' sizes in between. They kicked him, they scratched him an' they spit on him.

While all of this was happenin', an angel came up an' started whackin' at Luther with a cleaver.

"Now Luther was screamin' for his life an' tryin' to get to th' door. Th' angels knocked him down 'gain an' he crawled out of th' door hollerin' for a police to save him. He saw a red box on th' side of a building an' opened it, thinkin' it was a police telephone. He pulled down a lever an' let it stay down. Th' angels had followed him into th' streets. Soon, fire trucks started comin' from every direction – patrol wagons from th' riot squads an' th' emergency squads came. Policemen in cars an' on foot came to th' scene like they were being rained down from th' sky. Still th' angry angels kept chargin' at Luther. The commotion tied up traffic for ten blocks.

"It took more than one hundred policemen to rescue Luther from them angry angels. They had hit him every place including under his feet. The policemen had to take him to th' hospital before they could take him to jail. When he was well enough for his trial, th' judge threw th' book at him an' said he was sorry that he did not have a much bigger book. Life in jail changed Luther. He was, indeed, a new man when he came out. He was upright, law abidin' and he refused to drink anything stronger than coffee.

"So, fellas, I give you the case of Luther Jackson as my proof that a man who has been a drunkard most of his life can straighten himself out and become a pillar of respectability an' a credit to his community.

"Now Luther is a foreman of a stevedore group down on th' docks an' he's also an officer in th' union. He sent down south for his wife an' children an' he made a good home for them right here in Harlem. He is a church goin' man too an' a senior deacon. Nowhere in this land would you find a more peaceful an' law abidin' citizen than Luther Jackson. Since th' day of that fracas with those angry angels to this day, he never again touched another drop of likker."

The opposition had conceded defeat long before the fat man finished the story. A rebuttal was unnecessary.

From Prince Hall to Marcus Garvey West Indian Partisans in the Fight for Freedom

John Henrik Clarke

Negro Digest, June 1966, pp. 18–25

West Indians have been coming to the United States for over a century. The part they have played in the progress of the Afro-Americans in their long march from slavery to freedom has always been an important factor. More important is the fact that the most outstanding of these Caribbean-Americans saw their plight and the plight of Afro-Americans as being one and the same.

As early as 1827 a Jamaican, John B. Russwurm, one of the founders of Liberia, was the first colored man to be graduated from an American college and to publish a newspaper in this country; sixteen years later his fellow countryman, Peter Ogden, organized the first Odd-Fellows Lodge for Negroes. Prior to the Civil War, West Indian contribution to the progress of the Afro-American life was one of the main contributing factors in the fight for freedom and full citizenship in the northern part of the United States.

In his book, "Souls of Black Folk," Dr. W.E.B. DuBois says that the West Indians were mainly responsible for the manhood program presented by the race in the early decades of the last century. Indicative of their tendency to blaze new paths is the achievement of John W.A. Shaw of Antigua, who, in the early 90's of the last century, passed the civil service tests and became deputy commissioner of taxes for the County of Queens in New York State.

In 18th century America, two of the most outstanding fighters for liberty and justice were the West Indians – Prince Hall and John B. Russwurm. When Prince Hall came to the United States the nation was in turmoil. The colonies were ablaze with indignation. Britain, with a series of revenue acts, had stoked the fires of colonial discontent. In Virginia, Patrick Henry was speaking of liberty or death. The cry "No Taxation Without Representation" played on the nerve strings of the nation. Prince Hall, then a delicate-looking teenager, often walked through the turbulent streets of Boston, an observer unobserved.

A few months before these hectic scenes, he had arrived in the United States from his home in Barbados, where he had been born about 1748, the son of an Englishman and a free African woman. He was, in theory, a free man, but he knew that neither in Boston nor in Barbados were persons of African descent free in fact. At once, he questioned the sincerity of the vocal white patriots of Boston. It never seemed to have occurred to them that the announced principles motivating their action was stronger argument in favor of destroying the system of slavery. The colonists held in servitude more than half a million human beings, some of them white; yet they engaged in the contradiction of going to war to support the theory that all men were created equal.

When Prince Hall arrived in Boston that city was the center of the American slave trade. Most of the major leaders of the revolutionary movement, in fact, were slaveholders or investors in slave-supported businesses. Hall, like many other Americans, wondered; what did these men man by freedom?

The condition of the free black men, as Prince Hall found them, was not an enviable one. Emancipation brought neither freedom nor relief from the stigma of color. They were free in name only. They were still included with slaves, indentured servants, and Indians in the slave codes. Discriminatory laws severely circumscribed their freedom of movement.

By 1765 Prince Hall saw little change in the condition of the blacks, and though a freeman, at least in theory, he saw his people debased as though they were slaves still in bondage. These things drove him to prepare himself for leadership among his people. So through diligence and frugality he became a property owner, thus establishing himself in the eyes of white people as well as blacks.

But the ownership of property was not enough. He still had to endure sneers and insults. He decided then to prepare himself for a role of leadership among his people. To this end he went to school at night, and later became a Methodist preacher. His church became the forum for his people's grievances. Ten years after his arrival in Boston, Massachusetts, he was the accepted leader of the black community.

In 1788 Hall petitioned the Massachusetts Legislature, protesting the kidnapping of free Negroes. This was a time when American patriots were engaged in a constitutional struggle for freedom. They had proclaimed the inherent rights of all mankind to life, liberty and the pursuit of happiness. Hall dared to remind them that the black men in the United States were human beings and as such were entitled to freedom and respect for their human personality.

Prejudice made Hall the father of African secret societies in the United States. He is the father of what is now known as Negro Masonry. Hall first sought initiation into the white Masonic Lodge in Boston, but was turned down because of his color. He then applied to the Army Lodge of an Irish Regiment. His petition was favorably received. On March 6, 1775, Hall and fourteen other black Americans were initiated in Lodge Number 441. When, on March 17, the British were forced to evacuate Boston, the Army Lodge gave Prince Hall and his colleagues a license to meet and function as a Lodge. Thus, on July 3, 1776, African Lodge No. 1 came into being. This was the first Lodge in Masonry established in America for men of African descent.

The founding of the African Lodge was one of Prince Hall's greatest achievements. It afforded the Africans in the New England area of the United States a greater sense of security, and contribute to a new spirit of unity among them. Hall's interest did not end with the Lodge. He was deeply concerned with improving the lot of his people in other ways. He sought to have schools established for the children of the free Africans in Massachusetts. Of prime importance is the fact that Prince Hall worked to secure respect fort the personality of his people and also played a significant role in the downfall of the Massachusetts slave trade. He helped to prepare the groundwork for the freedom fighters of the nineteenth and twentieth centuries, whose continuing efforts have brought the black American closer to the goal of full citizenship.

In his series of articles entitled "Pioneers in Protest," Lerone Bennett, Senior Editor of EBONY Magazine , has written a capsule biography of John B. Russwurm, the distinguished West Indian who was a pioneer in Afro-American Journalism. The following information has been extracted from this article, "Founders of the Negro Press," *Ebony Magazine*, July 1964:

> "Day in and day out, the Negroes of New York City were mercilessly lampooned in the white press. In the dying days of 1826, the campaign of vilification and slander reached nauseous heights. The integrity and courage of Negro men were openly questioned. Worse, editors invaded Negro homes and impugned the chastity of Negro women... This was a time of acute crisis for all Negro Americans and the New York leaders were agonizingly conscious of the forces arrayed against them... More ominous was the creeping power of the American Colonization Society which wanted to send free Negroes "back" to Africa.

> "John B. Russwurm and Samuel E. Cornish, two of the youngest and most promising of the New York leaders, were assigned the task of inventing a journal that could speak forcibly to both the enemy and joint friend without and the 'brethren' within the veil."

Samuel E. Cornish, who is virtually unknown today, was born about 1795 in Delaware and raised in relatively free environments of Philadelphia and New York. He organized the first Negro Presbyterian Church in New York City. Russwurm, who is generally credited with being the first Negro graduate of an American college, was a Jamaican, the son of an Englishman and an African woman. His father neglected to inform his white wife of the sins of his youth; but after his death, the widow learned about his existence and financed his education at Bowdoin College where he was graduated in 1826.

Russwurm and Cornish made an excellent team, despite the difference in their backgrounds. In prospectus for the proposed paper they idealistically stated: "We shall ever regard the constitution of the United States as our polar star. Pledged to no party, we shall endeavor to urge our brethren to use their rights to the elective franchise as free citizens. It shall never be our objective to court controversy though we must at all time consider ourselves as champions in defense of oppressed humanity. Daily slandered, we think that there ought to be some channel of communication between us and the public, through which a single voice may be heard in defense of five hundred thousand free people of color..."

On Friday, March 26, 1827, the first issue of Freedom's journal, the first Negro newspaper in the Western World, appeared on the streets of New York City. In their ambitious first editorial Russwurm and Cornish struck a high note of positiveness that still has something to say to the Afro-Americans in their present plight. It read, in part: "We wish to plead our own cause. Too long have others spoke for us. Too long has the republic been deceived by misrepresentations, in things which concerned us dearly, though in the estimation of some mere trifles; for though there are many in society who exercise toward us benevolent feelings; still (with sorrow we confess it) there are others who make it their business to enlarge upon the least trifle, which tends to discredit any person of color; and pronounce anathema and denounce our whole body for the misconduct of this guilty one...Our vices and our degradation are ever arrayed against us, but our virtues are passed unnoticed...

"It is our earnest wish," the first Negro newspaper said, "to make our Journal a medium of intercourse between our brethren in different states of this great confederacy."

The timeliness of this editorial, written over a hundred years ago, and the dynamics of its intellectual content, is far ahead of most editorials that appear in present-day Afro-American newspapers.

During the later years of his life John B. Russwurm moved to a position that today would be called black nationalism. After receiving his Master's degree from Bowdoin College in 1829 Russwurm went to Liberia in West Africa, where he established another newspaper, the Liberia Herald, and served a s superintendent of schools. After further distinguishing himself as the governor of the Maryland Colony of Cape Palmas, this pioneer editor and freedom fighter died in Liberia in 1851.

The same year John B. Russwurm died, another west Indian, Edward w. Blyden, went to Africa and established himself in Liberia. He was destined to become the greatest black intellectual of the 19th century. He concerned himself with the plight of African people the world over the eventually built a bridge of understanding between the people of African origin in the West Indies, the United States and in Africa. More than anyone else in the 19th and during the early part of the 20th century, Edward W. Blyden called upon the black man to reclaim himself and his ancient Africana glory. The concept now being called Negritude started with Blyden.

Blyden was born in the then Danish West Indian island of St. Thomas in 1832, but reacted against treatment of his people in the New World by emigrating to Liberia in 1851. He was convinced that the only way to bring respect and dignity to the people of African decent was by building progressive new "empires" in Africa whose civilization, while remaining basically African, would incorporate useful elements of Western culture.

It was the great Edward W. Blyden, who, with the immortal Frederick Douglass, placed before the bar of public opinion in England and other countries in Europe the case of the black man in America.

As far back as 1881, the renowned scholar and benefactor of West Africa, Dr. Edward Wilmot Blyden, speaking on the occasion of his inauguration as President of Liberia College, sounded the note for the organized teaching of the culture and civilization of Africa and decried the fact that the world's image of Africa was not in keeping with Africa's true status in world history. I quote from his address on this occasion: "The people generally are not yet prepared to understand their own interests in the great work to be done for themselves and their children. We shall be obliged to work for some time to come not only with out the popular sympathy we ought to have but with utterly inadequate resources.

"In all English-speaking countries the mind of the intelligent Negro child revolts against the descriptions of the negro given in elementary books, geographies, travels, histories...

"Having embraced or a t least assented to these falsehoods about himself, he concludes that his only hope of rising in the scale of respectable manhood is to strive for what is most unlike himself and most alien to his peculiar tastes. And whatever his literary attainments or acquired ability, he fancies that he must grind at the mill which is provided for him, putting in material furnished to his hands, bringing no contribution from his own field; and of course nothing comes out but what is put in."

Blyden made several trips to the United States and to his former home in the West Indies. With the Gold Coast nationalist, J.E. Casely Hayford, Blyden developed the idea of a federation of West African states. He died in 1912.

Of all the West Indians who influenced the Afro-American freedom struggle, the most colorful and the most controversial was Marcus Aurelius Garvey. Among the numerous black Manassehs who presented themselves and their grandiose programs to the people of Harlem, Marcus Garvey was singularly unique. He was born in Jamaica in 1887, the grandson of an African slave-a fact that was his proudest boast. He had grown up under a three-way color system-white, mulatto and black. Garvey's reaction to color prejudice and his search for a way to rise above it and lead his people back to Africa, spiritually, if not physically, was the all –consuming passion of his existence.

Marcus Garvey's glorious, romantic and riotous movement exhorted the black race and fixed their eyes on the bright star of a future in which they would reclaim and rebuild their African home land and heritage. Garvey came to the United States as a disciple of Booker T. Washington, founder of Tuskegee Institute. Unfortunately, Booker T. Washington died before Marcus Garvey reached this country. Garvey had planned to raise funds and return to Jamaica to establish an institution similar to Tuskegee. In 1914, he had organized the Universal Negro Improvement Association in Jamaica. After the failure of this organization, he looked to the United States where he found a loyal group of followers willing to listen to his message.

Garvey succeeded in building a mass movement among American Negroes while other leaders were attempting it and doubting that it could be done. He advocated the return of Africa to the Africans and people of African descent. He organized, very rashly and incompetently, the Black Star Line, a steamship company for transporting people of African descent from the United States to Africa. Garvey and his movement had a short and spectacular life span in the

United States. His movement took really effective form in about 1921, and by 1926 he was in a Federal prison, charged with misusing the mails. From prison he was deported home to Jamaica. This is, briefly, the essence of the Garvey saga.

The self-proclaimed Provisionally President of Africa never set foot on African soil. He spoke no African language. But Garvey managed to convey to members of the black race everywhere (and to the rest of the world) his passionate belief that Africa was the home of a civilization which had once been great and would be great again. When one takes into consideration the slenderness of Garvey's resources and the vast material forces, social conceptions and imperial interests which automatically sought to destroy him, his achievement remains one of the great propaganda miracles of this country.

The deportation of Marcus Garvey and the decline of his movement marked the ender o an era-an era when West Indians and Afro-Americans worked together and saw their plight as one and the same. In spite of the contributions that West Indians continued to make to the Afro-American freedom struggle, the relations between these two basically African people deteriorated. There are indications that the present freedom struggle in Africa, the Caribbean area and in the United States will become the basis for a new era of understanding and cooperation.

References

"Prince Hall." By Lerone Bennett, Jr. Ebony Magazine, April 1964.

"Pioneers in Protest" series, No. 2.

"Founders of the Negro Press." By Lerone Bennett, jr. Ebony Magazine, July 1964. Pioneers in Protest series, No. 5.

"The Ghost of Marcus Garvey." Lerone Bennett, Jr. Ebony Magazine, November 1960.

"A New World A-Coming." By Roi Ottley. Houghton, Mifflin Co., Boston, Mass. 1943.

"Black Nationalism: A Search For an Identity in America." By E.U. Essien-Udom. Dell Publishing Co., Inc., NYC 1962.

"Black Moses: The Story of Marcus Garvey and the Universal Negro Improvement Association: By Edmund David Cronon. University of Wisconsin Press, 1957.

"Garvey and Garveyism." By Jacques Garvey. Published by the author 1963. 12 Mona Road, Kingston 6, Jamaica, W.I.

"Harlem: Negro Metropolis." By Claude Mc Key . E. P. Dutton and Company, Inc. 1960.

"Nineteenth-Century Negritude: Edward W. Blyden." By Robert W. July.

"Edward w. Blyden: Pioneer West African Nationalist." By Hollis R. Lynch.

John Henrik Clarke, author of "West Indian Partisans in the Fight for Freedom," is the associate editor of Freedomways, a quarterly review of the Negro freedom movement. The author of many articles of a historical nature, Mr. Clarke is a reviewer for African World Bookshelf in New York and last year edited the anthology Harlem: A Community in Transition. He is currently compiling an anthology of representative short stories by Negro writers.

Reports from the Black World Towards Pan-Africanism

John Henrik Clarke

Report from *Addis Ababa, Ethiopia,* December 1973
The Third International Congress of Africanists
Black World, March 1974

The greatest achievement of this Third International Congress was the coming together of scholars from regions of the world to present papers on economic, social, scientific, cultural and political development of Africa. The International Congress of Africanists was formed in 1963 in Ghana. Formerly, the International Congress of Orientalists met to discuss scholarly issues on Asia and Africa, but when several African countries became independent, it was agreed that the African continent required an organization devoted solely to African matters – an organization which would hold its meetings on African soil. Thus, at the invitation of the Ghana Government, and with additional financial support from UNESCO and U.S. foundations, the First Congress was held in Accra in December 1963. Hundreds of scholars from all over the world attended this first session where statutes of the Congress were drawn up, and many learned papers on Africa were read. The President of the First Congress was Dr. Kenneth Onwuka Dike of Nigeria. The Secretary-General was Dr. Nana Kabina Nketia IV of Ghana. The opening address was given by the late Dr. Kwame Nkrumah, then president of the Republic of Ghana.

At the invitation of the Senegalese Government, the Second Congress was held in Dakar, Senegal, in December 1967. Again, many scholars participated and many papers were read. The President of the Second Congress was Dr. Alioune Diop of *Presence Africaine* and the international Society of African Culture. The

Secretary-General was Professor Glassane N'Daw of Senegal and the University of Dakar. President Leopold Senghor welcomed the delegates.

In spite of the fact that the first two Congresses were held in Africa, they were dominated by white scholars, mainly from the U.S. based organization, the Africa Studies Association. No papers by Black American scholars were presented at the First Congress and only one at the Second Congress. Behind the scene, white scholars manipulated both the First and Second Congresses. This is why the Third International Congress was exceptional – at last. The Africans took over, and the Afro-Americans played a major role and presented papers in a number of the sessions; (and one) Afro-American was elect – (elected to) the Permanent Council that (will cover) the Congress for the next (five years) and plan future meet – (meetings.) Afro-Americans participated (on all) levels of this conference.

(The) Afro-American delegation, (led by) Professor James Turner, director of the Africana Studies and Research Center, Cornell University, was a representative and (well) balanced group that consisted of Patricia Karouma, Milfred (Fierce), Mae King, Shelby Smith, (Steven) McGanns (graduate student), John Henrik Clarke, Asa (Davis), Rukudzo Murapa, Len and Rosalind Jeffries, Issac Akinyobin, Josceph Harris, Walter Rodney (Tanzania), Ahmed Mohiddin (Makerere University) and Elliot Shinner.

Before the conference officially began, a meeting was arranged between the two major American African historical organizations attending this conference: the African Studies Association (ASA), mostly white, now with a Black president, the South African scholar, Absolom Vilakari; and the African Heritage Studies Association (AHSA), all Black, headed by Professor James Turner. There was some fear that there might be, now on African soil, a reoccurrence of the conflict of October 21, 1969, when a large number of African and Afro-American scholars broke away from the white-dominated African Studies Association and formed the African Heritage Studies Association.

At the annual meeting of the African Studies Association in Montreal, Canada, in 1969, a "black caucus" of militant students and educators called for equal Black representation in the association. The caucus contended that the ideological framework of the association perpetuated "neocolonialism." The conflict of 1969 was avoided at Addis Ababa in December 1973, because the president and other officials of ASA agreed that AHSA was entitled to equal representation in all matters pertaining to the American delegations' relationship to the Third International Congress of Africanists.

The Congress was officially opened on Monday, December 10, with an address by His Imperial Majesty Haile Selassie. In his remarks he called attention to this fact:

> "The weight of historical evidence attests that since the earliest times the civilization and progress of man has been based on knowledge gained through study and research rather than on that based on gratuitous assumptions. It is now generally acknowledged that for development and economic growth, study and research constitute a basis of proven worth: There can be no doubt that you, the scholars who have devoted your (life) works to study and research (on) Africa, will, aside from (your) contributions to human knowledge in general, also make contributions that will form the basis for the growth and development of Africa."

In further remarks the Emperor observed that the status of African scholars in the field of African studies was changing for the better when he said:

> "It cannot be denied that in the past the conduct of study and research on Africa was in the hands of non-Africans. The nature and content of such study and research was therefore primarily determined by non-African needs and interests. The (time) has now come when Africa, having abandoned the subservient status, is guiding her own destiny in the political and economic spheres. In the academic sphere, as well, the time (seems) to have come when Africans (can) abandon the role of subservience and embrace that of ful and equal participation. A clear demonstration of this is the fact (that) among you, the scholars assembled in this hall today, (there) is a greater number of African scholars than at any time in the past, all ready and able to participate in deliberations pertaining to their continent. While it is true that, as we pointed out earlier, scholarly research recognizes no political boundaries (yet) it cannot at the same time be denied that Africans need to carry a greater share of the study and research on their continent than they do at present. Their greater participation can no doubt help to re-direct Africanist research into areas of greater relevance to Africa's needs and interests. We are convinced that the work of scholars can have great relevance to the struggle that our continent is now waging against poverty, ignorance and disease."

The afternoon sessions began with the reading of papers on the history of Northeast Africa and of Africa in general. This history still is in great dispute. It begs for good answers. What is history and what is its meaning in the life of people in general and African people in particular? Why is there now a national and international fight over the history of African people, and who will interpret and control this history? White "historians" and "authorities" on the development of nations and civilizations, who for the past 500 years, in most cases, have said that African people have had no history, now are fighting to control the interpretation of the history they once said we did not have. What is this fight really about? To understand it, we might have to look backwards and forwards at the same time, while using the present as our vantage point. It was o accident that Professor Roland Oliver of England, a member of the old guard and the old school of interpreters of African history, was chairman of this first session on African history. There now exists a form of academic neo-colonialism that intends to control African social thought. It would surface very early at this conference, and, fortunately, the Africans would prove to be equal to combating it.

Many of the papers on African economic and political development dealt with African problems in the abstract as though a new African reality did not exist. The presenters of these papers and the other delegates had to be reminded of the existence of *apartheid* and the overall southern African problem of racism and oppression. They also had to be reminded of the fight against the Portuguese in Angola, Mozambique and Guinea-Bissau, where hundreds of people are dying daily.

In the sessions on social and cultural development, many of the often neglected dimensions of African life, history and culture were analyzed. Particularly outstanding were the following papers presented in the first sessions in the cultural development section: "Considerations of Some Ideological Problems in Ethiopia Today," by Girma Amare; "African Literature and Cultural Re-evaluation," by Ernest N. Emenyonu; "Toward and Operational Philosophy of African Education," by Patricia Kaurouma; "Africa as the Origin of Early Greek Theatre Culture," by Tsekaye Ghedre Yedhin; and "The Influence of African Cultural Continuity on the Slave Revolt in South America and in the Caribbean Islands," by John Henrik Clarke.

In the first of a number of keynote addresses, Professor L.K.H. Gama, of the University of Zambia, called attention to the "Scientific Underdevelopment of Africa" and pointed to the opportunities in this field that are still begging for more trained Africans.

In the second keynote address, "The Study of African History: The Present Position," by Dr. Kenneth Onwuka Dike, the still unresolved problems of writing and teaching African History were outlined. The closing sessions of the conference was devoted to a discussion of resolutions, chosing the sight for the Fourth International Congress of Africanists, and in electing new members to the Permanent Council that will handle the affairs of the International Congress (now renamed "The International Congress of Africanists") for the next five years. The leader of the Black American delegation, Professor Turner, had insisted from the beginning of the discussion that, insasmuch as a member of the African Studies Association (ASA) had been the American representative on the Permanent Council of the Council for the past 10 years, the next permanent member should be from the AHSA. Behind the scenes meeting on this matter lasted for days – in fact, throughout the entire period of the Congress. The candidate for the Permanent Council, who was finally elected, was John Henrik Clarke, the past president of AHSA, who is presently professor of African History in the Department of Black and Puerto Rican Studies, Hunter College, New York City. This election gives the Black Americans a decision making position in the International Congress of Africanists for the first time.

The President and presiding officer over this Third International Congress of Africanists was Dr. Aklilu Hable, President of Haile Selassie I University. The Secretary General was Dr. Nicholas Otieno of Kenya.

Africa and the American Negro Press

John Henrik Clarke

Reprinted from *Journal of Negro Education*, Vol. XXX,
Winter 1961, pp. 64–68

The American Negro Press has been more consistent in its coverage of African news than any other news media in the United States. This would indicate that its coverage has been adequate. Quite the contrary. While the quantity of this coverage could be accepted as adequate, the quality leaves much to be desired. In fact, the American Negro Press, like the American Press in general, have missed or mishandled the story of emergent Africa. I believe the emergence of Africa to be the greatest news event in the age in which we live. In the handling of news relating to Africa, there seems to be a reoccurring multiplicity of errors that can be traced to one error – the inability or reluctance of the present interpreters of Africa to recognize and understand Africa's historical past. Contrary to a still prevailing concept, the Africans did not wait in darkness for the Europeans to bring the light. What we are now witnessing is neither the first nor the second emergence of Africa. This is an elementary fact, yet the "Johnny Come Latelys" who have *lately* discovered Africa, do not see to be aware of it.

The awareness of Africa by the men who built and developed the American Negro Press, goes back to the hectic and heroic beginning of Negro journalism in this country. Some of the back issues of these old papers show their editors' keen awareness of Africa and its importance.

In the publication: *Douglass Monthly*, edited for the Anti-Slavery Society by Frederick Douglass, the following news item appeared in the issue of January 1862, under the heading: The Future of Africa. Miscellaneous: by Rev. Alexander Crummell, BA, of Liberia, West Africa.

The undersigned proposes to issue in twelve volumes of about 300 pages, orations, addresses, and other papers, mostly prepared for National and Missionary occasions in Liberia, West Africa; and pertaining to National Life and Duty.

The following is a list of the articles:

1. The English Language in Liberia.
2. The duty of a rising Christian State to contribute to the World's well-being and civilization.
3. Address on laying the corner stone of St. Mark's Hospital, Cape Palmas.
4. Duty and relations of free colored men, in America to Africa.
5. Eulogium of the life and character of Thomas Clarkson, Esq.
6. God and Nation — an anniversary Sermon.
7. The fitness of the Gospel for its own work — a Convocational Sermon.
8. The progress and Prospects of the Republic of Liberia.
9. The progress of Civilization along the West Coast of Africa.
10. The Negro Race not under a curse — from the London Christian Observer of August, 1853.

This volume will be printed on good white paper, in clear type, neatly bound, and at $1.00 per copy.

As it is published to help repair serious losses by fire in Africa, and to secure the education of children, it will not be published until 400 subscribers are obtained.

The aid of generous friends is requested, at an early day as possible as the subscriber is anxious to return, very soon, to his duty in Africa.

Alexander Crommel, Missionery
311 Spring Street
New York, NY
December 12th, 1861.

Alexander Crummell, founder of the African Academy, friend and contemporary of Dr. Edwin W. Blyden, the great West Indian scholar and benefactor of West Africa, was one of the first of our early writers to call attention to Africa through the American Negro Press. He was the dean of the black scholarly and literary group, in the closing quarter of the nineteenth century. The life of Dr. Crummell later fired the imagination and redoubled the vigor of Dr. W.E.B. DuBois, whose sharp and penetrating pen burned its own path in National and international affairs from the early nineties to the present day.

DuBois, inspired by Alexander Crummell made the subject of Africa a burning issue in the American Negro Press. In 1915, the Home University

Library brought out a small book "The Negro," in which DuBois outlined the program that must be followed in order to deal properly with the whole field of African life and history.

Carter G. Woodson came forward with his researches and publications which blossomed forth into the widest popularization of the subject. Quietly African scholars like J.E. Moorland, Arthur A. Schomburg, J.A. Rogers and William L. Hansbery led the field in gathering material.

After the first World War, DuBois again accelerated the American Negro's interest in Africa by organizing a series of Pan-African Congresses. At a time when the news about the aspirations of Africans for self government was being ignored throughout most of the world, the American Negro Press gave full coverage to this subject.

In the pages of these newspapers we learned of the activities of outstanding African personalities stubbornly keeping alive the dream of eventual independence for all African nations.

The South African writer, Sol Plaatje and the trade unionist, Clement Kadalie made tours of the United States in 1927 and 1928. Now the story of Africa's struggles was brought directly to us by two able Africans. This occasion went unnoticed by all, except the American Negro Press.

From the reports on the Pan-African Congress we learned of other Africans of caliber. Dr. J.E.K. Aggrey had lived in the United States for a number of years and returned to the Gold Coast (now Ghana). The career of his fellow countryman, the Honorable Casely Hayford had been well reported by the American Negro Press. Again from the Pan-African Congress reports the names Blaise Diagne, of French West Africa, a member of the Chamber of Deputies, Paul Panda of the Belgian Congo and Rene Maran of French Equatorial Africa, became identified with Africa's awakening.

The coverage of news relating to Africa was revitalized by the American Negro Press during the Italian-Ethiopian War. In the reporting of this conflict the American Negro Press was fortunate in having at least two reporters who had been well schooled in African History in particular and World History in general. In his dispatches from Ethiopia, J.A. Rogers gave an astute analysis to the Pittsburgh *Courier*, of the war, together with a commentary on the political intrigues in Europe that led to this conflict. Later, in a small book, "The Real Facts About Ethiopia," he digested his reports and produced the most revealing document of the Italian-Ethiopian War that has so far appeared in print.

Dr. Willis N. Huggins, a high school history teacher, author of a remarkable book, "Introduction to African Civilizations," went to Geneva and reported on the League of Nations meetings concerning the Italian-Ethiopian War, for the Chicago *Defender*. Here again the American Negro Press in its coverage of African news was fortunate to have on the scene of conflict a keen observer who could see through the subterfuge and pretenses of European powers in their frantic schemes to keep their African colonies. Both Rogers and Huggins saw behind and beyond the headlines and foretold the future repercussions of Ethiopia's betrayal. Their reports were a highwater mark in American Negro journalism.

While the coverage of African news by the American Negro Press was increasing, in the years since the Italian-Ethiopian War, the caliber of this coverage was sadly declining. Today, most of the news about Africa that appears in the Negro Press, consists of press release handouts from the various colonial Information Centers, re-written news items from white newspapers, and an occasional article of group of articles by a nonjournalist traveler, recently returned from a trip to Africa. Very little on the scene and behind the scene coverage of African news is being done. The few exceptions I will mention later.

The coverage of African news by the American Negro Press was accelerated when the rise of independence movements in Africa became international news. This acceleration reached some kind of ceremonious plateau the week the Gold Coast gained its independence and took back its ancient name, Ghana. The occasion was well observed by the American Negro Press. Most of the major Negro papers published special supplements, saluting the new state of Ghana.

For many years the Pittsburgh *Courier* has been ahead of all other Negro newspapers in its coverage of news relating to Africa. Their special supplement of the occasion of Ghana's independence was the most intelligently edited of the many that were published. In an article, "Ghana... The Empire in the Sudan," George S. Schuyler wrote a capsule history of the old Empire of Ghana and briefly appraised the significant events leading to the establishment of the new state. In other articles by J.A. Rogers, Marguerite Cartwright, and the editor of the *Courier*, the history and importance of the new state were presented in a manner that could be understood by readers who had no prior knowledge of the subject matter.

Here again an American Negro newspaper proved that was capable of presenting African news on a high journalistic level. Unfortunately the American Negro Press has never been consistent in maintaining this high standard.

The largest Negro newspaper published locally, in New York City, *The Amsterdam News*, did not do as well as the *Courier* in its Ghana Independence Supplement, lacking the experienced writers on Africa that the Pittsburgh *Cou-*

rier has nearly always had. Their writer picked at and wrote about the subject, without showing any real understanding of it. His contribution lost my interest when he digressed in his article in order to explain how a Ghanaian male persuades a Ghanaian female to say "yes" to that ancient and obvious question.

The flurry of interest in African news continued somewhat abated. Kwame Nkrumah, Prime Minister of Ghana, became a national hero to the American Negroes, who were presently very short of heroes. Now he has a place in the right side of our heart, alongside Martin Luther King.

The Pittsburgh *Courier* continued to lead all other Negro newspapers in its coverage of African news, particularly in reporting the news as it relates to African history.

From September 7, 1957 to March 8, 1958, the *Courier* published a twenty-seven-week series of articles under the title: "Famous African Chiefs." This was the longest series of this nature ever to appear in an American Negro newspaper. This series of articles were drawn from a completed book: "The Lives of Great African Chiefs." The book consists of twenty-one short biographies of outstanding African Chiefs whose lives and activities have influenced the direction of African history in the years between the early part of the 18th century to the middle of the 20th century.

Now permit me to digress long enough to make one thing clear: commendable as the Pittsburgh *Courier* may be, I do not mean to imply that its coverage of African news is adequate. There is no really adequate coverage of African news by any newspaper in this country.

In the November 16, 1957 issue of the *Courier* another impressive Special Supplement was published on Africa. All the material for this supplement, except an article, "Africa's Peaceful Revolution" by George S. Schuyler, was prepared by the French Press and Information Service here in New York City. This supplement was informative in spite of being completely pro-French. After reading this one-sided recitation on the "achievement" of the French in Africa, an uninformed person could easily conclude that the French imperialists were angels who came to Africa to bring milk and honey. A well-informed person could easily conclude that this was not the case. The major weakness of the American Negro Press in its coverage of African news is plainly shown in the publication of this supplement. All too often, news relating to Africa is published without question, examination or analysis.

In May 1958 the pro-French leaning of the Pittsburgh *Courier* was continued in a more direct way. George S. Schuyler, New York editor of the *Courier* made a tour through the French colonies in West Africa and wrote a series of revealing articles, titled: "In Brightest Africa." To me the articles revealed among other things: the French were obviously paying Mr. Schuyler's traveling bill and he was obviously seeing what they wanted him to see.

Once more, French imperialism was washed whiter than snow. I traveled through some of the same colonies last summer, paying my own traveling bill, and my eyes saw an entirely different picture. There is much to admire in French colonial administration and much to abhor; and snow is figuratively and literally whiter than anything I saw.

Another major weakness of the American Negro Press in its coverage of African news is the lack of a dynamic approach in presenting the African story. Indeed, *they view with alarm* as the unpredictable Africans move rapidly from one stage of transition to another. This alarm should be converted into a new and dynamic journalism that will present the story of emergent Africa in a manner that will summon both attention and respect.

First the standard sitters of the American Negro Press will have to learn what makes a good African story. New and more interesting ways must be found to tell the African story, which indeed is the story of the new age of man.

A case in point: last year Tshekedi Khama, son of the great Bechuana Chief of the same name died in London where he had gone for medical treatment. The name Tshekedi Khama has been in the news at regular intervals for more than twenty-five years. In addition to being the son of one of the greatest men born in Southern Africa, Tshekedi Khama was an able and defiant African leader who lived under British rule without ever really accepting it.

In 1933 Tshekedi Khama tried and punished a misbehaving Englishman for molesting some Bechuana girls. The incident made headlines around the world. The thought of a white man being tried and punished by an African, in an African court, shook the then prevailing colonial structure. Tshekedi's tribe, the Bamangwata, and others in Bechuanaland, were on the brink of revolution. The British muddled through this crisis by slapping Tshekedi's wrist lightly and carefully. Their reprimand was tantamount to a retreat.

After the passing of this crisis, Tshekedi Khama resumed his responsibilities as Paramount Chief of the Bamangwata Tribe of Bechuanaland – following in the footsteps of his distinguished father. In the years that followed, he developed into one of the most able tribal rulers in all Africa. When he objected to his nephew's, Seretse Khama's, marriage to an English girl, he was back in trouble again, and back in the headlines.

The death of this outstanding African personality went almost unnoticed by the American Negro Press. This is what I meant when I said: "The standard sitters of the American Negro Press do not seem to know what makes a good African story." In addition to needing a new way to evaluate the African story, they also need a new way to re-evaluate the relations between the emergent African and the status of the people of African descent in the Western World.

Admittedly, the American Negro Press in its coverage of African news have been more consistent and thorough than any other news media in the United States – all the more reason why their present inadequacy cannot be excused. The African story is bigger than all the story tellers, and it is forever changing. No one is expected to tell it as well as it needs to be told. The many dimensions of the African story have made the collective efforts of all of its present day interpreters appear like a mole hill that leaves a mountain to be desired.

African Culture as the Basis of World Culture

John Henrik Clarke

Reprinted from *Presence Africaine*, nos. 117–118 (1st and 2nd Quarters, 1981): 123–129

Introduction

Within the last year, in both national and international scholarly circles, the role and impact of African people on the history and culture of the world is being reconsidered. This reconsideration has been brought into being by the publication of new works of depth and insight by both black and white scholars. After many years of neglect and distortion, African history and culture is at last being put into proper perspective as it relates to world history and the culture of the world. The publication in the United States of the book *The African Origins of Civilization: Myth or Reality*, by Cheikh Anta Diop, brought new light to this subject. This was followed by two of his other books in English: *The Cultural Unity of Black Africa* (1978) and Black Africa: *The Economic and Cultural Basis for a Federated State* (1978)*

In this preliminary paper, the main focus of my attention will be on the struggle of black Americans for causes in African world history and culture that respects all the known facts in the matter. I have called this struggle – A Dilemma at the Crossroads of Cultural History.

I. General Remarks

a) "Black Studies, the Dilemma at the Crossroads", has long historical roots and there is no way to understand this dilemma if we look at it only as a current event. The demand for Black Studies grew out of the demand for

Civil Rights. Out of these demands the concept of "Black is Beautiful" and "Black Power" was born.

b) There is a need to look, at least briefly, at the events in history that brought this dilemma into being. I must again go back to the period of the second rise of Europe. All the world was changed to accommodate this event which was followed by the European conquest of most of mankind. This conquest was achieved by the astute use of two political instruments-the Bible and the gun. The Europeans, in addition to colonizing the world, in turn colonized the writing of world history. Now world history lost its broad definition and became a rationale for European control and a means for the glorification of European people at the expense of other people and nations, whose civilizations were old before Europe was born.

The first European attack was on African culture. The next move was to deny that this culture had ever existed. A look at this culture will show, in part, what Black Study programmes are about or should be about.

c) Africans were great story-tellers long before their first appearance in Jamestown, Virginia, in 1619. The rich and colorful history, art and folklore of West Africa (the ancestral home of most Afro-Americans) present evidence of this, and more.

d) Contrary to a misconception which still prevails, the Africans were familiar with literature and art for many years before their contact with the Western world. Before the breaking up of the social structure of the West African states of Ghana, Melle (Mali) and Songhay, and he internal strife and chaos that made the slave-trade possible, the forefathers of the Africans, who eventually became slaves in the United States, lived in a society where University life was fairly common and scholars were beheld with reverence.

e) There were, in this ancestry, rulers who expanded their kingdoms into empires; great and magnificent armies whose physical dimensions dwarfed entire nations into submission; generals who advanced the technique of military science; scholars whose vision of life showed foresight and wisdom and priests who told of gods that were strong and kind. To understand fully any aspect to Afro-American life, one must realize that the black American is not without a cultural past, though he was many generations removed from it before his achievements in American literature and art commanded any appreciable attention.

f) I have been referring to the African origin of Afro-American literature and history. This preface is essential to every meaningful discussion of the role of the Afro-American in every major aspect of American life, past and present. Before getting into the main body of this talk, I want to make it clear that the black race did not come to the United States culturally empty-handed.

g) I will elaborate very briefly on my statement to the effect that the "forefathers of the Africans, who eventually became slaves in the United States, once lived in a society where University life was fairly common and scholars were beheld with reverence." During the period in West African history from the early part of the fourteenth century to the time of the Moorish invasion in 1591, the city of Timbuktu, with the University of Sankore in the Songhay Empire, was the intellectual center of Africa. Black scholars were enjoying a renaissance that was know and respected throughout most of Africa and in parts of Europe. At this period in African history, Sankore was the educational of the Western Sudan. In his book *Timbuktu the Mysterious,* Felix DuBois gives us the following description of this period: "*The scholars of Timbuktu yielded in nothing to the saints in their sojourns in the foreign Universities of Fez Tunis and Cairo. They astounded the most learned men of Islam by their erudition. That these Negroes were on a level with the Arabian savants is proved by the fact that they were installed as professors in Morocco and Egypt. In contrast to this, we find that the Arabs were not always equal to the requirements of Sankore*".

h) I will mention only one of the great black scholars referred to by DuBois. Ahmed Baba was the last Chancellor of Sankore. He was one of the greatest African scholars of the late sixteenth century. His life is a brilliant example of the range and depth of West African intellectual activity before the colonial era. He was the author of more than 40 books: nearly everyone of these books had a different theme. He was Timbuktu when it was invaded by the Moroccans in 1592 and was one of the first citizens to protest against this occupation of his beloved home town. Along with other scholars, he was imprisoned and eventually exiled to Morocco. During his expatriation from Timbuktu, his collection of 1,600 books, one of the richest libraries of his day, was lost.

West Africa then entered a sad period of decline. During the Moorish occupation, wreck and ruin became the order of the day. When the Europeans arrived in this part of Africa and saw these conditions, they assumed that nothing of order and value had ever existed there. This mistaken impression, too often repeated, has influenced the interpretation of African and Afro-American life in history for over 400 years.

i) All Black Study's programmes, when they are properly run, are restoration projects. The objective is to restore what the slave-trade and the colonial system took away. The objective is also the establish a new definition of what black people have been, what they are, and what they still must be. In his new book, *The Challenge of Blackness*, Lerone Bennett, Jr. states that, "if black people are not what white people said they were, then white America is not what it claims to be. What we have to deal with here, therefore, is a contestation at the level of reality. We are engaged in a struggle over meaning, in a struggle over the truth."

The struggle that Bennett refers to is both national and international. Out of this struggle the future of mankind will be decided. When people decide who they are, they also decide what they have to do about their condition. First, they look backward in order to look forward; then try to find out how they were lost from history in the first place.

II. Background

Some assumptions that confuse and distrort the study of African History and world history in general

a) The assumption that the people of African descent had no culture prior to the European contact.
b) The assumption that Ancient Egypt was a pseudo-white nation and that its culture was European or Asian and not African.
c) The assumption that Africa made no contributions to the early development of Europe.
d) The assumption that slavery was to the Africans a blessing in disguise.
e) The assumption that the Africans had no civilization and made no contribution to mankind prior to its contact with Europe.

III. Afro-American History: Main Currents and Missing Pieces.

a) Background to this course: "The African People: Their Influence on World History; Africa, the Beginning of the Troubled Years, 1400–1492."
b) The pre-Columbian presence of the Africans in the so-called "New World", and their first impact on it.

c) Extension of the slave-trade; slavery in the American colonies from 1619 through the American Revolution.
d) American independence and American slavery after the Revolution; a review of the contradictions; the impact of the Haitian Revolution on the slave systems of the "New World".
e) Resistance movements in the first half of the 19th century; the massive slave revolts; the impact of David Walker's "Appeal" on the thought and action of the Abolitionist's Movement after 1829.
f) The impact of the black *elite* of the Abolitionists' Movement (Frederick Douglass, John Russwurm, Samuel Ringold Ward, Samuel Cornish and Henry Highland Garnet). Martin Delany and the concept of African redemption and repatriation.
g) Haiti after the revolt; the making of a black nation; revolt in Jamaica.
h) The Civil War; emancipation; the new "freedom" and new illusions; black political power, brief and fleeting, to 1875; Reconstruction; black political power, a short day in the sun.
i) The betrayal of Reconstruction; the emergence of Booker T. Washington, 1875–1900: the making for black institutions before and after the betrayal.
j) The impact of Booker T. Washington on his times; the impact of W.E.B. DuBois on his time.

IV. Some Prefaces to the Present

a) The black American enters the 20th century; new dreams and new illusions.
b) Pan-Africanism, nationalism and survival; the emergence of W.E.B. DuBois; the first Pan-African Conference (London, England, 1900); the rise of the new Black radical elite (W.E.B. DuBois, W. Monroe Trotter and others). The creation of the Niagara Movement in 1906 and that of the NAACP in 1909.
c) The end of the Booker T. Washington era (1915); the emergence of Marcus Garvey (1916–1925) and the challenge to the leadership of W.E.B. DuBois.
d) The black American between the wars; the Harlem Renaissance period, 1920–1930; the great Depression and the rise of a new protest movement.
e) New days and new illusions. The black Americans in the post-war world (1946 to the present). The rise of new leadership (Martin Luther King, Jr.);

the new and last period of A. Philip Randolph; black protest and Black Power.

V. The Black Studies Explosion and How it Grew

a) The concept was reborn during the Civil Rights Movement.
b) It grew out of a new search for identity, definition and direction.
c) It led us to where we are, standing on the ground Black and Beautiful.
d) Where do we go from here?

VI. Conclusion.

In his book, Tom-Tom, John W. Vandercook states that "*a race is like a man: until it uses its own talents, takes pride in its own history and loves its own memories, it can never fulfill itself completely*".

As a teacher of African and Afro-American History, my main mission in life is to teach black youth (and the adult who will listen) to use their talents more creatively in the struggle for total liberation and nationhood. To do this, of course, they must also be taught to take pride in their own history and love their own memories. This search for self history that I call the "Black and Beautiful Plateau". This position is both good and bad. It is good because all the talk about blackness, Pan Africanism (the world union of African people) and "Nation Time" has made black people reconsider themselves as human beings and their place in world history past and present. It is bad because a large number of black people, especially in America, have used the "Black and Beautiful" phase of our history as a cop out. They have wallowed in black fantasy and made no contribution to black liberation.

At this juncture, we need to take a good look at the past with the hope that it can illuminate the present and indicate the future. How did we arrive at this state of self-discovery and self-deception?

When Europeans recovered from their long night of internal strife and confusion in the fifteenth century, the Africans, not knowing of their intentions, invited their future conquerors to dinner. This act reveals something about the Africans' humanity, about their traditional hospitality to strangers beginning of African's time of trouble.

During the slave-trade and the colonization period that followed, Europeans would not only colonize most of the countries of the world but they would also colonize the teaching of history itself. Human history was rewritten or rearranged to make it appear that the world waited in darkness for the Europeans to bring the light. In the meantime, these Europeans destroyed civilizations that were well developed and old before respectful commentary of history in order to justify the expansion of Europe. The image of the African as being black and ugly emerged. This is the image that the "Black and Beautiful: phase of our present day history is trying to destroy. The war against this image is what has brought us to the "Black and Beautiful Plateau". The question now is: How do we move beyond this plateau to our next state in history that is nation building? First, we will have to take serious shouting "Nation Time" committed to the hard work that goes into bringing a "Nation Time" committed to the hard work that goes into bringing a nation into being and maintaining it? How many of the shouters for "Nation Time" know how to make an airplane fly? How many can cure stomach aches? And how many can make muddy water drinkable? At what point will we finish convincing ourselves that we are "Black and Beautiful"?

This is a highly complex world. It can only be ruled by blackness nor beauty. It can only be ruled by people who know how to handle power. The powerlessness of black people is more of a deterrent to their fight for freedom, direction and definition than their blackness. In this kind of world being "Black and Beautiful" means nothing unless, ultimately, you are also *black and powerful.*

John *Henrik CLARKE*

Conclusion

As this volume comes to an adjourn and completion, I would like to offer some parting thoughts on the life and times of John Henrik Clarke. Using some selected principles from the Nguzo Saba, I wanted to focus on five key areas to describe and evaluate the lasting contributions of this historical "*Jelle*." First, throughout the writings of Clarke, he consistently urges the idea of African unity. This takes place in the form of global and continental Pan Africanism. Additionally, Clarke used examples from a micro to a macro analysis, with emphasis on unity, referring to the development and institution of the Black family. In summary, all of these attributes play a vital role in Africana people developing an ethos towards understanding the singular and plural concept of unity.

Second, probing the notion of faith – one of the enduring commentaries which Clarke argues is that African people have made a way, out of no way. Some refer to this vernacular coining the term *waymakers*. In this sense, Clarke borrowed folklore and the ideas from classical periods in African history, with direct reference to empires in the Nile Valley and Western Sudanic regions. Many of these Kingdoms established nation states, agency, and governance. Equally important, the motif of faith, is regulated through Clarke's narrative voice making the clear distinction between spirituality and religion. While aggregating his philosophical thought, Clarke points out the polytheistic and humanistic attributes of Africans ability to seek redemption and salvation through faith and not reciprocity for their captivity.

Third, in addressing collective work and responsibility, Clarke, is an ardent scholar activist, who engages the campus and community with alternative ideas concerning the regulation and dispensing of Africana agency. Hence, his discussions in the articles presented in this volume provides a context for: locating Africana people as involuntary migrants; the need for a collaborative work ethic;

and the relevance of networking being a vital component for the existence and maintenance of Africana people in the diaspora and on the continent.

Fourth, examining the issue of cooperative economics, Clarke acknowledges that all people must answer to a name that identifies and describes: *land, history*, and *culture*. From this point, once a people know their rightful name, they can then locate themselves to have a cultural ethos. Furthermore, the ethnos of a group is a lens that assist them in understanding their world, reality, and historical precedents. Continuing on, when a people or group has a understanding of themselves in this historical and cultural context, their concepts on the issue of economics adheres to a prioritization dictated by their cultural norms. Therefore, economics or should I say, the construction and develop of economics, is centered and defined by the mores and normative attributes of the culture.

Finally, purpose, Clarke while making his transition in 1998, still challenges the African world community with concern to the implementation and exhibition of a Pan African perspective in a technologically driven society. Indeed, three general query come to mind: first, what role will Africans in diaspora play in the United States and Africa foreign policy relations; Second, how will nation states on the continent of Africa interact and trade with each other and those African nations in the Caribbean; and Third, who will define and direct the future of continental Africa's imports and exports over the next decade. Moreover, the query are not to be answered in this volume, but rather to be examined and addressed in the body of literature that grows out of Africana studies research and scholarship. In closing, Clarke made an enormous contribution to the academy of higher learning and the Africana world community. Let us remember his words, his spirit, his work ethic, and his persistence to advance the cause and condition of African people.

Biographical Summary and Selected Research Publications of John Henrik Clarke (1915–1998)

YEAR	EVENT
1915	Born of January 1915 in Union Springs, Alabama to the parents of John (farmer) and Willella (Mays) Clarke.
1933	Travels to New York City and begins studying creative writing at the League of American Writers.
1941	US Army Air Forces, 1941–45; became master sergeant.
1948–52	Attended New York University
1948	Publishes book of poetry titled, *Rebellion in Rhyme*, Dicker Press, 1948.
1949	Edited a weekly syndicated poetry column.
1950	Clarke along with Rosa Guy, John Oliver Killens, and Walter Christmas founded the Harlem Writers Guild.
1949–55	Association for Study of African American Life and History (executive board member, 1949–55).
1949–50	Clarke becomes the co-founder and associate editor of the Harlem Quarterly.
1950	Publishes an article titled, "*Askia Mohammed's Return from Mecca*," *Negro History Bulletin* (now, the *African American History Bulletin*), 1950, Volume 13, no. 5.
1954	Founder of *Freedomways*.
1956–58	Attended the New School of Social Research
1956	New School for Social Research, New York City, occasional teacher of African and Afro-American history, 1956–58.
1957–59	Developer of African Study Center, 1957–59

YEAR	EVENT
1957–58	Feature writer for the *Pittsburgh Courier*, Pittsburgh, PA.
1958	Founder of the African Heritage Studies Association.
1958–60	New School for Social Research, New York City, Assistant to Director, 1958–60.
1958	Travels to Ghana during the summer of 1958 and spends three months.
1958	Feature writer *Ghana Evening News*, Accra, Ghana.
1959	Research Director for African Heritage Exposition in New York City, 1959.
1959	During the early part of 1959, Clarke is on record as having traveled through West Africa.
1961	Married Eugenia Evans (a teacher) on December 24, 1961.
1962–82	Serves as Associate Editor of *Freedomways*.
1962	Founder of the National Council of Black Studies.
1964–69	Director, Haryou-Act (teaching program), 1964–69.
1964	*Harlem USA: The Story of a City within a City*, Seven Seas Books (Berlin), 1964, revised edition, 1970.Collier.
1964	Malcolm X announces the formation of the Organization of Afro-American Unity. Clarke assists in the writing of the charter of this organization.
1965	Begins teaching as a lecturer at Hunter College of CUNY.
1965	Publishes the edited volume titled, *Harlem: A Community in Transition*, Citadel, 1965, 3rd edition, 1970.
1966	Publishes the edited volume titled, *American Negro Short Stories*, Hill & Wang, 1966.
1967	Member of board of directors of Langston Hughes Center for Child Development, 1967.
1968	During the fall of 1968, Clarke gives a lecture titled,"Afro-American Search," at the African Studies Association meeting 11th annual conference in Los Angeles, California.
1968	Coordinator and special consultant to Columbia Broadcasting System, Inc. (CBS-TV), television series, *Black Heritage*, 1968.

YEAR	EVENT
1968	Carter G. Woodson Award, 1968 for creative contribution in editing, and 1971, for excellence in teaching.
1968	Publishes the edited volume titled, *William Styron's Nat Turner: Ten Black Writers Respond*, Beacon Press, 1968, reprinted, Greenwood Press, 1987.
1967–70	Carter G. Woodson Distinguished Visiting Professor of African History, in the Africana Studies and Research Center, Cornell University 1967–70.
1969	Lecturer in teacher training program, Columbia University, summer, 1969.
1969	President of African Heritage Studies Association, 1969–73.
1969	Member of advisory board of Martin Luther King Library Center, 1969.
1969	National Association for Television and Radio Announcers citation for meritorious achievement in educational television, 1969.
1969	Publishes the edited volume titled, *Malcolm X: The Man and His Times*, Macmillian 1969, Africa World Press, 1991.
1970	Awarded an Honorary Doctorate L.H.D., University of Denver.
1970	Publishes the revised edition of the book titled, *Harlem* USA: *The Story of a City within a City*, Seven Seas Books (Berlin), 1964, revised edition, 1970. Collier.
1970	Co-Editor with Vincent Harding, *Slave Trade and Slavery*, Holt, 1970.
1970	Publishes, *Harlem: Voices from the Soul of Black America*, (short stories), New American Library, 1970.
1970	Hunter College of the City University of New York, New York City, Associate Professor of African and Puerto Rican studies, beginning 1970, became professor emeritus, 1985.
1970	Publishes the co-edited volume titled, *Black Titan: W.E.B. DuBois*, Beacon Press, 1970.
1972	J.A. Rogers, *World's Greatest Men of Color*, two volumes, Macmillian, 1972.

YEAR	EVENT
1972	Co-Editor with Amy Jacques Garvey, and author of introduction and commentaries) *Marcus Garvey and the Vision of Africa*, Random House, 1974.
1974	Writes the introduction and translates Chiekh Anta Diop classical work titled, *African Origins of Civilization: Myth or Reality.*
1974	In April, 1974 Clarke receives one of three Chicago's Kuumba Workshop 3rd Annual Awards for contributions to African people.
1974	In October, 1974, Clarke is honored by the New York Support Committee of the African Heritage Studies Association.
1977	Received the Marcus Garvey Annual; Lectureship Award a Pepperdine University in Malibu, California.
1978	Receives an Appreciation Award for Community Service from Rider University.
1981	Receives the Black Leadership Award from the National Council of Black Studies.
1983	Receives a Service Award from the Study-Activist Group, Sons and Daughters of the Sun, in New York City.
1983	Receives the Thomas Hunter Professorship for Academic Excellence, Hunter College.
1983	During the fall of 1983 Hunter College sponsors a tribute to Dr. Clarke.
1984	Receives the Leo Hansberry – J.A. Rogers Award from the Institute of Pan African Studies in Los Angels, California.
1985	Receives an Achievement Award from the National Association of Black School Educators.
1985	Retired from CUNY – Hunter College, ranked as Professor Emeritus.
1985	Cornell University's Africana Studies and Research Center named their 9,000 volume library, The John Henrik Clarke Africana Library."
1987	Receives the first Visiting Scholars award from Prarie View A&M University for the Benjamin Bannaker Honors College.
1986	During the summer of 1987 Clarke gives a lecture on Marcus Garvey at the Schomburg Center for Research in Black Culture.

YEAR	EVENT
1988	Receives Distinguished Service Award from the Department of African American Studies at Temple University. In the fall of this year, Temple University establishes the first doctoral program in African American Studies in the Unites States.
1989	In April of 1989 Clarke gives a lecture on African American history and culture in Chicago.
1991	Publishes the volume titled, *Africans at the Crossroads: Notes for an African World Revolution*. Trenton, NJ: Africa World Press, 1991.
1991	Produces the audio aid, *African Diary Reflections of John H. Clarke*. East Point, GA: Waset Educational Productions, 1991, audiovisual.
1991	Publishes the volume titled, *Lectures of Dr. Yosef ben-Jochannan and Dr. John Henrik Clarke*, Trenton, NJ: Africa World Press, 1991.
1992	Awarded an Honorary Doctorate Litt. D., University of District of Columbia.
1992	Publishes an edited volume, *Christopher Columbus and the African Holocaust*, A&B Books, 1992.
1992	Receives an award of a certificate of recognition from Congresswoman Maxine Walters, 29th Congressional District of California.
1992	Authors with the edited assistance of Barbara Adams an oral history project titled, *An Oral Biography of Professor John Henrik Clarke*, United Brothers and Sisters Communications Systems, 1992.
1992	Al Sharpton receives an endorsement from Clarke during his campaign for the U.S. Senate seat in New York.
1992	During the summer of 1992, Clarke appears as a witness before the subcommittee concerning the African Burial Ground in New York City.
1993	Completes Doctorate of Philosophy Degree at Pacific Western University in Los Angles, California.
1993	Receives the first annual award given in the name of Chancellor Williams for Critical Scholarship by the Association for the Study of Classical African Civilization.
1993	Awarded an Honorary Doctorate from Clarke-Atlanta University.

YEAR	EVENT
1993	Publishes the edited volume titled, *African People in World History*, Black Classic Press, 1993.
1994	In November of this year, Clarke and Yosef ben-Jochannan are honored at Boys and Girls High in Brooklyn, New York.
1994	Receives the Phelps Stokes Fund Aggrey Medal for his service as a public philosopher.
1994	Clarke gives a lecture on the topic, "*Who Betrayed the African World Revolution*," at Kent State University in Ohio.
1995	Receives the Carter G. Woodson Medallion, which is the highest award presented from the Association for the Study of African American Life and History.
1996	The 95 minute film documentary titled, John Henrik Clarke: A Great and Mighty Warrior was released. The film was directed by Saint Clair Bourne and narrated by Wesley Snipes.
1997	Publishes the book titled *The Second Crucifixion* of Nat Turner, Baltimore, MD: Black Classic Press, 1997.
1997	Dr. Iva Carruthers conceives and commissions the John Henrik Clarke Ancestral Shield. The art work is created by Mitchell Melson on January 1, 1998 having been accepted and approved by Dr. Clarke.
1998	Publishes the volume titled, *My Life in Search of Africa*, Chicago, IL: Third World Press, 1998, 1994.
1998	Receives Doctorate of Humane Letters from Medgar Evers College.
1999	Cornell University Black Alumni Association Incorporated established the goal of a development campaign to raise $250,000.00 to endow two fellowships in the name of John Henrik Clarke.
2000	New York City Mayor Rudolph Giuliana signed a bill commissioning 137th street be renamed to Dr. John Henrik Clarke Place.

Data retained from the following sources:

- Anna Swanston, *Dr. John Henrik Clarke: His Life, His words, and His Works*, I AM Unlimited Publishing, Incorporated: Atlanta, Georgia, 2003.
- Barbara E. Adams, Editor, *John Henrik Clarke: Master Teacher*, A & B Book Publishing, 2000.

- There are complete bibliographies and additional biographical data on the subject located on various internet web sites. A researcher would need to search under the subject heading of John Henrik Clarke.

Selected Publications by John Henrik Clarke

Rebellion in Rhyme (poetry), Prairie City, IL: The Dicker Press, 1948. Reprinted, Trenton: Africa World Press, 1991.

The Lives of Great African Chiefs, Pittsburgh: Pittsburgh Courier Publishing Co., 1958.

Africa, Lost and Found, with Richard Moore and Keith Baird, (Audio) New York: Harlem Freedom Schools, 1964.

Harlem, USA: *The Story of A City Within A City*, (An Anthology), Berlin: Seven Seas Publishers, 1965. Revised American Edition – New York: Collier Books, 1971. Harlem abridged translation of Harlem, USA), Budapest: Kossuthe Konjukiado, 1967. Preprinted – A & B Book Publishers, NY, 1995.

American Negro Short Stories, (An Anthology), New York: Hill & Wang, Inc., 1966.

Reprinted, *A Century of the Best Black American Short Stories*, Hill & Wang, Inc., 1992.

Curriculum Guide for the Study of Afro-American History, New York: Haryou-Act, 1967.

William Styron's *Nat Turner: Ten Black Writers Respond*, (An Anthology), Boston: Beacon Press, 1968.

The History and Culture of Africa, Aevec, Inc., Educational Publishers. NY. 1969.

What's it all About, with Vincent Harding, New York: Holt Rinehart & Winston, 1969.

Malcolm X: The Man and his Times, (An Anthology), New York: Macmillan, 1969.

Slavery and the Slave Trade, edited with Vincent Harding, New York: Holt Rinehart & Winston, 1969.

Harlem: Voices from the Soul of Black America, (An Anthology), New York: New American Library, 1970. Reprinted- New York: A & B Book Publishers, 1996.

Black Titan: W.E.B. DuBois, edited with the Editors of Freedomways Magazine, Boston: Beacon Press, 1971.

World's Great Men of Color, Vol. I & II, by J.A. Rogers, (Revised and updated with commentary), New York: Collier-Macmillan, 1972.

Marcus Garvey and the Vision of Africa, New York: Random House, 1973.

Black Families in the American Economy, an ECCA publication, Washington, DC: Community Counselors Associates, 1975.

Black-White Alliances: A Historical Perspective, Chicago: Third World Press, 1975.

Black Families in the American Economy, an ECCA publication, Community Counselors Associates, Inc., Washington, DC, 1975.

Paul Robeson: The Great Forerunner, with the Editors of Freedomways Magazine, NewYork: Dodd, Mead & Co., 1978.

Pan-Africanism & The Liberation of Southern Africa: A Tribute to W.E.B. DuBois United Nations Centre Against Apartheid & The African Heritage Studies Association, NY, 1979.

Dimensions of the Struggle Against Apartheid: A Tribute to Paul Robeson, United Nations Centre Against Apartheid & The African Heritage Studies Association, NY, 1979.

The State of the Race, Los Angeles: The Pan-African Secretariat, Los Angeles Chapter, 1980.

The End of the Age of Grandeur and the Beginning of the Slave Trade, New York: New York University Institute of Afro-American Affairs, 1981.

Thoughts on the African World at the Crossroads, Guyana, South American: NERAC Educational Pamphlet, 1980.

Can African People Save Themselves, Detroit, MI. Alkebulan, Inc., 1990.

New Dimensions in African History Trenton: Africa World Press, 1990.

African People at the Crossroads: Notes for an African World Revolution, Trenton: Africa World Press, 1991.

Columbus and the African Holocaust: Slavery and the Rise of European Capitalism, A & B Distributors, NY, 1992.

African People in World History, Black Classic Press, Baltimore, 1993.

Africans Away From Home, Washington, DC Institute for Independent Education, 1988. Revised and expanded, 1993.

My Life in Search of Africa, Africana Studies and Research Center, Cornell University, Ithaca, New York, 1994. Republished. Third World Press, Chicago, IL 1999. Reprinted, Trenton: Africa World Press, 1991.

CONTRIBUTORS

James L. Conyers, Jr., Ph.D., is the Director of the African American Studies Program and University Professor of African American Studies at the University of Houston. He is currently at work on an intellectual biography of Charles H. Wesley.

Raymond R. Patterson (1929–2001), was a Poet, Writer and Professor of English at New York City College. He is the author of: *26 Ways of Looking at a Black Man and Other Poems* (1969) and *Elemental Blues* (1983). Additionally, he was the founding Director of the Langston Hughes Festival in New York city from 1973–1993. On April 5th of 2001, Professor Patterson made his transition to become an ancestor.

Julius E. Thompson, Ph.D., is the Director of the Black Studies Program and Professor of History and Black Studies at the University of Missouri at Columbia. He is the co-editor of this volume.

Ahati N.N. Toure, is the Assistant Director of the African American Studies Program at the University of Houston and a doctoral candidate in Afrikana and United States World History at the University of Nebraska at Lincoln.

Index

G

H

I

J

K

L

M

N

P

Q

R

S